D0971708

HANGING BY A TWIG

*Understanding and Counseling Adults with
Learning Disabilities and ADD*

Also by Carol Wren
Language Learning Disabilities: Diagnosis and Remediation

Also by Jay Einhorn
Leadership in Health Care and Human Service Organizations

A NORTON PROFESSIONAL BOOK

HANGING BY A TWIG

*Understanding and Counseling Adults
with Learning Disabilities and ADD*

Carol Wren, Ph.D.

with psychotherapeutic commentary
by
Jay Einhorn, Ph.D.

W. W. Norton & Company
New York • London

HANGING BY A TWIG: Understanding and Counseling Adults with Learning Disabilities and ADD by Carol Wren, Ph.D., with psychotherapeutic commentary by Jay Einhorn, Ph.D.

Composition and book design by Paradigm Graphics
Manufacturing by Haddon Craftsmen

Library of Congress Cataloging-in-Publication Data

Wren, Carol T.
Hanging by a twig : understanding and counseling adults with learning
disabilities and ADD/Carol Wren ; with psychotherapeutic
commentary by Jay Einhorn.
p.   cm.
"A Norton professional book."
Includes bibliographical references and index.
ISBN 0-393-70315-0
1. Learning disabled—Mental health.
2. Learning disabled—Counseling of. I. Einhorn,
Jay. II. Title.
RC394.L37 W74 1999
616.85'889—dc21   99-043411

W. W. Norton & Company, Inc., 500 Fifth Avenue, New York, N.Y. 10110
www.wwnorton.com
W. W. Norton & Company Ltd., 10 Coptic Street, London WC1A 1PU

1 2 3 4 5 6 7 8 9 0

For Mary, Mark, Kerry, Dominic, Sonja, and Hannah, who shared themselves so that others with LD can benefit

and

For Alice

Contents

·················

Acknowledgments

Carol: This book has had quite a long gestation period, and I have benefited greatly from the ideas and assistance of many people since its conception in 1987. Thanks to Barbara Hoskins for her contribution to the original proposal; it was our shared concern for the emotional health of LD adults that has sustained this effort over the years. I benefited also from Jacqueline Rondeau's readiness to map out and discuss early versions of this manuscript and from her participation in conducting two of the interviews in the book. Thanks as well to Warren Rosen, who was willing to contribute the insights of a neuropsychologist to the project. A very large thank you to Jay Einhorn, who has added so much to the book. And certainly to Tom Wren: *mille grazie* for his unflagging support, ingenious suggestions for solving some technical writing problems, and his talent for wielding the red pencil.

Thanks to Jimmie Shreve who gave permission to quote from his book *A Square Peg in a Round Hole* (1993, Square Peg Enterprises), especially the title and epigraph for Chapter 4.

I'm also grateful to several therapists and counselors who read early chapter drafts: Sarah Yogev, Joseph Palombo, Warren Rosen, Myrna Orenstein, Steven Tovian, Duncan Sylvester, and Sr. Frances Ryan. I was able to do much of the writing of the book thanks to a research leave from DePaul University. Finally, a most heartfelt expression of gratitude goes to the six individuals who contributed their stories to this book.

Jay: Laura Lehtinen Rogan, colleague of Alfred Strauss and pioneer in the education of children with learning disabilities, began the

Cove School in Evanston and thus started a tradition of excellence in learning disabilities education that continues to this day. (When asked at Cove's 50th anniversary celebration how she had done it, Laura, by then retired, replied, "I was just doing my thing.") Libby Noell, who as Cove's Executive Director hired me to work there, provided vital encouragement and support in my work with children and adults with learning disabilities, as well as a model of selfless dedication, exceptional competence, zest for educational leadership, and sheer good-humored collegiality. Barbara Gadeau and Phillip Jackson, III, today's Co-executive Directors at Cove, continue this work with great dedication.

Carol Wren conceived and carried out a wonderful project and has been a consistently cheerful, constructive, and openminded collaborator. Thanks, too, to Susan Munro, our editor at Norton, for her vision and support.

Eugene Eliasoph, Harold Balikov, and Arthur Deikman have helped me to learn something of the art and craft of psychotherapy.

Robert Ornstein's work in presenting the research and thinking of others, as well as his own, has made the difficult job of learning about psychology considerably easier.

Several people read this work at various stages and made invaluable comments, among them Eugene Eliasoph, Mary Nicholas, Margit Kir-Stimon, George Peranteau, and Libby Noell. Thanks to them all.

My wife, Cynthia, helped keep my life going and kept up consistent good-natured support, notwithstanding the mess that crept into the living room. Thanks, too, to my father, Martin Einhorn, my original exemplar for doing a job right.

My clients have taught me an enormous amount about learning disabilities and psychotherapy. Special thanks to the members of the Therapeutic Support Group of the Cove Center for Adults, with whom I have met nearly every week for ten years.

All valuable work is done on the shoulders of many others, mostly anonymous, whose work provides the platform for ours. The pioneers of neuropsychology, learning disabilities education, and psychotherapy have made it possible for us to make our contribution. May it help others as we have been helped.

Preface

I learned firsthand about the emotional consequences of learning disabilities (LD) when I founded Project Learning Strategies (PLuS), a support program for college students with learning disabilities at DePaul University, and began working with students who had been diagnosed with this difficulty.[1] In addition to their learning disabilities, depression and anxiety often interfered with their ability to study, to do well on tests, and to interact with college faculty. Insecurity and poor self-concepts plagued them. Academically and emotionally they were "hanging by a twig," as our book title suggests. Hoping to provide access to counseling as part of the services of the PLuS program, I tried to learn more about the emotional problems of those with learning disabilities and began searching for a therapist who was familiar with the needs of adults with LD. These tasks proved much more difficult than I had expected, and it was my frustration that provided the original impetus for writing this book. The investigation was not entirely fruitless, however. In the course of the search I met a small group of competent and concerned therapists in the Chicago area who work with adults with LD, among them Jay Einhorn, a clinical psychologist in private practice and Director of the Cove Center for Adults (a program for adults with LD), who has collaborated with me on this project.

A review of the literature revealed that very little had been written about counseling the adult with learning disabilities. To gather more information, I asked those of my students who had sought therapy on their own to share their experiences and impressions with me. I discovered that many had quit therapy prematurely and that most felt that they had not benefited significantly from the experience. Typically, they felt that their problems were either dismissed or misinterpreted. As a result, therapists were charged with "not really listening" and "not really hearing what I'm saying." Further conversations with other learning disabled adults verified that unsatisfactory counseling experiences extend beyond the college years and suggested that their reasons for quitting were not entirely defensive. These adults reported that they gained a measure of relief from the immediate crises that led them to therapy, but quickly reached a plateau and thus either stopped therapy or were referred elsewhere. This book provides insight into why this happens and what therapists can do about it.

The book is not a manual or a research text, however. Jay and I have not tried to write an "A to Z" of learning disabilities, diagnostic evaluation, or psychotherapy, since most readers will have some familiarity with most of these topics. Nevertheless, we have tried to include enough material to orient those who are unfamiliar with any of these topics. We provide guidelines and suggestions both for diagnostic assessment and for therapeutic intervention, but we do not espouse a specific theoretical approach to therapy, since both experience and research have shown that the personality of the therapist is far more important than her theoretical approach. Our point is that, whatever the therapist's personal approach to treatment, she can only be of very limited assistance without a working knowledge of the nature of learning disabilities and how the disability has affected the patient's life.

Because an empathic understanding of the experience of living with a learning disability is critical to successful therapy, each chapter of the book is structured around a personal story told by an individual with a learning disability. However, the chapters are more than just stories, since I weave into the narratives related information about learning disabilities. Then Jay discusses the therapeutic implications. Since diagnosis is so important in understanding an individual's learning disability, we each discuss diagnostic issues as they arise in each chapter.

Each of the six people who tells his or her story in this book is a real person. The names have been changed to protect confidentiality, except in the case of Mary Grigar, who is a published author and has given me permission to use her real name. They all have dramatic stories to tell. But they are—in a twist on the title of Pirandello's play—six characters in search not of an author, but of a reader who is open-minded enough to consider the possibility that cognitive disabilities can underlie a wide range of emotional problems.

I began collecting the interviews that form the basis of the book in 1985, as individuals expressed a willingness to have their stories tape-recorded in order to help convey to various audiences what it is really like to have a learning disability. In fact, they were all extremely eager to share their experiences, precisely so that others with LD would not have to suffer as they have. I have used portions of these interviews for lectures and public presentations, as well as for a series of booklets about learning disabilities. Jay is currently the psychotherapist for two of these people.

The language of the interviews was edited only to remove that jerky and repetitious quality of oral conversation that seems so natural when one hears it but is so annoying when one reads it in transcribed form. However, the interviewees' own vocabulary and syntax were retained as much as possible, not only to preserve the charm of their own often highly original modes of expression, but also, where applicable, to preserve the evidence of their oral language learning disabilities.

It is worth acknowledging that in these narratives we are listening to a purely one-sided account of the life of each of the interviewees. By limiting ourselves to their own self-reports, we lose whatever objectivity might have been gained from a more comprehensive evaluation. Of course, their own perceptions are quite valuable, since they help us gain an empathic understanding of what it is like to live with a learning disability. In treatment, however, therapists may need to help their clients confront what may well be inaccurate perceptions in order to become more responsible for their choices and to make those choices more successful ones. Jay's comments indicate how some of these perceptions might be supported and others challenged.

Jay's psychotherapeutic commentary is based on an integration of cognitive-behavioral and psychodynamic models. These models provide ways of focusing on what people think, how they feel, how thoughts and feelings interact, how all that affects what they do, and how all *that* emerges from their developmental history. It is rooted in two beliefs: (1) that human behavior always makes sense—no matter how it sometimes seems not to—when its developmental ante-cedents are understood in the context of human nature and a particular person's life story, and (2) that it is nearly always possible to make progress toward improving one's inner and outer life if one really wants to do so and can find competent help. There are, of course, many ways of approaching counseling and psychotherapy, and many different ways of explaining the same phenomena. Here we are particularly concerned about the interactions between learning disabilities, the development of attitudes toward self and life, and the clinical problems of personal and emotional adjustment. The developmentally stunting effects of educational and clinical misperception, misdiagnosis, and mistreatment come into focus as we listen to the life stories of particular individuals and try to help them outgrow the damage that has been done to them by the cultures that were supposedly there to support their healthy maturation.

Though the book is primarily written for counselors and therapists, we expect that it will be useful to other readers from both the professional and nonprofessional ends of the spectrum. We hope that scholars will find it useful as a stimulus for thinking about future research questions. However, we also hope that adults with LD will find it readable and will recognize themselves, gaining reassurance and insight into their own lives. Perhaps some will share the book with their counselors or therapists so that they can work together more comfortably. Learning disabilities specialists who read the book will discover a new and broader perspective that can help them make more timely referrals for psychological counseling and might stimulate ideas on how to work more closely and effectively with the therapists whom their patients may be seeing. Of course, this last point applies to therapists working cooperatively with LD specialists as well. We also hope the book will prove useful to students of counseling, clinical psychology, social work, and rehabilitation, if only to stimulate them to read more about learning disabilities as they begin to understand the relevance of LD to emotional problems in some clients. We expect that most people with learning disabilities and those who try to help them will identify with certain issues almost immediately. We invite you to correspond with us about your own experiences and reactions to our case presentations at jay@psychatlarge.com.

Hanging by a Twig

*Understanding and Counseling Adults with
Learning Disabilities and ADD*

CHAPTER 1

Misunderstood, Misdiagnosed, Mistreated

Introduction to the Problem

"You look worried," I remarked to Matt, a good friend and therapist, as we finished lunch one recent afternoon. "Is there something wrong?"

"No. Well, yes. I just finished a tough session with a patient who has me very concerned. I don't know where to go next," Matt said dispiritedly. "Ethically I probably should refer him elsewhere, but it seems I don't understand his problem well enough to know what kind of referral would meet his needs. I never like to contemplate failure, but this client has made very little progress and I'm more worried about him than usual."

Why do some clients fail to make expected progress in therapy? Are they undermotivated or overly defensive? Has the counselor failed to establish a therapeutic alliance? Or could a learning disability have been missed or misdiagnosed?

An estimated 3% (perhaps as high as 10%) of the adult population has a learning disability (LD). These individuals are at very high risk for emotional problems and disorders for two related reasons. They are at risk because they struggle with the disability itself. They are also at risk because they are misunderstood, mistaught, misdiagnosed, and mistreated not only in school but also in psychotherapy and in life. Because of the increased probability of serious emotional difficulties, it should not be surprising that many people with learning disabilities find their way to counselors and therapists. For example, in a well-known follow-up study of learning disabled children, Rogan and Hartman (1976) found that 75% of them later sought therapy or counseling.[1] In fact, given these statistics, it seems likely that every counselor and therapist will treat some individuals with learning disabilities over the course of his or her practice, though in some cases the disability remains to be diagnosed.

Even competent and conscientious therapists may overlook learning disabilities, because many of the behaviors associated with LD can be easily misinterpreted as symptoms of sensory, intellectual, or emotional problems. Although people with learning disabilities often suffer from emotional distress and could benefit from therapy, their experiences in therapy are often far from satisfactory. In fact, learning disabilities may be a significant factor in many more cases of failed therapy than we might expect, as my experience with Matt, a good friend and experienced counselor, illustrates.

Though he had done some reading in hopes of finding a more appropriate approach to working with his client and had even consulted with one of his former internship supervisors, Matt was becoming discouraged. "What do you think?" he asked. "Maybe you could help me take a fresh look at this."

Although my perspective as a professor of learning disabilities seemed rather remote in the context of our conversation at that point, I suggested that Matt tell me about his client, whom we will call Stephen. "He's quite depressed," he told me. "After some initial relief of his symptoms two years ago, he hasn't made any progress to speak of. He has been in therapy for longer than I would have expected and now he's starting to have suicidal thoughts. I've thought of referring him elsewhere, but in this context it's probably unwise to change therapists. So I need help."

"Do you want to fill me in on the details?" I asked.

"Stephen is 39 and unmarried. He lost his job a couple of years ago and has been unemployed since then. He's been unable to formulate any concrete goals and has no career direction. Previously he had a fairly stable career with a newspaper. He was in the editorial department, but the division was reorganized and he was unable to adjust. He was seen as unmotivated and subsequently fired. No one said it in so many words, but an unacknowledged contributing factor was that people just didn't like him. He lacked social skills and didn't fit in.

"Originally when Stephen came to see me, he was entirely unmotivated. He had lost his job a few months earlier and had all the symptoms of depression—irritability, sleep disturbance, lack of motivation, sad mood, low tolerance for frustration. After a reasonable time, his symptoms were alleviated to some degree. Not that all of a sudden he was a ball of fire, but he became motivated at least to some extent and wanted to replan his life, seek a new career. But no real plan materialized and he had continual difficulty getting himself back in the job market. It's very hard to put my finger on this, but he seems to have difficulty imposing some sort of structure on his life, finding a strategy. More recently, as I told you, he has had some suicidal ideation because he doesn't seem to be able to solve his problem. I'm not sure if he can't solve it or just doesn't have the motivation to solve it. In any case, he's not even looking for a job right now."

Matt's comment about Stephen's difficulty imposing a structure on his life piqued my interest. "Can you give me the highlights of his history?" I asked.

"He's an only child and apparently got along with both parents, who had a stable marriage. He had been quite dependent on his mother until she died about four years ago. She shielded and protected him quite a bit, and he lived at home even as an adult. Father, who is still living, is the just the opposite. He's a driven, ambitious, outgoing, gregarious individual, and he wants his son to accomplish things. He's frustrated right now with a son who won't perform. He tells Stephen, 'It's been over two years; get up and do something.' The mother, had she been there, would have found excuses and said, 'It's all right, son. Don't worry.'

"Even though Stephen is a sensitive individual, he never had any intimate friends, only an acquaintance or two. He avoids people, has little need to be around them, and doesn't seem interested in making friends, either male or female. Of course, his introversion comes partly from the fact that he has been rejected by other people, and it's clear that he experiences acute emotional pain because of his poor social skills."

Keeping in mind Stephen's social awkwardness and his difficulty imposing a structure on his job search, I asked how he did in school. "Well, of course his main difficulties were social. He didn't fit in, didn't have friends, and had a difficult time relating to his teachers and then to his professors in college. Math was his worst subject; he really struggled with that. He did better in English and history, though he was never anything more than an average student in college. Verbally he seems quite strong. Well, he was an editor, after all, and he did quite well on some of the verbal subtests of the WAIS two years ago when he was initially evaluated: He got a 15 on both Vocabulary and Digit Span, although his overall IQ was average. He's fairly articulate."

"How was his Performance Scale?"

"Low average, although he got a 4 on Block Design. . . ."

"Matt," I interrupted, "have you ever considered the possibility of a learning disability?"

"Oh, he was tested for that back in high school. There was some suggestion that he might have some sort of LD but the report was vague, and they thought his problems were emotional. The main recommendation was for counseling, although there was no follow-through. The test results suggested he was intelligent, and they didn't see any other reason why he would have so much difficulty in school."

"I think you should consider a reassessment for LD, one that would be much more thorough."

"But he can read! He was a newspaper editor. He's not learning disabled."

"Dyslexia isn't the only kind of learning disability, Matt. Some types of LD involve nonverbal abilities that affect math skills and even social skills, instead of verbal ones that affect reading and writing."

"I'm not sure I understand, Carol. Even if he had some kind of math disability when he was a kid, he's been out of school for nearly 20 years. Math isn't the issue; his problems are much deeper. He's depressed and can't function. His life may be at stake, not his report card."

"I think you underestimate the harmful aspects of LD, Matt. It can have a critical impact on an adult's ability to function, and leads to serious emotional problems more often than you might think. The cognitive problems, such as perception or memory, that underlie those reading or math problems don't entirely go away. Those residual problems can undermine an adult's ability to perform well at work. Then failure can lead to depression."

"As I see the case," Matt said, "his depression stems from an extended bereavement. His mother was overprotective and he was quite dependent on her. He's still mourning her loss. Then his resulting depression and loss of motivation led to his failure at work.

His early progress in therapy—I mean the lifting of some of the depression and his temporary regaining of a little motivation—occurred as we worked through some of these issues of mourning, but the process is incomplete. He doesn't have learning problems; he just hasn't adjusted to the loss of his mother on whom he was so dependent."

"Yes, but let me go back to my point for a minute, Matt. Adults with LD typically do continue to have learning problems. As adults, all of us still have to learn many social and vocational skills, and people with LD often have lots of difficulty learning these skills for truly cognitive reasons. These cognitive problems are not reducible to emotional problems or vice versa, but the two sorts of problems interact in very powerful ways."

"I guess I still need help to understand what this has to do with my client. I still don't see that Stephen has any serious learning disabilities."

"The sort of learning disability that I suspect Stephen may be dealing with doesn't show up as severe reading or writing problems. The sort of LD I'm thinking of can be very subtle and primarily affects one's ability to accomplish myriad everyday tasks. Just for the sake of hypothesis, let's assume that some nonverbal learning disability is preventing him from dealing with many day-to-day problems and causing difficulty with planning, organization, and finding a job search strategy. This lack of competence can in turn affect his confidence and sense of ability to cope. If so, this wouldn't be unusual. People with this nonverbal type of LD really can't solve many day-to-day problems, so a panicky feeling of inefficacy arises, often coupled with a low frustration tolerance. Then his sense of helplessness leads to hopelessness and depression. If you look at it from that perspective, then his depression and lack of motivation have a very different meaning."

"Are you telling me that his motivational problems don't have anything to do with his relationship with his mother?"

"No, I'm not saying that, but there are different perspectives from which we can view the same behaviors. His relationship with his mother was quite important, as was her death. But it might be helpful to ask yourself why his mother was so overprotective in the first place. Even his parents' behaviors are typical of families with children who have LD. You may have your own explanations as to why the mother-son relationship was enmeshed, but let me try to explain it from the perspective of undiagnosed learning disabilities. The typical father, who wants to believe there is nothing wrong, pushes the son and is always telling him, 'You can do it,' but at the same time senses that no matter what he does he can't push hard enough to ensure his son's success. So he—the father, that is—is frustrated, and very impatient. But even more important is the reason for the mother's behavior. From this perspective, the mother isn't overprotective because of some pathological need of her own; instead she sees a genuine need to protect the child and compensate for all his deficiencies. So we get this unhealthy triangular relationship with the father pushing too hard and the child becoming more and more dependent on the mother. So of course Stephen falls apart when his mother dies—a real midlife crisis! Without her to rely on, his meager coping and planning skills are inadequate, and so when he loses his job he feels overwhelmed and has very real problems making a plan to find another one."

"That makes sense, Carol, but I still think that the reason he hasn't developed better coping skills is that his mother smothered him and didn't allow them to develop, and that his lack of motivation is based on unresolved grief. I just can't find a way to help him address these issues productively."

"If my hypothesis is correct, it's even more complex than that. I suspect that grief for his mother is interacting with his learning disability. He probably understands, perhaps in a nonreflective way, that he had a very special niche at the newspaper. Then he lost it due to poor social relationships, and I think he knows that too. It's not going to be a simple task at all to find another niche. Occupational change of any sort is going to be very difficult, not only because the learning disability restricts his freedom to explore a wide variety of possibilities, but also because he doesn't have the structure his mother provided."

"Well, I'm going to have to reflect on this a bit more, but I begin to see what you're driving at, and I think you might be right that something else is operating here. I guess I've suspected for a while that something else is going on, that there's some piece of the jigsaw puzzle that I've not been able to find."

*   *   *

Stephen's recent reevaluation, which resulted in the diagnosis of nonverbal learning disability, has allowed Matt to find that missing piece of the puzzle. However, instead of abandoning his interpretation of Stephen's depression, Matt now works from a richer understanding of the dynamic relationship between Stephen's cognitive limitations, his feelings of helplessness in the face of those limitations, and his grief over his mother's death. His client is making slow but noticeable progress in therapy and has taken a first step toward seeking employment.

People with learning disabilities have often been referred to as "puzzle people." They are puzzles to themselves, to their families, and often to their therapists as well. In my experience working with learning disabled adults, it is not surprising that clients like Stephen fail to make progress in therapy, though this need not be the case if therapists interpret behavior from both a learning disabilities perspective and from their own psychotherapeutic perspective. It is important for counselors and therapists to be sensitive to both the psychosocial difficulties and the cognitive problems of adults with LD. Treatment issues will be pervasive because the impact of the learning disability extends into family, work, and leisure pursuits. If therapists understand how cognitive dysfunctions affect the expectations and demands of marriage, interpersonal relationships, parenthood, vocational success, household management, and leisure time, the net result can only be therapeutic for this population (Bender, 1994).

The point of this story about Matt and his client, however, is not to discuss intervention strategies just yet. The point here is to alert therapists to a very real problem and to suggest that when LD is overlooked they may lose a key opportunity to help. In the next section, Jay's Psychotherapeutic Commentary, we see a second clinical situation in which an LD diagnosis was missed and then provides some preliminary thoughts about therapy.

Psychotherapeutic Commentary

Mrs. Redmond recently brought her son, Jason, a high school senior, to me for diagnostic evaluation. She had read a newspaper article on nonverbal learning disabilities and recognized some of Jason's characteristics: not knowing how to behave in social situations, lack of normal relationships with peers, and great difficulty with English, social studies, and science classes, even with private tutoring, although he spoke and read well. He did well in mathematics.

Two years ago Mrs. Redmond told Jason's high school advisor, a social worker, that she suspected her son might have a learning disability. The social worker attributed Jason's social and academic difficulties to emotional problems, particularly anxiety and low self-esteem. He saw Jason as suffering under the pressure of his parents' high academic expectations. Jason had no apparent difficulty in reading or speaking (although he rarely said more than a few words at a time, and then nearly always in response to a question), and was earning passing grades in his classes (although he had to work hours every night and receive tutoring to get C's). The situation seemed plain to Mr. Wells, the adviser, who saw nothing to indicate that this child had anything other than an emotional problem and overly demanding parents. He did wonder whether Jason had an attention deficit disorder, but an assessment was vague and inconclusive. Jason was referred for counseling, but gave it up as irrelevant after a few sessions. The counselor kept waiting for Jason to initiate conversation about his emotional problems, and Jason kept waiting for the counselor to tell him what he should talk about, so it didn't go anywhere. He continued to struggle for the next two years, passing with mostly C's despite hours of homework and frequent tutoring. Both the student and his parents thought that his academic problems were due to his being "lazy."

Quite a different picture emerged as a result of my evaluation, which led to the diagnosis of a severe nonverbal learning disability. There was a nearly 30-point difference between Jason's verbal IQ, which was average, and his nonverbal IQ, which was very far below average; this is a huge difference. His memory for both verbal and nonverbal content was quite seriously impaired. Assessment of his reading showed that, while his ability to decode (sound out the words) was well above high school level, his ability to comprehend what he read was considerably below, so that he often couldn't answer relatively simple questions on reading passages above the seventh grade level. Jason's memory problem was of course a contributing factor here, but it seemed significant that he did much better when the reading passage was concrete or explicit, and much worse when the reading passage featured interpersonal dynamics and the comprehension questions required inferential reasoning.

In the light of the evaluation results, we can see that:

- His mother was right.
- Whoever evaluated his possible "attention deficit disorder" completely missed a serious learning disability.
- The counseling that was provided was just as irrelevant as the child thought it was; how could it not be, when the counselor had no idea of his cognitive pattern and thus no real diagnostic understanding of him?
- He suffered needlessly through his junior and senior years after his mother suggested that he might have a learning disability (not to mention the years he had suffered needlessly before that!).
- He and his parents were completely unprepared to make appropriate decisions about which colleges he should consider applying to or what kinds of support he may need. His high school was likewise completely unprepared to provide appropriate advice and guidance.

When Mr. Wells learned about the results of my evaluation, he was sorry that he hadn't followed through more completely on the mother's suspicion that her son might have a learning disability. He told me that the diagnosis he'd made at the time—anxiety due to excessive family demands and consequent low self-esteem—was entirely consistent with his training, and seemed to account for all the apparent problems. His professional training had included nothing about learning disabilities.

I wasn't surprised at his limited training and lack of awareness of learning disabilities. My own training in clinical psychology had included nothing about learning disabilities until an unexpected opportunity occurred to do psychological testing on a vocational evaluation unit for adults with all kinds of disabilities. This was under the supervision of Vernon Tracht, Ph.D., himself afflicted with cerebral palsy and by then near the end of a long and distinguished career. Vernon had received an award from John F. Kennedy for services to disabled Americans by using forms of testing that identified strengths in disabled persons whose abilities might otherwise be ignored by standard tests. The unit was directed by Curt Kohring, who had a master's in psychology and was himself an experienced evaluator who was deeply concerned about helping disabled adults find vocational niches that fit their patterns of ability and disability. The experience of working on the evaluation unit with Vernon and Curt led me into neuropsychological testing and an interest in discovering individual cognitive styles. It was one of those coincidences that might easily not have happened— the internship showed up in the psychology department office just as I was looking for a placement. Had I been placed in a more traditional internship site, I might have learned, like the school social worker, to perceive all behavioral problems as the result of emotional dysfunction due to psychodynamic or family problems. I might never have learned anything about individual cognitive strengths and weaknesses, how those patterns can be detected, or how a counselor or psychotherapist must take those facts into account in working with persons with learning disabilities.

Jason stayed on to work with me in psychotherapy after his evaluation was complete, but my treatment of him was very different than it would have been had he been a cognitively normal senior with a primary diagnosis of anxiety disorder, low self-esteem, and dysfunctional family issues. If he had been a cognitively normal, anxious patient, his treatment goals might have been more or less as follows:

- Finding ways to manage his anxiety in the short term.
- Understanding the causes of his anxiety in terms of the interaction between environmental stressors and his own developmental history, identity, attributional system, etc. Conflicts between himself and his parents would certainly be a part of this.
- Utilizing the therapeutic relationship, insight development, and cognitive/behavioral skill training to provide longer-term attitudes and strategies for successfully negotiating potentially stressful situations. This would include developing a more realistic self-esteem based on self-acceptance rather than feelings of failure based on his family's expectations.

Instead, in light of his learning disability diagnosis, his treatment goals included:

- Helping him to understand his functional strengths and weaknesses as a student.

- Helping his parents understand this also.
- Helping him and his parents understand the kind of college program that he would need in order to be successful. In this case, this entailed helping them to make the transition from academic excellence as the primary consideration to having the right kind of learning disability support program as the primary consideration.
- Helping him to adjust his understanding of himself and his history—that is, his identity or self-concept—to incorporate the reality of his cognitive disorder. One of the reasons for his low self-esteem is that he has struggled for years with an undiagnosed learning disability and attributed his academic difficulties to personal shortcomings.
- Helping him to understand his anxiety at least partly in the context of the disparity between expectations of how he should perform—his own, his parents, the school's—and the reality of his cognitive disorder.
- Helping him to understand the connection between his cognitive disorder, with its deficit in social perception, and his lack of social relationships.
- Helping him to develop methods of compensating for his academic and social deficits. Academically, this entails using strategies such as tape recording lecture classes and amending his notes based on the recordings. Socially, it means learning to negotiate social situations much more verbally than nonverbally, since he lacks the perception of nonverbal cues upon which the understanding of most social situations normally depends.
- Emphasizing that, both academic and socially, and later vocationally, he will need someone to help him understand the situations he is in and what he is expected to do in ways that more cognitively normal persons would be expected to just "get." He will need both coaching and a longer adjustment period to new situations.

Therapeutic Empathy and Learning Disabilities

By another lucky coincidence, during my undergraduate career at Goddard College I had met the distinguished social worker Eugene Eliasoph (who later became President of the American Society for Group Psychotherapy and Psychodrama). Because off-campus field studies are an important part of education at Goddard, I was able to accept Gene's invitation to study with him for undergraduate credit. The main thing that Gene emphasized was the necessity for the therapist to empathically intuit the patient's experience and to form a relationship with her that included and developed that knowledge.

As Gene's young apprentice, I got to accompany him to various centers and hospitals around New Haven (where he is a leading therapist, group leadership trainer, and psychodramatist) as well as work with him at the New Haven Center for Human Relations, which he co-directed. Time and again, Gene would send me to sit next to someone he was working with in a group as an "auxiliary ego" or "double," the psychodramatic role for someone who helps the person the director is working with by trying to "enter his skin," understand his or her experience and express some aspect of it that is present but which the person is not expressing. Time and again, the bunch of young therapists-in-training around Gene would ask him for theoretical frameworks, but he would always decline. The message was: "First gain some understanding of the person's experience, then make a relationship with him."

This is the attitude that I brought into my vocational rehabilitation work with clients with disabilities. The difference was that my role, and the role of the evaluation unit on which I worked, wasn't psychotherapeutic; rather, the focus was on identifying the strengths and weaknesses of individuals with disabilities and helping them to succeed in vocational training and placement. Working with adults with disabilities of all kinds, some congenital and others acquired, I learned that I needed to understand more than just a client's disability. I needed to know what it meant to her, how it affected her perception, communication, self-esteem, and worldview. Among my clients were those who had severe learning disabilities or who had suffered traumatic brain injuries due to accident or illness. Their disabilities were powerful but invisible, and they often caused distortions in how the clients perceived themselves and their situations in life. To help them find jobs and progress toward personal independence, it was necessary to identify and support their strengths and to identify and somehow compensate for their weaknesses.

Years later, when I became the clinical psychologist at Cove School, one of America's oldest schools for children with learning disabilities, I realized that it was only by understanding as much as I could about the nature of the cognitive strengths and weaknesses of the children that I could be the kind of therapist that Gene Elia-soph had taught me to be—one who understands another's experi-ence and makes a therapeutic relationship with him based on that understanding.

Whether it is called empathy, congruence, or whatever, what makes all psychotherapy effective—aside from whatever authority the patient attributes to the therapist and faith the patient brings to treatment (Frank, 1974)—is the psychotherapist's ability to know something about the experiential world of the client and to estab-lish an emotionally healing relationship with her based on that knowledge. When a patient has a learning disability, it is necessary for the therapist to have some understanding

- that the patient does have a learning disability;
- of approximately how that learning disability affects the patient;
- of approximately what the patient's cognitive strengths are;
- of approximately how having the learning disability has affected the patient's development of a sense of identify or self; and
- of approximately how the learning disability affects how the patient perceives and processes communication with the thera-pist.

Contributions of the Diagnostic Evaluation to Psychotherapy

A psychotherapist doesn't need to be an expert on testing in order to know what test results say about her client's learning abilities and disabilities, and what that means in terms of how her client does in everyday and special situations. That understanding is based on the diagnostic evaluation. A good-enough diagnostic evaluation will tell a good-enough therapist what she needs to know to begin to incor-porate the client's learning disability and related issues into her treatment goals and to design a treatment strategy that incorporates how her client's mind works and learns.

In Jason's case, the following information stands out:

- There is a very substantial discrepancy between his primarily ver-bal and primarily nonverbal intellectual functioning, indicating that he has a nonverbal learning disability. This means that the client will not be able to perceive and understand lots of things that we normally take for granted, both in his life in general and in his relationship with his therapist in particular. The therapist will have to help compensate by spelling them out explicitly. In particular, there is almost no recognition of nonverbal affective information in social situations.

- Memory tests showed that, although he learned slowly and needed lots of repetition, his memory remained stable once information was stored. This meant that there would be a need for lots of repetition in learning, both in school and in therapy, but that his therapist could be confident that information, once learned, would be likely to be retained.
- Testing also showed that his listening comprehension for speech was lower than his ability to speak, which was quite high. The therapist should know that this client's ability to understand what the therapist says to him is not on the same level with what he can say to the therapist. Obviously, this is counterintuitive; we would expect a person's ability to understand what we say to him to be on par with the level of what he says to us. But in this client's case, that wasn't true.

Obviously, there is important knowledge here for the psychotherapist working with him. First, since he has a nonverbal learning disability, everything will have to be made explicit for him. The therapist should avoid assuming that this client has an implicit understanding of social behavior or an intuitive understanding of self or others. Second, this young man will likely need lots of repetition of information in therapeutic conversation, as he will in school. Third, the psychotherapist will have to adjust the difficulty level of his communication somewhat below what the client seems able to receive, since his expressive level of speaking is above his level of comprehending speech.

The diagnosis disproves some of Jason's negative opinions about himself and provides the therapist with important information with which to correct his misperceptions about himself. For example, Jason has concluded that he is "lazy," not because he doesn't put in study time—he puts in hours—but because his grades don't correspond with his expectations about what they should be for the amount of time he puts in. The equation here is: low grades = laziness. In psychotherapy, we can now advise him that his trouble is not due to laziness; in fact, he works pretty hard. The problem is that he has a certain kind of learning disability that causes him to have difficulty acquiring new information. This means both that he will have to spend extra time and that he will have to use compensatory strategies, such as tape recording lectures, in order to get by in college.

It turns out that he did tape record some lectures in high school, at his mother's insistence, and this did help him in those classes, but he stopped doing it. The reason he gave for stopping tape recording is that he felt that he didn't need to any longer. In fact, it is probable that he wished not to stand out as different from his peers and didn't want to acknowledge that he had a problem. Poignantly, this suggests that he already recognized at some level that he did have a problem, but wished to avoid it.

For a psychotherapist, the evaluative information about this young man provides a completely different view of him than if one did not know it and had to formulate a diagnostic impression and treatment strategy just from his behavior in psychotherapy sessions and the information that he was not doing as well in school as he and his parents thought he should. Now it becomes an entirely different kind of case, one in which the client's adjustment to the facts of his learning disability—what it means to him and what he can do about it—becomes central to the psychotherapeutic treatment. The psychotherapist needs to take into account this client's communication issues—listening and speaking, memory and learning, what he can readily understand and what he can't.

In the following chapters, we will meet several persons with learning disabilities of different kinds. We will meet them through their stories and learn about their histories, and we will consider the implications for their psychotherapeutic treatment. We hope that readers will glean something of the quality of psychotherapeutic work with clients with learning disabilities. In some ways, it's just the same as doing psychotherapy with anyone: We relate empathically and form a diagnostic impression, a strategy, and a therapeutic alliance. In other ways, though, there is a world of difference between treating a person with a learning disability, especially one whose LD has become a major clinical and personal issue, and treating someone without a learning disability.

Readers who have little knowledge of learning disabilities and wish to begin with a theoretical framework for psychotherapy with adults with LD are invited to turn immediately to Chapter 8. Those who are familiar with basic concepts in these fields and who want to immerse themselves in the experiences of people with learning disabilities should continue with Chapter 2.

. . . .

CHAPTER 2

Hanging by a Twig
LD and Development of the Self

In America the philosophy is you've got to do better. Inside, though, there is that fear, because of that "Yes, you can, yes, you can." And you're afraid that you're falling off a ledge on the side of a canyon and you're hanging on to a twig. The "Yes, you can" people are telling you that you can jump across the canyon to the other side, but the LD person is hanging by this twig, over the edge, and because they tell you to try harder, you always are trying harder, so you're always hanging by some twig. Oh, some people think that if they say "No, you can't," that you'll try harder, but that doesn't work at all. Some LD people when they hear "No, you can't" do try harder, but all they do is pull the roots of the twig further out of the ground and hang a little further down the canyon.

—Mary Grigar

For Mary, telling her story is enjoyable work. She has traveled across the country for over ten years, talking about her life and lecturing about learning disabilities. "I've been to and spoken at most of the learning disabilities conventions, from California and Rhode Island to Texas and Ohio." Mary has been interviewed on television and in the newspapers, and a number of years ago when learning disabilities was a new concept her life story was featured in *Family Circle* and condensed in *Reader's Digest.* "When I give talks, my purpose is not to teach special methods for working with the learning disabled," she says. "My purpose is to have people know that this problem [learning disabilities] does exist. I *never* want another child to suffer through this problem." Mary has been extremely successful in carrying her message about learning disabilities to educators and the general public across the country, using a variety of formats, including personal presentations, video presentations, a major exhibit at the Chicago Museum of Science and Industry on learning disabilities, and most recently her book called *A Day to Cry*. Yet Mary Grigar reads at about a fifth grade level and spells at a third or fourth grade level.

Mary's professional accomplishments are all the more significant because she barely graduated from high school. "Everybody's saying go back to college. But it's just . . . it's not possible. There is no part of my body that would ever allow me to sit in a classroom again," she says emphatically. "I would start crying. And the only sad part about it is that I will never get the degree, if that is the sad part. No. The sad part is that much of society will never see what I do have to offer."

Mary's life is full of inconsistencies, such as being quite intelligent but failing to get a degree. She is an excellent listener, who successfully served as a peer counselor to learning disabled adolescents, yet she would have difficulty reading a transcript of those same peer counseling sessions in which she listened so empathically. With her wit and imagination it is no wonder that she has been a dynamic, effective, sought-after speaker, yet she still has difficulty writing a sentence without errors in spelling and grammar. "All those 'ly's' and 'ing's'—those are things that you throw on at the end, you know. I've memorized all the endings, and then when I write I leave a space between the words so that I can fit in an 'er' or an 'ed' or an 'ing.' When I go back I see it from another angle, and I think maybe I should add another 'er' or an 'ed' or an 'ing.'"

One purpose of this chapter is to explore the pervasive impact such cognitive inconsistencies have on development of the self. In spite of her achievements, Mary has never fully recovered from the early damage to her sense of competence. An equally important purpose of the chapter is to provide useful information about learning disabilities. Although the term "learning disability" had not yet been coined when she was a child, Mary's story gives us a context within which to understand LD both now and in the early days of the field. It also gives us an opportunity to make plain the defining features of learning disabilities.

Historical Context

The concept "learning disability" is only slightly more than thirty years old, although research that formed the foundations for this concept has been reported since the nineteenth century. During the 1800s, studies by neurologists such as Gall, Broca, Wernicke, Jackson, and Head indicated that damage to isolated parts of the brain could produce specific types of functional difficulties such as problems with oral language comprehension or production, reading, spelling, and so on. Then, during the first half of the twentieth century, several individuals (e.g., James Hinschelwood, Samuel Orton, Alfred Strauss) began working in clinical and educational settings with children who had extreme difficulty learning specific academic skills. They hypothesized that these skill deficits were due to defective learning processes, which were in turn often attributed to "brain damage." Helmer Myklebust, as well as Samuel Kirk, investigated deficits in auditory and linguistic processing as causes of problems in spoken and written language. Drawing on these observations and hypotheses, Kirk proposed the term "learning disability" (more simply, LD) to bring together the seemingly heterogeneous population of children "who have disorders in development in language, speech, reading, and associated communication skills needed for social interaction" and who have inherent limitations in their ability to process certain kinds of information necessary for these skills (Kirk, 1963, pp. 2–3). Central to the concept of a learning disability is the notion that a weakness or deficit in one or more cognitive processes such as perception, memory, or reasoning interferes with the acquisition of various academic and life skills. Of course, there are still many gaps in our knowledge of how all this takes place, and different views exist about the scientific status of the construct of "learning disabilities."[1]

In spite of unresolved theoretical controversies, Mary and others like her give us a clear picture of what it like to *live with* LD. Mary laughs heartily, enjoying her recollections of stories about her early childhood. "I was hyperactive. But my mother tells me—there were eight of us kids—that she saw my behavior as perfectly normal! But she did talk about tying all the chairs to the table so they wouldn't be knocked all over the dining room, and she called me 'helium butt' because I would always be on top of the table. I was singing, dancing, performing all the time. And everybody just liked having me around because I was full of energy. When my oldest brother went into first grade in our parochial school, I went with him even though I was only three. The nun liked me and she would let me stay in the back of the room. I could sing the alphabet and the rest of them couldn't. I could recite a poem and the other kids couldn't. So I started out on a high like you wouldn't believe. I knew I was smart before I ever got into school."

Defining Features of LD

Learning disabilities are characterized by their specificity, in contrast to generalized deficits in mental functioning or low overall intelligence. As a young child, Mary was developmentally well ahead of many of the older children, especially in oral language and social development. Today, her intelligence is immediately apparent in her ability to converse readily on a wide range of topics, and her accomplishments are clear evidence of intellectual ability. Yet by the time she was in grade school, many teachers thought that she was "dumb" and incapable of learning. In fact, learning disabilities have consistently been confused with lowered intelligence and mental retardation.

In spite of the many thorny issues still surrounding the measurement of intelligence, it is still important to distinguish, on the one hand, individuals in whom there is a discrepancy between intellectual ability and level of achievement (the LD population) and, on the other hand, those who are learning at a level and rate consistent with their lowered intellectual ability (the mentally retarded). Unfortunately, even today, children and adults who have specific learning disabilities are all too frequently regarded as "slow," less intelligent, incapable of learning, or retarded, in spite of ample evidence from the lives of many learning disabled adults that difficulty in processing specific kinds of information does not necessarily result in generalized mental impairment.[2]

People with LD have average intelligence in at least some areas. In Mary's case, scores on standardized intelligence tests range from very high in some cases to very low in others. However, even severe learning disabilities cannot suppress her quick wit, her keen ability to "read" other people, and her perceptive and often profoundly moving reflections on her past experiences.

To be sure, such discrepancies (between level of intelligence and level of achievement) can be the result of problems other than cognitive processing difficulties. Individuals may have difficulty learning for a *wide variety* of reasons other than LD, including lack of motivation, inadequate academic preparation, poor teaching, language or cultural differences, sensory or physical disabilities, or a broad spectrum of personal and social problems. Thus unexpected underachievement (i.e., a discrepancy between potential and achievement) is properly considered only a part—though an important one—of the concept of LD. Learning disabilities are characterized by the additional notion that the underachievement in question is related to difficulty with one or more specific cognitive processes such as perception or memory or the ability to process spoken or written symbols. That is, cognitive processing difficulties can interfere with learning.[3]

At this point it is important to note what is not being claimed. Many—probably most—cases of underachievement or learning difficulty in children and adults are due to personal, sensory, physical, or social problems, and these difficulties are *not* learning disabilities per se. These social and physical problems certainly can accompany and exacerbate a learning disability, but they are conceptually different.

What, then, do we mean by cognitive processing difficulties? Johnson (1987) proposes a broad schema of multiple systems in the brain receiving and abstracting information from the environment. This schema includes central processes of attention, perception, memory, symbolization, conceptualization, and intersensory integration (p. 21). When one or more of these processes are weak or dysfunctional, they affect the ability to learn basic academic skills as well as many skills of daily living. The stories of the adults with LD in this book illuminate these processing difficulties more effectively than any didactic explanation or scholarly text. Mary's story is valuable to counselors and therapists precisely because through her own words we can begin to get a sense of the nature of certain specific cognitive processing difficulties and how they affect both the development of self and the quality of a person's life.

Reflecting on her early school experiences, Mary continues, "When I got into kindergarten, I could already sing the ABC's. I was a star. And I was still in the spotlight at the beginning of first grade. No matter what they asked me to do, I could do it, at least at first. But soon they knew something was not right. I was really fortunate though, because there was an affection for me, where for a lot of kids the teacher felt frustration and anger. But I had such a warm fuzzy feeling starting off. There was an affection for me, because I wasn't fighting it. I wanted it. Oh, I wanted it so bad!

"By the end of first grade I still couldn't read, and my parents were panicking. They even went out and bought me alphabet wallpaper," Mary laughs heartily, and goes on to explain how alphabet wallpaper only added to her confusion. Was B for *rabbit* out in the woods or was B for *bunny,* a fuzzy toy you put on the bed? "People don't realize that there's an alligator and a crocodile, and for all I knew there was a K in *crocodile.* You have A for *apple* which is always OK, but then you have B for *rabbit,* maybe K for *crocodile.* And once that sets in it's hard to change. Even though I could sing the alphabet, when I looked at the printed letters they got all mixed up. I not only confused 'b' and 'd' but also the 'g's' and 'p's' and also the 'r's' and the 's's,' but at the time I didn't realize it. So panic really set in. Then anger. Not on my part, on the teacher's part. On my part there was just total amazement. I sat there and I was asking myself, 'Why are they yelling at me?'

"I saw a picture recently, an illustration on the cover of a professional photographer's journal called *Photo Methods.* In this picture the photographer had deteriorated the letters of several words into oblivion, to create a visual effect. And that's what happened when I tried to remember the letters—they fell apart. It still happens to me, even today. The 'r,' it's round, so it turns into an 's.' Of course, 'm's' would always be 'n's' and printed 'a's' become 'e's' because the circles get screwed up in my mind.

"The next few years are a blur. I remember crying. All the time crying. I remember punishments of writing every spelling word 50 times. If there was a test of 25 words, I would miss 22 and have to write them all 50 times. I couldn't say the words. I couldn't read them. And I didn't know what I did wrong, so I made up these little games where I would write the first letter 50 times down the side of the page. Like if the word was 'I'm' I would write I, I, I, I, asterisk, asterisk, asterisk, asterisk [here she means *apostrophe*], m, m, m, m, all the way down the page. I couldn't read the word 'I'm' that I was supposed to be learning. To me they were just letters. And that's all I ever did. I never did any homework.

"By sixth grade I was considered a crybaby. You know, 'Sit out in the hall.' By then it was just total depression." Mary's early sense of self-efficacy has been seriously eroded. "In sixth grade the teachers were mean, just absolutely cruel, because by then I couldn't read at all. Whatever I had learned, I had lost it. If I could read at all it was maybe at a third grade level.

"There was a woman at a cocktail party that I met years later, after my story came out in *Family Circle* and *Reader's Digest*. At this cocktail party they had all read the article and this woman came up to me. . . ." At this point, Mary's face reddens. "I'll start crying," she says softly. But she looks up and continues. "This woman had tears in her eyes. We had gone to grammar school together. Her name came after mine alphabetically, so she sat behind me in school. You know how everybody would correct the paper of the person in front of them. She told me she used to change my answers, put the right answers in when she corrected my papers. She said, 'I did it because I couldn't stand them yelling at you.'

"At this point, because of the total depression, my parents took me to the Child Guidance and Reading Center at Loyola University. Whatever that psychologist did and that reading teacher did was helpful, because I got some confidence back. But they did 'phonics' me to death at this reading center. I still can't do phonics. I can't hold one sound in memory long enough to add another sound to it. When I put them together—like trying to sound out 'cat'—I lose the first *k* before I can add the *a* to it. Was that a *k* or a *ch* to add the *a* to? If you can't hold sounds in your memory, you can't blend them together. If you can't blend them together, you can't do phonics.

"So I went to the Loyola clinic for three years. Then in eighth grade my father taught me to tell jokes. I just became a comedian. If they tried to discipline me I would have to tell a joke, otherwise I would be in tears. So with my dad's help and some counseling and the remedial reading some of my confidence came back.

"In high school, having that sense of humor really was a blessing and they adored me again, because I never got angry. And I decided to learn *my* way. I would talk with someone about every subject I needed to learn, because I couldn't read very much. My biology teacher was absolutely fabulous because she lectured. She was a very precise, very organized teacher. I know all about the trees and the plants. But with her lecturing and the students asking questions, we never got to discuss the human body and we had to *read* those chapters. And I think I was married about four years before I had any idea about where all the important body parts were or what they were called, because I never did read the chapter on reproduction!

My Latin teacher taught all the derivatives of Latin before she taught Latin. She showed us 'aqua' in Latin, 'agua' in Spanish, words like 'aquatic' in English. When she was teaching us 'amo, amas,' she read us love stories and mythology. So Latin was absolutely wonderful. I failed it! But she gave me something. My English teacher double-graded my papers. She gave me an A for my ideas— the first time in my life I knew I had ideas—and then F for my spelling. I came out with mostly 70's in high school. I got a few 68's. And failed the Latin."

Learning Styles

Mary was fortunate to have some teachers whose instructional style happened to match her unique learning style. She learns best by listening, and then being able to talk about what she has learned to fix it in her memory. Oral language is Mary's strength, and the more concrete, the more narrative, the more dramatic the language is, the more likely she is to learn and retain it. Her fifth grade teacher, the "rote" teacher, was good for Mary, although today educators frown on learning anything by sheer memorization. Similarly, the lecture method of her biology teacher, although also out of fashion, matched her learning style, as did the narrative style of the Latin teacher, who made the language come alive for Mary by telling stories from mythology. However, these were the exceptions. Most of her schooling involved a decided mismatch between teaching and learning styles. Such mismatches make learning much more difficult and filled with anxiety for any pupil, but especially for the learning disabled.

Each of us has cognitive strengths and weaknesses, which combine with personality variables to form a preferred learning style. However, most of us can adopt other learning styles as the situation demands. We can flexibly adapt to a phonics method of learning to read or to a whole word method. In the morning we adapt to a teacher who lectures and in the afternoon to one who uses a Socratic method. The learning disabled individual, however, has fewer options because cognitive processing weaknesses make certain avenues of learning unavailable. It was for this reason that Mary had so much difficulty with teachers whose main teaching strategy was assigning chapters from books and requiring papers or written exams.

Continuing her story, Mary says, "And then I decided to be a nun, so I lived in the convent my junior and senior year in high school. There was a uniqueness to that experience in the sense that the convent provided a consistent learning structure. It created a magnificent inside clock. I was able to learn a self-discipline that very few people have. So you know I really say I was blessed all along."

But Mary didn't stay in the convent. "The nun that was in charge of the novices came up to me when I was 18 and she said 'Are you happy?' And I said, 'I thought it was supposed to be a sacrifice, you know, penance.' She said, 'If you're not happy, you can't do a decent job, and then you make everyone else around you miserable, so it's OK not to stay around. And I always remembered that. Later, whenever I got to that point where I couldn't do the job, I would leave, but I never felt like a failure."

After high school, with her characteristic enthusiasm and energy, Mary was eager to find work. "When I graduated and left the convent, there was no thought that I would have trouble getting a job. I mean that never entered my mind. I taught preschool and I was fabulous, because I don't talk in abstracts, and I don't use 25-cent words. I organized my lessons around a theme, like obedience. The entire week had to do with obeying laws, and policemen, and dogs obeying their masters. I was great at observing my kids. I had one girl who they wanted to take to a therapist because she would sit on the rocking horse during play time, while everybody else played. It turned out that at home she had a two-year-old and a three-year-old sibling that messed things up. 'This is why she's not playing with the rest of the kids,' I told them. 'She doesn't want to clean it up!' There were incidents with three or four of my kids that they were worried about, and I was able to figure out why they were doing what they were doing."

But Mary did have some difficulties at the preschool. "They wanted records kept on all these kids. I couldn't write reports on those kids. My memory was so bad, I never even learned their names! There were 24 of them with names like Adele, and Esther, and Fideles, and Alphonso. Hah! They were 'Punkin,' and 'Sweetheart,' and 'Honey.' They never had names; they were 'Darling' and 'Dear.'"

Learning Disabilities in Adults

Clearly, Mary's LD interfered with her ability to function at work just as it did in school. Although learning disabilities may first be identified in grade school, they usually continue to have an impact throughout life. With a lot of hard work people with LD may learn to read and spell fairly well, but the underlying processing problems (in Mary's case, problems with perception and memory) remain and surface in new ways. For example, in grade school Mary had enormous difficulty with phonics since it required her to remember and then associate two things: the shape of the printed letters and their sounds. Since neither the visual shapes nor the sounds would stay in her mind, it is no wonder that she had problems making connections between them. Later, as a preschool teacher, she had a similar difficulty connecting her children's names with their faces, since neither would stay in her memory. For several reasons, including difficulty keeping records, Mary eventually quit the preschool job. "I was tired. You can imagine having to organize all this stuff and not being able to keep any notes or any records or anything. I had to keep it all in my head and I got exhausted."

Mary then worked at Sears. "I had to work this old-fashioned adding machine with rows of six 1's, six 2's, six 3's, six 4's, with an arm that pulls down. And well, I never learned how to do it, but I cleaned desks real good! Made coffee every morning. Everybody loved me, but I knew they would have to get rid of me because there was no way I could figure out this job. As soon as I knew that I had hit the point where they were catching on that I couldn't do the job, I would quit and go on a new adventure."

Mary did indeed go on new adventures. After she left Sears she worked with the Franciscan missions, on the Navajo reservation in Arizona. "I was housemother for fifty women between 18 and 27. I also taught religion. Fabulous. I could go on for hours with Bible stories. Never had to write a thing. There was no paperwork except to schedule these people's jobs and I was a great organizer.

"The frighteningest thing was coming back from the Navajo reservation. I couldn't work at Sears because in the meantime they had put in a test that I had to take when I was being interviewed. I had to pass a written test for wrapping packages! I had taught two years of preschool and a year in the missions, so I had three years of teaching background, with non-English-speaking children, and I couldn't get a teaching job because by then you needed two years of college just to be an aide.

"For a while I kept house for a priest, and eventually I got a job—because they didn't give tests—ordering parts for a heating company. And at the end of a year, after I got laid off, the girls I worked with told me that they corrected all my mistakes. The guy that let me go told me that I had lost more money for the company than I had made, probably because I transposed numbers on the orders. So obviously, the other girls in the office did not catch *all* my mistakes!" But even *that* was not a failure. I'll tell you why.

"While I was working there, I volunteered to teach creeping and crawling to orphans at Angel Guardian Orphanage in the evenings. They figured they were going to get those orphans to read better. So they started to teach them creeping and crawling—that was Doman and Delacato's reading method. And one evening I started laughing with one of the nuns and said, 'I should be down there on the floor crawling around with the orphans because I can't read either.' At that point I really *couldn't* read. I was 23, and I couldn't read. She knew nothing about learning disabilities, but when I started to read to her an alarm went off in her head and she said, 'I don't think you can see right.' She knew of a specialized optometrist, and sure enough through the examination they did find out that my eyes were not functioning well, so the doctor gave me glasses and exercises. "So even though I was let go from the heating company, I wasn't devastated, because during this time I discovered something very reassuring—I needed glasses. I was feeling so good because that was the first realization that it wasn't really my fault. There was just something wrong with my eyes. So my boyfriend and I would do these eye exercises—you know, holding a pencil up, and bringing it closer to your eyes. And his ears would turn red, and my ears would turn red, because you know you get awful close to that person when you're doing those exercises, so we just had to get married!"

The years Mary spent raising her six children were both satisfying and demanding. "Now I mean, I had really won! I had six kids. I had my *own* preschool! I was supermom. I did 45 minutes a day of yoga. I kept a perfect house, had a handicapped kid that needed every part of his body exercised [Mary's second son had spina bifida and died during childhood], but I was doing fine, just fine. My downfall came when my first child started school. That was my first real sense of failure. There was no way I could fake doing homework with my child. And I'd cry every morning when he'd leave for school. I became neurotic. There was no other word for it. Petrified. I couldn't talk to the teachers. Intense anger, to the point where I would throw chairs, and break windows, and throw furniture. And my mouth would just rattle on, and awful words would come out. Petrified. Fear. Everything came back." Therapists will recognize the devastating and lasting consequences of those early experiences in which the development of self was so powerfully affected. "And even now when I talk about it," she says softly, with a catch in her voice, "everything comes back. It doesn't go away." Here Mary's eyes fill with tears, and she takes a moment to compose herself before going on. "It was exactly like when I went to school. Everything was the same. But I had to function. I had to be a mother, care for the kids, keep a nice house, and try to keep everything organized and all that. I had absolutely no control. David left for school, and I was filled with the fear that all the rest of them were going to have to go too. Oh God! It's a blur because it was so painful.

"So when David started school, I . . . it . . . getting through that . . . I have no idea how . . . it was harrowing." And as if having to deal with the issues left over from her own difficult time in school was not enough, her son began having problems as well. Even David's learning disability was not recognized for what it was, because there was still no concept of LD. He has what are now called auditory memory and comprehension problems. Mary says, "He was able to read just fine, but he couldn't listen to or remember anything that was going on. He has a really poor short-term memory. So he was accused of lying when he didn't do his homework and said that he didn't know what the assignment was. They would say, 'You're punished; you have to stay in at recess.' So he would leave to go to recess and they'd say, 'You're punished because you weren't supposed to go to recess,' and he would say, 'You didn't say that.' That's scary because those are the things that destroy your self-esteem. And they did dumb things like accusing him of 'stealing' milk, because he didn't remember hearing about paying for it.

"At the time I didn't know what David's problem was. I didn't even know I was LD at the time. I figured he had an emotional problem. I figured that having the handicapped brother, Marky, who was then dying, was what was causing David to screw up in school. So then Marky died—he was 7—and maybe 6 months later I grew very,

very concerned about David. He wasn't getting any better, and the homework wasn't getting done. I mentioned this to the social worker at Children's Memorial where I had taken Marky for therapy, and she got a psychologist to come to our house and we had lunch together. My kids were their usual—you know, walking on the couch and sticking raisins in their nose—and I was thinking, 'Oh God, she's going to think I'm a failure as a mother.' But what she told me was, 'The kids have adjusted very well to your son's severe handicap and his dying, but I think you have miminal [sic] brain dysfunction.' [Mary means *minimal.*] I said, 'Great, just what I need. I just had a son die. I just had a new baby, and you tell me I have miminal [sic] brain dysfunction!' I couldn't even say the word, and I just kind of laughed at her. She suggested being tested—no she didn't actually suggest being tested; that came later. She just mentioned the word dyslexia. But that was a start."

Even these experiences were what Mary would call "a gift," since it was through seeking help for her son that she eventually learned about her own learning disability. After several months, Mary finally worked up her courage to have an evaluation, which revealed that, regardless of her intelligence, she had very severe processing deficits. "Dr. Nyhus, the guy who tested me, said, 'I hope you never sign anything in your life.' I mean he was really scared for me. He said I had fifth grade reading, third grade math, third grade spelling, and I had a six-year-old visual memory. And I said, 'Sixth grade visual memory?' And he said, 'No, six-year-old visual memory.'"

These results were a revelation to Mary. "What he came up with is the fact that I don't really have much visual memory at all. Everything in my world is lost after a short time. And that's true. Remember I told you about the cover of the photographer's magazine? When I look at something, like a letter or a word, and then close my eyes, I see the letters disintegrating into nothingness. So once I realized this, I started hanging my purse on the curtain rod inside the front door. I tied my brush to the bathroom sink. My keys never left my hand. My shoes were always in the same place. Within two months 80% of the anger I had been living with was gone! I finally understood that whenever I lost things, I couldn't see them in my mind's eye, and that was why I couldn't find them. It was a revelation. I used to think that my kids' little Fisher-Price people were taking the vacuum cleaner pieces and hiding them in different places. Oh God, was I excited! And I said to myself, *that's* why I can't type.

I can't remember what I'm supposed to be typing. I mean, all this realization! I was like a newborn [born-again?] Christian. *That's* why taking information off the chalkboard onto a piece of paper is difficult. There were so many things that were answered."

Cognitive Strengths and Weaknesses

The results of a comprehensive assessment of one's cognitive abilities can be assembled into a descriptive "profile" of individual strengths and weaknesses, which may differ significantly from person to person. Mary's strengths are in the area of oral language and meaning. She learns by listening and then talking about what she has heard in order to secure it in her memory. Narrative and drama are media for learning and communicating that fit well with her strengths. With her wonderful sense of humor and dramatic flair, it is easy to see why she is such a successful speaker.

In contrast, Mary does not visually perceive the world in the way most of us do. "The first time I really understood this was looking at a photograph that a woman showed me. To me it looked like a cathedral, but she said, 'No, it's an old broken down barn with the light shining through the broken slats and lots of shadows.' And I thought, *'That's* what I don't see.' I don't see shadows as shadows. And it's true that unless I go to the right or to the left of something, it doesn't come into perspective." Mary understands the concept of shadows intellectually, but for her, shadows are just another part of the landscape. She does not perceive them as being related to the objects that create them. Nor is she able to easily connect all the different appearances of a single object into an abstract visual concept, an ability we call visual constancy. "I think my world is more exciting than anybody else's, because I see the whole world differently every time light puts a different shadow on it. Every time I walk out of the house at a different time of the day, the tree or the lamp post has a different shape. Everything is always new to me." For Mary shadows continually change the appearance of objects so radically that she has difficulty correlating all these different appearances. For this reason, she does not readily perceive objects as constant regardless of seemingly incidental changes.

In addition to her problems with visual perception and visual memory, she also has short-term auditory memory problems with certain aspects of language, especially with isolated letter-sounds.

Mary found it nearly impossible to learn phonics in school because she couldn't, and still can't, hold onto the component sounds of a word long enough to blend them together into a single word. Nor can she easily remember the sequence of similar sounds within a multisyllable word like "dyslexia" or "minimal."

Of course *all* of us have relative strengths and weaknesses in cognitive processes that influence the ways we receive and express information, and so LD is a matter of degree. Those with learning disabilities experience more extreme weaknesses in some areas that then interfere with learning to a significant degree. Because of these difficulties in processing information, people with LD often become less flexible and rely much more on their strengths to compensate for those weaknesses. Limitations in the pathways through which people with LD can process information first have an impact on learning in school, and later influence how they interact with the adult world emotionally, physically, socially, and vocationally.

Patterns of LD

Most experts agree that "learning disability" is not a unitary concept, but rather an umbrella term for many types of cognitive processing weaknesses. However, there is little agreement on how to categorize them. This section highlights several common patterns of LD, each of which consists of (1) a cognitive processing dysfunction and (2) the skills that are predictably affected by the dysfunction (i.e., reading skills, social skills, etc.). The patterns discussed below are identified by this second feature. Learning disabilities are not limited to these varieties, but they are the most typical configurations found in adults (based on epidemiological data from studies such as Johnson & Blalock, 1987), and those that are most necessary for therapists to understand and recognize.

Written Language Problems

Written language problems are generally thought to be the most common pattern of LD (85% of Johnson and Blalock's adult subjects were poor readers). Reading problems such as Mary's are typically referred to as dyslexia, which often involves problems in both reception (reading) and production (spelling, writing) of written language. Dyslexic adults frequently have difficulty with word attack skills, with accurate oral and silent reading in context, with comprehending what they read, and with spelling and writing.

When severe, either visual processing problems or auditory processing deficits are enough to make learning to read very difficult,[4] since an automatic association must be made between the spoken and printed word. In Mary's case (sometimes called "mixed dyslexia"), visual and auditory weaknesses combine to make it extremely difficult for her to remember both the printed letters and the spoken words. Because reading and spelling are such complex activities and require a wide variety of cognitive processes, not all those with dyslexia will exhibit exactly the same profile of processing strengths and weaknesses.

Oral Language Problems

Mary's son David exhibits a second common variety of LD, namely difficulty with oral language. In David's case, his problems with auditory memory made it difficult for him to listen to, understand, and recall spoken language. Johnson and Blalock (1987) found that nearly 80% of their LD adults had some degree of oral language problem, which can involve difficulty with receptive language (listening), as well as expressive language (speaking). The language of the adults in their study was characterized by frequent misperceptions, misunderstandings, incorrect word usage, mispronunciations, faulty syntax, and poor organization. Their language abilities tended to be uneven rather than generally low-level. Both receptive and expressive problems interfered with interpersonal communication, and although these adults had good ideas and a desire to communicate clearly, precise expression required much conscious effort on their parts.

Oral language problems are often quite complex. Johnson and Blalock analyzed many cases in which other processing deficits such as thinking and conceptual problems, attention deficits, and nonverbal disorders also contributed to poor oral language. The faulty explanations, long pauses, and poor conversational skills of these adults were the result not only of specific problems with the language system itself but also of more basic difficulties in selecting, retrieving, and organizing relevant information. As one woman said to them, "I know I talk it, but I really don't know my language" (1987, p. 83).

Nonacademic Problems

In contrast to the more academic nature of the patterns of LD discussed above, many adults with learning disabilities have significant problems with skills related to daily living, independence, and social maturity. Research suggests that nonverbal processing problems (involving tactile and visual-spatial perception and judgment) often underlie this nonacademic variety of LD (Casey, Rourke, & Picard, 1991).

Difficulty learning social skills is one of the most important of these nonacademic problems because of its impact on psychosocial development. Bryan (1998) characterizes LD children and adolescents as less socially competent and less well liked than their normal counterparts. Reiff and Gerber (1994) suggest that in LD adults certain cognitive characteristics inherently associated with learning disabilities lie at the root of some social skills deficits. These may include problems with perception and interpretation of facial expressions, gesture, body language, inflection, and tone of voice. They may also include the inability to make central inferences in social situations, poor judgment of mood or attitude, and problems discriminating the response requirements in social situations. However, as Mary's story illustrates, not all learning disabled individuals have social difficulties. Many have adequate or even very strong social skills. They may excel in the social and interpersonal realm, sometimes using these skills to compensate for other weaker ones.

Attention and Organization Problems

A fourth pattern, one that is closely related to learning disabilities, are problems of attention and organization.[5] Attention deficit disorder is generally recognized as a syndrome of characteristic problems, the most central being limited attention span, distractibility, and impulsivity. An additional characteristic, hyperactivity, frequently accompanies and contributes to attention difficulties. The fluctuation in terminology in various editions of the *Diagnostic and Statistical Manual (DSM)* over the last several years reflects attempts to classify diagnostically useful "subtypes" of this complex syndrome.[6]

Regardless of the specific terminology used to identify subtypes, adults with ADD have been described as forgetful, nervous, argumentative, erratic, and temperamental. They tend to procrastinate, be late, get lost, and lose things. They have been called "space cadets," and typically don't seem to be "tuned in." But they also have many positive qualities, including "spunk, resilience, persistence, charm, creativity, and hidden intellectual talents" (Hallowell &

Ratey, 1994, p. 25). Closely associated with attention deficits are organizational difficulties. ADD individuals with organization problems are frequently unsystematic and messy, have problems with planning, problem-solving, and follow-through, and always seem to be behind schedule. They appear to be forgetful, but are often too disorganized to remember (Hallowell & Ratey, 1994). At work they miss deadlines, lose important papers and files, and have difficulty planning and using time efficiently.

These patterns of LD (written language problems, oral language problems, and nonacademic problems, as well as problems with attention and organization) were found by Johnson and Blalock (1987) to be among the most common complaints of their adult subjects. But, of course, not every person who experiences difficulty with a specific cognitive process is identified as learning disabled. Some individuals (particularly those who are highly intelligent) may compensate so well that the reading, writing, or other problems never seem severe enough to be identified as disabilities. Others may have specific processing problems that surface in areas that are not critical for success in mainstream Western culture. Though they may have serious problems in developing certain skills, these difficulties are not identified as LD. Thus, most current conceptions of LD have an implicit cultural dimension. For example, those who are "tone deaf" or who have little sense of rhythm may not be successful at learning to play an instrument or learning to dance, but these skills are seen as "extras" in our society. Literacy, however, is not only essential in terms of financial independence, but also virtually synonymous with self-respect. Its opposite, illiteracy, is associated with highly-charged negative features such as stupidity, laziness, high school attrition, and even criminality. [7]

In spite of her many successes, Mary was not entirely unaffected by the stigma society places on those who cannot learn the "important" academic skills. Unfortunately, as the cultural role of women changed in the 1970s and '80s, feminism began to create new problems for maintaining her self-respect. "Over the next several years I was just raising the kids and working in the photo studio with my husband [a commercial photographer]. So I kind of just stayed at the same level, speaking at meetings and doing in-services in schools. But in the last four years, I haven't done any of those things, except the exhibit at the Museum of Science and Industry. And that feeling of not wanting anybody to know about my LD is back again. I've gotten to this stage now, where I'm trying to hide my LD again. I haven't quite figured this one out yet, but I think it's all the yuppies that have moved into our neighborhood. And it's like I have a different status. Before, I was the sharpest dresser on my block and for years I was sort of like king of the mountain, the neatest Mom. And now the yuppies are coming in and they have careers *and* kids. It's a real tough place to be. I'm patronized because I don't have a 'mainstream' career. Now it may not have anything to do with the LD. It may be a feeling of women my age across the board, but more so in my case, because I don't see myself going back to school, having a career, and that kind of thing.

"So during this period—and I've had other periods like it, but never this long—it's like I have to learn to be self-sufficient. I've always had to have somebody for help, for support. And you know that happiness is only going to come from within. Not until last year did it all fall apart, where I wasn't happy from within. I've become insecure again. I imagine the empty nest is playing into it too. [Mary's children are now all grown.] And the LD isn't helping me get through this stage either. But I know something will have to come. I will have to do something to be accomplished, to feed my ego, to last until I'm 100, you know. Something will have to happen."

Has Mary found that "something" to last her until she is 100? After more searching and feeling insecure, Mary has indeed landed in a place where she excels. A volunteer position turned into a full-time job caring for babies who have been exposed prenatally to crack or cocaine. She has fared well in this job, loving those babies and quickly establishing a reputation as the one who best knows how to comfort and feed them, even when they are most distressed. As always, with her quick intelligence, she has developed imaginative compensatory techniques, and has readily found ways to adapt to the demands of the job. She has described some of them in her autobiography, *A Day to Cry* (1994). When she has to write notes and reports on the babies, she says, "I make cards showing the words I need to write in the reports. Words like 'volunteer,' 'diaper rash,' 'congestion,' and 'stomachache' (that's my hardest word). I first started using 'cue cards' for job applications and shopping lists. I know where to find the words I need to use. 'Weather' is on the front page of the newspapers. 'Potatoes' is in the grocery store ads. Sometimes I need to do some research. When I needed 'chicken pox' for the teacher, the ads only used 'fryer' so I had to turn to Dr. Spock. From then on my kids only had diarrhea because that word was on the medicine bottle." Reflecting on what it is like to live with a learning disability, Mary writes, "I guess I have been using cue cards all my life" (p. 130).

Psychotherapeutic Commentary

Mary's life history shows how learning disabilities can affect the development of self in a child and an adult. Self-confident and precocious at three years old, her sense of her own competence was seriously damaged by age six, and she has never really fully recovered from this injury. The story of the rest of her life, from her own point of view, has been that of a series of alternations between the devastation of incapacity and the elation of overcoming impairments to express herself effectively and capably.

This pattern of emotional alternation between the desperation of "hanging by a twig" and the elation of mastery is ripe for diagnostic misinterpretation. If we didn't know Mary's life history or LD status, we might easily misperceive her as primarily suffering from an affective disorder, perhaps bipolar or cyclothymic.[8] But treatment for a primary chronic affective disorder will not help Mary. It won't change her cognitive profile (of "peaks and valleys," relative strengths and weaknesses of different cognitive functions). It won't help her to adapt to the personal challenges that she is confronted with as a result of her learning disability, of how she is treated because of it, and of what all that means to her.

For a psychotherapist, the diagnostic challenge of a person with a learning disability is to understand both the nature of the learning disability affecting the person and the nature of the person being affected by the learning disability. Each of these understandings is grounded in a different context.

Cognitive Framework for Learning Disability

The concept of "learning disability" is grounded in a concept of the brain as an organ of thought and perception in which learning disabilities are the result of organic malfunctions that cause learning and performance to suffer. As we have pointed out, the existence of learning disabilities was first noted by neurologists who recognized that some children with learning problems seemed very similar to adults who had been normal before sustaining brain injuries. These children were called "minimally brain damaged (MBD)" as a result. The term "learning disabilities," which was promoted by the great learning disabilities educator Samuel Kirk, was an attempt to help educators see MBD children in terms of what they *can* learn instead of what they can't.

The growth of special education training programs divorced from the neuropsychological foundations of the profession made it possible for fully trained LD professionals to say such things as, "Just because he has a processing disorder doesn't mean that he has a brain disorder," tempting me to ask just where those professionals thought the "processing" was taking place. The growing availability of so much information about brain function, both within education and outside of it, and the lively interest of so many educators in applying new knowledge about brain function and learning to education, is helping to bring the temporarily separated fields back together again. Someday, all education will be seen as brain training for life.

Developmental Framework for Personality

The concept of "personality" is grounded in the context of the development of an individual's sense of self or identity. It is here that the psychotherapeutic tradition at its best has much to offer, for it values the study of the individual's history, her family and community culture (with its own history), and her developmental experience within it, as an essential part of the emotionally healing psychotherapeutic relationship.[9]

Psychotherapy's most important contribution to our understanding of human nature may be in the pioneering of methods for the meticulous study of how individuals have been affected in their development by their environments. How we perceive ourselves and others, what we expect of ourselves and others, and the habits of attitude and emotion that so often underlie our behavior and undermine our success in life are often best understood in the context of an individual's development within a family, neighborhood, and community. Within the family, the role and identity of the child are profoundly affected by how she is perceived and treated in the neighborhood and community. For most children and families, school is the main institution through which the community reaches out to integrate and prepare children for eventual membership as adults.[10]

When a child has a learning disability (or any other kind of disability), it plays a key role in how she is perceived and treated in school, which in turn can profoundly affect how she is perceived and treated at home. Thus, the existence of a learning disability plays a profound role in the developing child's fundamental experiences of life and self, which do so much to shape the personality of the growing child. (See Chapter 8.)

Some idea of natural type or predisposition is an essential part of our understanding of personality. Infants vary from birth, and even prenatally, in their dispositions. Any hospital nursery worker or parent of several children knows that newborns vary considerably in their level of arousal, interest in and reaction to their environment, and quality of emotional responsiveness. They may be happier or crankier, may welcome stimulation or react with discomfort and defensiveness. Emotionally, some of us seem to be predisposed to become inhibited and depressed when stress overloads our abilities to cope, while others tend to become hyperaroused. Some people are predisposed to alcoholism, others aren't. Some are more preoccupied with internal stimuli, others with the environment (Ornstein, 1993).[11] Various proposals defining genetic temperamental types have been put forward, though all seem to fall short of providing reliable contributions to individual-specific diagnosis. Probably we just don't know much that is reliable about genetic emotional predisposition yet. But any diagnostic impression of use in psychotherapy includes some idea of the natural type of the patient, although it may be expressed more intuitively than explicitly—for example, in how the therapist relates to the patient and how she chooses to focus on issues.

There are different forms of diagnosis. One is the formal, categorical type of diagnosis, which may be important for establishing eligibility for receiving special education services, pharmacologic or psychotherapeutic intervention, or legal protection against discrimination in job or housing situations. Nowadays in America this is always taken from the *Diagnostic and Statistical Manual of Mental Disorders, Fourth Edition* (American Psychiatric Association, 1994). The other is an individualized description of the patient's problems, which is really more important for understanding the patient as an individual and for the interpersonal treatment of psychotherapy.[12]

Mary

In Mary's case, we can see that for this gifted and precocious toddler, already an accomplished performer at age three, school was not the door to the future but the barrier to it, not the road but the roadblock. The consequence of her learning disability was that Mary's developmental process was profoundly disrupted from the time she began school by the daily, powerful disconfirmation of her self-efficacy. This disconfirmation persisted throughout her childhood and adolescence. Indeed, the forms of intrapersonal and interpersonal conflict engendered by Mary's learning disability and how she was treated because of it have continued to influence, shape, and bedevil her development as an adult. As a result, she tends to oscillate between situations in which she can position herself in such a way that her disabilities are irrelevant and she can apply her strengths to their best advantage and those in which she finds herself, once again, as if back in grade school and in despair, regarded by herself and others as hopelessly incompetent. She is often a winner, often a loser.

In Mary's case, as in the case of many adults who are both gifted and learning disabled, the development of a sense of self had been confused by the gap between her cognitive strengths and weaknesses. Such clients' consciousness tends to be configured around the seesaw of cognitive mastery versus incompetence. What they need therapeutically is to develop a sense of self that is detached from or, so to speak, "behind" the cognitive aspects or functions of self.

Psychiatrist Arthur Deikman calls this the "observing self," linking it with the mystical tradition, and it is toward the development of such an "observing self" that psychotherapeutic effort is largely directed (Deikman, 1982). This is because choices about being, responding, or doing things differently arise from the awareness of opportunities, moments when we can either automatically reproduce a previously learned dysfunctional pattern or respond with a consciously selected or mediated choice. Such awareness is based on the activity of a sense of self that is independent of the usual contents of consciousness.

There is a need for detachment from the turmoil of changing emotional states. Here, incidentally, we can note an important difference between psychotherapy and medication treatment. Medication may reduce turmoil, but typically does so at the cost of some deadening of the self, which may be necessary in cases of severe emotional turmoil. Psychotherapy, however, can lead to detachment in which the mind can heal itself through the consciousness. The self, instead of being deadened, is enlivened and matured.

Imagine being the therapist with whom Mary consults in a crisis. She walks in your office door, an energetic and forthright woman in middle age who makes a strong impression. Despite her record of achievement as an author and speaker in the field of learning disabilities, she describes a history of always trying to be like others, or to be herself as she really could be, which she achieves only sporadically and temporarily. As she describes her history of trying, failing, achieving, failing, sometimes with ironic wit, sometimes in tears, sometimes sad, and sometimes upset, diagnostic impressions begin to form in your mind. "The focus on one theme seems to dominate her consciousness, she seems fixated on it; perhaps she is compulsive." "Her sense of herself is centered around an emotional injury; perhaps she has a narcissistic disorder." "Her affect changes rapidly from laughter to tears; perhaps she is bipolar, maybe a rapid cycler."

Compulsivity of thematic focus, narcissistic injury, rapid emotional cycling there may be, but they all emerge from a definite, specific set of causes—the combination of her giftedness and her learning disability, how she has been treated because of that in the various environments in which she has developed, and what those experiences have meant and continue to mean to her. Failure to recognize this will result in failure in psychotherapy. It will also mean failure with Mary, because she is too aware of this herself to remain with a therapist who attempts to treat her without acknowledging her learning disability as a central fact of her life.

Mary is not just learning disabled; she is gifted and learning disabled. This combination brings special problems of its own. In a very practical and cognitive manner, it is as if the person were split into two parts—one bright, quick, and capable, and the other dull, slow, and impaired.[13] The polarities of Mary's life are not just normal versus slow; she is also fast, often the quickest person in the room to grasp something important about a situation that's unfolding. Gifted learning disabled people often have the understandable wish to be gifted only, to be able to operate at their highest and best all the time. Instead, they are gifted sometimes, average sometimes, impaired sometimes, and they have little control over when and where, because it all depends on what kinds of thought and perception events require of them. Inexplicably and uncontrollably, they find themselves ahead of others in some situations and lagging far behind in others.

This polarization within the personality between cognitive superiority (and the feelings associated with ease of comprehension) and cognitive deficit (and the feelings associated with failure to grasp what others can learn fairly easily) can lead to terrible frustration with oneself, and often to self-hatred. Alternately, it can produce grandiose overvaluation of one's strengths, and the attitude that nothing is worth doing that can't be done with one's best attributes—which, for an LD person, can include a lot of territory to turn one's back on.

Thus, when providing psychotherapy for a patient like Mary, important goals would include:

- Establishing a treatment relationship in which her learning disability and its effects on her self (or identity) are explicitly acknowledged.
- Proceeding to investigate within the treatment relationship the myriad specific ways in which her learning disability and its social ramifications have affected her development as a person. Understanding her emotional reactions to certain situations in terms of the attitudes, beliefs, and habits of emotion and behavior that originate in interactions between the growing child, with all her cognitive gifts and learning disabilities, and her world.
- As part of this process, clarifying the polarity between her giftedness and learning disabilities, and helping her to develop a more detached attitude and stable emotional state toward her cognitive functioning, however it may vary in different situations. This involves the development of some degree of self-observation as a skill in itself (a major goal of psychotherapy), and of a consequent sense of self that is not merely dependent on moment-to-moment fluctuations in cognitive ability to cope with situations, but rather anchored in a more durable existential sense of self.
- Such psychotherapeutic work leads toward the development of a sense of self that is not defined by learning disability: "I am a person with learning disabilities" rather than "I am a learning disabled person" or "I am my disability."

- Realizing that her cognitive issues are only part of her story. Like everyone else, Mary has a personal history engendered by her family and community of origin and her developmental processes, blocks, experiences, etc., within those contexts. By exploring the problems they would have had anyway, regardless of their learning disabilities, people with learning disabilities can see themselves as fundamentally connected to the larger human community, which is a healthy identification, while working through their particular issues.

CHAPTER 3

Naked Under the Desk
LD and Coherence of the Self

I knew I was smart. I knew I was intelligent, but yet I had to fake a lot. I had to bluff it, because you know that you're not like the rest of the kids. And I would have dreams, like reoccurring [sic] dreams, like for most of my young life. You're hiding this thing, this dark secret, which is not really a deep dark secret, but it feels like one. I would dream I was in a classroom, in the back of the class, completely naked, trying to hide under a desk.

—Mark Mitchell

Mark Mitchell leans back in his chair, unwinding from a long day, but his intense light blue eyes dart frequently around the room and his posture is still tense. He describes what he has been doing since he graduated from college with a business degree a few years ago. He works for a small company that originally hired him as a payroll clerk, "but I would say I'm more of a cost analyst." Tapping his thumb against his leg in a characteristic gesture, he explains that he has developed his own computerized program for the payroll of this small company. "I honed up the payroll process, sort of perfected it, and now it's just a duty that I do. It takes me Tuesday afternoons and Wednesdays, and then it's done, and the rest of the week I work on Lotus, formulating my own little strategies and plans, coming up with all kinds of neat little things for the boss to look at. He likes most of the stuff that I do!"

Mark seems to have done well in his career. He has his finger on the pulse of the company, has gained the boss's confidence, and has a secure job as the one who puts out the company payroll. But instead of relishing these accomplishments, he is afraid of failing. "It's kind of hard, you know, because of my learning disability. It's hard to work in a place where you're pushing a pencil. The hardest thing you can do is be accurate in pushing a pencil. I've got a problem with spelling, I've got auditory problems, language problems, and all kinds of stuff." One of Mark's most noticeable weaknesses is difficulty retrieving the exact word he wants to say when speaking. Sometimes he has difficulty retrieving any word at all, much like what we all experience from time to time when a word is on the "tip of our tongue." But in Mark's case, the problem is much more frequent and he often retrieves a word that sounds similar, such as *pacific* instead of *specific*, and has no idea he has used the wrong word. Mark's retrieval problems are reminiscent of Mrs. Malaprop, the comical character in William Sheridan's *Rivals* whose speech was full of malapropisms such as: "Sure, if I reprehend [apprehend] anything in this world, it is the use of my oracular [vernacular] tongue, and a nice derangement [arrangement] of epitaphs [epithets]" (Sheridan, 1879). Sheridan wrote his play two centuries ago, but it was only in our time that researchers began to understand difficulty with word retrieval in the context of language learning disabilities.

Mark was diagnosed as having language-based learning disabilities in his junior year in college. In addition to problems with word retrieval, he has subtle difficulties listening to and using language that in turn interfere with reading comprehension. Problems analyzing the sequence of sounds in words makes spelling especially difficult. These learning disabilities affect him at work just as they did in school. "Oh, tremendously. Across the board. You make mistakes. I'm going to be making these mistakes if I stay with the job for ten years, because the mistakes are just there, it's something you have to live with, like missing an arm."

Frequent malapropisms and spelling errors unquestionably affect other people's perceptions of Mark and lead them to assess his competence, intelligence, or level of education as relatively low. "People exhibit [he probably means *estimate*] you at a lower intelligence because your literary skills are not there." Furthermore, these disabilities affect Mark's *own* assessment of his competence, leaving him insecure and vulnerable. "Just writing a simple memo, I have to start looking in the dictionary. You can't ask other people at work. It's not a melancholy [does he mean *mellow*?] world. It's dog-eat-dog in the corporate world. You can't be asking, 'Oh, how do you spell this word?' If you want to be secure in your job, you have to create the illusion that you can make things happen, at least when you start up. Later on, you can tell the world. Everyone at work knows now that I'm dyslexic. But I didn't tell them until I was there six months, after I proved myself. Then I said, 'Hey, I've got this problem. It's no big deal. I can pound out reports and do stuff you probably can't even think about.' And I'm doing it. And then they forget about it. In a way it's challenging. I know that I can't be the Harvard graduate, the VIP, set the world on fire at 28, but I can be at the same time. I *can* be. It's like a double-edged sword. You can be and you can't be."

The Paradox of LD

"You can be and you can't be." How can a person seem so normal—indeed, *be* so normal, or even, like Mark, be clearly above average in many respects—and not be able to do certain relatively simple and basic things? How can one be so smart but so stupid at the same time? This incoherence is part of the very nature of a learning disability. The learning disability itself creates this conflict, and it is this phenomenon that makes LD unique. Mark's story is important because it helps us understand the contradictions and conflicting emotions of living with LD. The purpose of this chapter is to examine these contradictions in depth and show how they contribute to incoherence in the self. We will also explore the crucial but often overlooked implications of living with the LD paradox for diagnosis and therapy.

Mark grew up and went to school in a suburban working-class neighborhood on the outer fringe of New York City. He visibly shudders as he recalls those days in school. "I was always . . ." [and here he utters a long, anguished sigh] "always hiding, always having a shadow, a dark spot in the back." Since he sometimes has difficulty expressing himself orally it is not always clear how literally he is speaking. Does he mean literally hiding in the shadows? "Not actually hiding in the shadows, but living with a shadow or a dark spot in the back of my mind. Actually trying to, um. . . . See, I knew I was smart. I knew I was intelligent, but yet I had to fake a lot. I had to bluff it, because you know that you're not like the rest of the kids. And I would have dreams, like reoccurring [sic] dreams, like for most of my young life. You're hiding this thing, this dark secret, which is not really a deep dark secret, but it feels like one. I would dream I was in a classroom, in the back of the class, completely naked, trying to hide under a desk."

Mark's dream is an exceptionally apt metaphor for the compelling need to cover up this completely confounding inability to do seemingly simple things and the accompanying feeling that he was not like everyone else. "When I was young, it was easy to hide. I was in an elementary school where there was a big group of kids that were not heading for the stars, let's say. These kids, well, their parents never went to college. They were mechanics and plumbers, which is nothing bad. I mean you know, bliss is happiness [he probably means *ignorance is bliss*]. But there was less expected of you so I was able to hide because I was able to blend in. It wasn't very agonizing [sic]. I didn't even know I had a learning disability. Then in high school there was this clique called the burn-outs. I cliqued [clicked?] really good with them. They were smart people—just giving up and doing drugs and going about it like that. They would be in the dummy classes and be goofing off all the time. I just really fit in there. I could hide well, but I'd be *trying hard* just to get those D's and C's!"

But hiding out has unexpected emotional costs. Mark recalls one experience where he had to write a paper for U.S. History. "I found ways of doing what had to be done. I cheated and I still feel terrible about it. I had to write about the first 15 presidents, and I found a *Time* magazine that had an article about all the presidents up to date. I took a little paragraph from here and there, put them all together, and had a professional typer type it up for me. I had to get out of U.S. History to get out of high school."

Mark's intense need to hide his inexplicable problems in school had other costs as well. "It didn't do a lot for my social life. I didn't have a lot of girlfriends because of that. You couldn't have a real close relationship. I was always afraid it would get out. And that's where my insecurities would come in. So girlfriends were out of the question. You had to give everything to them. That was the nature of relationships when I was in school. I would have had to reveal myself too much."

Although he had thought about college, Mark never dreamed that he would be able to meet the admissions standards. "I didn't even know that I was going to go to college, but then they told me that I did well on my SAT's. The SAT's got me in and my mom looked at that like she'd won the lottery!" But what did Mark think of those test scores? Did he ever stop to think about where they came from if he were such a burnout? As is common with many learning disabled students who live with the paradox of a learning disability, he had no rational explanation. In school, hard work never yielded positive results. The few good grades he got came from cheating. His response? *"I got lucky."* Mark did go to college, but his burnout attitude would not serve him well in a competitive university atmosphere.

"Swimming. Swimming kicked me out of that. That changed me right away. I chameleonized. I grew up on a lake, and was always swimming, but I didn't know how fast I was. In high school I figured maybe I'll go out for the swim team, but the team really stunk, and the coach had a falling out with some of the team members. So I said the heck with it. I never swam competitively until I got to college.

"I just knew that I was going to be in trouble academically. I knew it right off the bat. So that's when I jumped into the swimming thing and just went full bore on it. Taking all these blow-off classes and swimming. It was kind of lonely, because I was with other guys that had been swimming for 12 years, very intelligent, hardworking, all-American-type guys. And it was a winning team; you were respected. And the coach found a place for me on the team. I wasn't a first place swimmer, he knew that. But he knew I had drive, and he knew where I was, my glitch [niche?]. I actually won a couple of matches. It wouldn't go down as me winning it, but everyone on the team would know it.

"Swimming did me a lot of good. It got me out of my burnout attitude. So now I was a jock for a couple years. I was in tremendous shape. Did a transformation. I went back to my high school and trained with the guys during the summers and I was like a star, you know! Where'd he come from? I'm the best thing that came out of that high school in recent history. It got my image going!"

Unfortunately for Mark, toward the end of his sophomore year the team got a new coach who emphasized academics and he was unable to stay on the team. With a better self-image and more maturity Mark decided to change schools and try a business major. He found himself at a large urban university at the beginning of his junior year. "But it was high level, and I went right back down again." Without adequate high school preparation he found himself struggling, but he was determined to make it. "I decided I really had to concentrate on academics. And then all of a sudden things started clicking. Things were very, very difficult, but I was able to figure them out and do them. And all it took was my realization that it's OK that things are going to be difficult. Not impossible, just difficult. Then I kind of built myself back up. Pretty soon I'm scoring all by myself, scoring on tests. Figuring out the accounting, working really well."

But not without enormous cost. "Yeah. Double studying. I'd have to study so I'd know the material like everyone else, and then I'd have to double study to memorize the words that were going to be on the test so I could spell them and *look* like everyone else. I'd have to put in six hours where other people would put in three hours. I couldn't figure it out. In one sense I was like the A students, because I was one of the boring guys up in the library all the time. But at the same time I'm thinking, 'I'm not an A student. I'm not like these guys." (Note the LD paradox in yet another form.) And he was puzzled and resentful when he observed some of his other classmates' behavior. "Is everyone else doing this? No! They're floating around at the bars, blowing off classes and going out, taking a week off from class. Why isn't everyone working this hard? If I'd taken even a *day* off, I'd be in deep trouble."

It was at this time that one of Mark's business professors referred him to the university learning disabilities center for an evaluation. Even now, five years after his graduation, he refers to this experience as being 'found out.' Like many learning disabled individuals who are deeply invested in hiding their inexplicable learning problems, he still reacts strongly to memories of his terrible, dark secret being uncovered. "I got detected in my junior year in college. They found me out because I went upstate for a weekend, I believe for a basketball game, and I only did three hours' worth of studying instead of six. So I took the test on Monday and I knew the material, but I couldn't spell any of the words. I got an 86 on it, but the words were all misspelled. And they couldn't figure out if I was a dummy or what. I was like one of the dolphins that got in with the tuna nets. You know, what's he doing here if he can't spell these simple words? And that's how I finally got detected. I was really at the end of my rope at that time. And that's where basically I learned about my DL [sic]."

Mark's story shows us that a learning disability is a contradiction not in the logical sense, but in the psychological or emotional sense that it contradicts very natural expectations on the part of society and the learning disabled individuals themselves. We normally expect that all of a person's basic competencies will be more or less equal—that someone who reads well will also write well, and so on. But learning disabilities involve very specific cognitive processing weaknesses and so defy such expectations. People with learning disabilities are competent in some ways but inexplicably incompetent in others. One person can do math but can't spell, another person can sing but can't learn to read the music, a third can fix anything but can't even begin to explain to someone else how to do so. The result of living continuously with these contradictions is that many LD individuals never develop a secure sense of who they are, what they are capable of. They constantly ask themselves, "Am I the competent person who can 'read' other people so well, or am I the dummy who can't read the newspaper?"

How does Mark understand his learning disability? It is not easy for him to grasp what specific aspects of language processing are difficult for him and why. But he does have a clear realization that he does not read like other people, does not learn like other people. He has thought a lot about how to explain how his mind works, but the subject is elusive. Mark does not have significant difficulty (although many dyslexics do) actually decoding the words on the page, i.e., figuring out what they "say," but because of his subtle language problems, he often has difficulty comprehending what he reads. He tells me, "Reading's been very hard. I can't just sit back and do it. I have to analyze it, pull it up, figure it all out. I have to actually see what I'm reading. I have to be pictographic. It's not like I'm reading and information is going in and just staying in. My mind's got like a little video camera that will click on and my imagination will take over. I don't mean I take pictures of the words themselves—my brother reads like that. He's got a little monitor going and the words are running in front of him, but if I'm reading 'lamp,' I'm seeing a lamp itself. I see the real thing in my mind. That's why reading is pretty hard for me, but it works, it works well."

Translating verbal information into nonverbal pictures may work well when he is reading about relatively concrete ideas or a narrative text. But what happens when he has to read something so abstract that he can't picture it? What does he do then? Mark explains his conscious, painstaking way of mapping out what he reads. "Then I start analyzing it, taking it apart, figuring it out. I go back to my sailing days. It's like the complete derigging and rerigging of the boat. I have to analyze the whole system. It's what I do with everything, the way I learn anything. The start-up time is very slow. It's agonizing. But that's because I'm like a computer sifting through everything. I can't just take a little piece, and lock it in and then go back ten weeks from now and remember it. It's got to be completely analyzed, taken apart and put back together again. But the beauty of it is that at some point everything comes together at the same time"

The symbols on the printed page are elusive for Mark, and do not easily convey meaning. Although highly intelligent, he has difficulty holding onto and wrestling with the purely linguistic symbols in his head. This is why a spreadsheet computer format such as Lotus is so helpful to him: it provides a graphic organizational structure that is logical and yet can be physically manipulated. "For me, Lotus really allows me to think the way I can think. Put this over here, take this out from here, break it down here, split this down to here. It's sort of like an extension of my brain. Everything is interconnected, the possibilities are phenomenal.

"If I read something, I have to interpret it my way. *I'll* understand it, but nobody else will. I'll be able to keep a logical explanation of it, but it would be completely out of syntax, completely out of the defined standards. I'm just a person, a normal human person, but I don't read like everybody else. Which is not bad, it's not a big deal. But it's like I was from another planet, and I came down and tried to figure out what this was all about. That's how I interpret my learning. Like I come from another planet. I don't have the same skills, the same abilities as other people. I'm just as smart as them, but *I'm not one of them*. The thing that I probably don't have to fall back on is this standardized mode of thinking. To be normal I have to be abnormal, so I can be with the main just [does he mean *gist? thrust?* or both?] of society." The importance of this notion of "paradox" cannot be overemphasized and is worth taking a look at in more detail.

Sources of the Paradox

When a person has a learning disability, the fundamental disparities in abilities give rise to different and conflicting aspects of self within the personality. Such conflicts can be expressed as dichotomies in feelings and beliefs about oneself.

Conflicting Feelings

A number of conflicting feelings are exemplified by the people who tell their stories in these chapters.

- *I want it/I fear it.* Mary expressed conflicting feelings of "desiring" and "fearing" the same thing. For example, she says of going to school, " I think I lived in total fear. All the time crying, biting my nails. . . . I wet my pants when I had to stand up to read, and punishments like writing every spelling word fifty times. They're yelling at me and screaming at me and punishing me and it's after-school classes and summer school every summer. My husband often said, 'It's too bad you hated school so much,' but I said, 'I loved it. I absolutely loved it.' I wanted it so bad. It's like, teach me, I want to learn everything."
- *I'm proud of myself/I'm ashamed.* Dominic, whom we will meet in Chapter 5, tells of his experiences playing practical jokes in high school. His considerable intelligence had no other outlet since his learning disability prevented academic success. Speaking of the many jokes he played, he says, "I felt ashamed at what I did. I wasn't proud of myself, but I was proud of myself to be able to establish that I could do it and not get caught."
- *I feel confident in myself/I have no confidence.* The conflict between a strong sense of self-confidence and an equally strong sense of feeling like a failure is not unique to those with learning disabilities, but people with LD have ample and undeniable evidence that they in fact are both successful in some ways and a failure in others. Mark says, "I'm trying to build my confidence, because people see that I have logical ideas. I know I have really good ideas—great ideas sometimes. But then I get scared. I get scared to the point where I don't even want to attempt things because I feel like a failure. I don't know if I'm afraid of success, afraid of my dreams coming true. If my dreams do come true, will they be nightmares? That's what worries me. And I think I'm like other people in that respect, but the difference is, *I don't have anything to fall back on.*"

Conflicting Beliefs

As a consequence of having to live continually with conflicting emotions, LD individuals draw certain conclusions about themselves as they reflect on their experiences, and these cognitive conclusions are then incorporated into the self-concept. Like conflicting emotions, these beliefs also reflect the paradoxical nature of learning disabilities, albeit in a cognitive rather than primarily affective way.

- *I'm smart/I'm dumb.* While discussing his early experiences in school, Mark brought up one of the most common conflicting set of beliefs that LD individuals experience. "I knew I was smart, I knew I was intelligent, but I was in a school where the kids were not headed for the stars." Then a few minutes later, when asked if he ever thought that he was dumb, Mark immediately replied, "Oh yeah, quite dumb. I thought I was flat-out dumb. You know, I had this feeling that there were certain things that were not expected. Like in high school, I didn't write papers. I mean people that are dumb don't write papers."

- *I'm lazy/I'm trying as hard as I can.* Another crucial conflict is between believing one is trying hard and believing one is lazy (or at least not trying hard enough). Having been called lazy all her life, and driven by feelings of guilt,[1] Mary now saves all sorts of chores, like folding the laundry, to do while watching TV in the evenings. She says, "Society in America is terrible. All we hear is 'Yes you can; you can do anything if you try.' Well, give me a break, sometimes you can't. Maybe you don't want to do it. Maybe you're not capable of doing it, but we're not respected for that. In America the philosophy is you've got to do *better*. Inside, though, there is that fear, because of that 'Yes, you can, yes, you can.' And you're afraid that you're falling off a ledge on the side of a canyon and you're hanging onto a twig. The 'Yes, you can' people are telling you that you can jump across the canyon to the other side, but the LD person is hanging by this twig, over the edge, and because they tell you to try harder, you always *are* trying harder, so you're always hanging by some twig. Oh, some people think that if they say 'No, you can't,' that you'll try harder, but that doesn't work at all. Some LD people when they hear 'No, you can't' do try harder, but all they do is pull the roots of the twig further out of the ground and hang a little further down the canyon."

- *I'm rational/I must be losing my mind.* Often in the midst of their confusion about themselves, people with LD wonder if they are "going crazy," even though they know they are thinking quite objectively. "I had periods when I couldn't function," Mary recalls. "I was afraid I might be going crazy. I was afraid I might commit suicide. I would talk about dying and not wanting to wake up. Like with the tree imagery, where you're hanging over the cliff on the twig. You want to quit, to let go. You want to die. It's not suicide though. Your brain is so overworked that you want to lie down and never wake up because you have overdone it. I mean, you're pulling scraps off the twig, and the roots are coming out. I actually thought I had a problem with suicide, but when I sorted it all out, I realized that I would feel this way at the peak of whatever I had accomplished. You know, like you're running the PTA bazaar and money is pouring in, and that's when you want to commit suicide? It didn't make sense. So the way I sorted it out was that I needed sleep. The vacuum cleaner might be in the middle of the floor, or I'm in the middle of a phone conversation. I say, 'I'll call you back.' I have to lie down for half an hour or 45 minutes, because I'm pushing so hard. Because I'm on the limb, and I'm still hearing, 'You can do it, you can do it if you try harder.' You know *The Little Engine that Could?* 'I think I can. I think I can?' I want to blow it up!"
- *I'm normal/I'm different.* All of these conflicting emotions and beliefs feed into the most central conflict of the LD experience: I'm normal/I'm different. Mark has given us the most explicit example of this conflict as he talked about his unusual method of reading comprehension. Recall that he said, "I'm just a person, a normal human person." And then just a few sentences later he remarks, "I come from another planet. . . . To be normal I have to be abnormal, so I can be with the main just [sic] of society."

Masking the Conflicts

The long-term effects of living with these conflicting feelings and beliefs can be quite detrimental, and it becomes more important than ever to hide the learning disability. Sally Smith, founder and director of a school for learning disabled children in Washington D.C., has identified numerous masks LD individuals wear to hide their learning disability: the masks of supercompetence, outrageousness, helplessness, invisibility, indifference, or boredom, the masks of the victim, the good Samaritan, the clown. They are "an elaborate subterfuge that make students feel worse about themselves. The masks protect the students from being thought of as 'stupid,' but isolate them from others" (1989, p. 28).

Such masks may be first identified in children, but they continue to be worn in adolescence and adulthood. Mark's adolescent mask was "the burnout." In high school he hung out with smart but rebellious boys who took drugs and were not invested in school. Once he got into college, he adopted another mask, "the jock." Handsome and naturally athletic, he could hide well behind this mask. He swam four hours a day, a perfect reason for not doing well academically. I ask Mark if there were any other ways he covered up his LD. "Oh, yes," he says, "losing my temper, subconsciously probably, because that deflects the issue, changes everything, clouds up everything." Did he find himself thinking, "I can't let anybody know?" "Absolutely. That was constantly in my mind."

It is important for counselors and therapists not to overlook the enormous emotional cost of hiding the learning disability. Substantial amounts of energy are invested in maintaining the facade, in Mark's case, for example, studying six hours instead of three. Individuals with LD are also prone to severe anxiety because they must also be ever watchful so they won't be found out. Each new situation must be assessed for its safety or, conversely, its potential for accidentally revealing the "dark secret." Strategies must be devised in advance for covering up inadvertent slips. Continuous vigilance is exhausting and ultimately destructive, diverting energy from learning, from productivity, from personal relationships.

The effects of the incoherence that is so central to LD extend to Mark's relationships with his family, peers, and girlfriends. "My family always sensed it; they knew more than I did that I had some kind of a handicap. Just for example, phone calls coming in, or someone needs to take a message, or something along that line. They'd say, 'Oh, don't give it to Mark. We'll take it, we'll do it.' Or if there was work in the shop that had to be done quickly, something like that, I was always brushed to the side, even though I was the oldest son. My brothers were allowed to say whatever they wanted about me, and do whatever they wanted to me, because I was hanging around with the burnouts, and I got caught with marijuana. My mother allowed them to think that they were the older siblings, but really they weren't.

"But now I'm reclaiming my birthright," he says fiercely. " I've started to do this in the last three or four years, almost with a vengeance in the beginning. I didn't give this thing away for a bowl of porridge. Like my brother was getting to the point where he was feeling very insecure about what he was doing with his life and I couldn't joke with him. I had to walk on eggshells every time I was around him. So I told him I wouldn't put up with it. And for him to come back at me and call me a couple of four-letter words in front of other people! But he'd been used to treating me that way. I tried to talk to him, but his insecurities were so strong, the more I said, the more he resisted. So finally I said, 'If I can't stop you from doing that, we're going to come to grips [has he confused *come to blows* and *come to grips with*?]. It never came to a fight, because he's a nice guy, but now our relationship is stronger, because I had to establish dominancy [sic]. Not dominancy, but like wolf cubs, or bear cubs, when they're young, they wrestle, and they fight, and they play, and they figure out where the levels are."

Mark feels confident in reestablishing what he sees as his rightful relationship with his brothers because he can look back and see that he has accomplished many things that genuinely deserve the respect of his family. "I got out of college, I paid off all my bills, and now I'm back up again. I'm back, and this time I have more than I ever, ever dreamed of—character, life experiences, it's all squared away. My education's out of the way. I know I can work, earn a living. I know I can do the family business. I know I can do this corporate thing downtown. And now what I'm working on is personal relationships. It's like my biggest goal right now—to find that person to go through life with, which is one of the most important things I'll ever try. But now I'm ready to do that, in a mature stance. Ten years ago, coming out of my jock phase, as a kid hiding under all these facades, I wasn't ready. I'm sort of questing in a way, in an orderly manner, a good manner about it. And that's my nirvana, it's coming all together."

But social relationships do not come easily, in spite of his outgoing charm. "The insecurities that come from the learning disability are tremendous. It's like I'm 20 or 21. I'm actually 28 years old, but I feel like I'm 21 in my thinking, in my ways, even in my personal relationships. It's kind of like a fountain of youth almost for me. I go out with girls that are eight or nine years younger than I am. They think it's really kind of unique, and I'm very open with them. You know, the 28-year-old girls, the 27-year-old girls, I can't get along with them. I'm just discovering all these things in life, and they've already been through the wringer. Most of these girls have had boyfriends since they were 14. I didn't even have a girlfriend until I was 24. I was out on the lake waterskiing, hunting turtles, fishing. After that, for the next couple of years, I was too busy studying and doing all these other things. And now all of a sudden it's relationships. That's my next thing I've got to do. But the maturity's coming. I can feel it coming now. People have even mentioned that to me."

Revealing one's learning disability is another aspect of the conflict of living with LD that interferes with social relationships. "Now it's one of the first things I tell people when I meet them. After I feel comfortable in a conversation I'll say, 'Yeah, I got a little problem there. I got a learning disability.' You know, you just get it out right away, man. Don't hide that stuff. I was always insecure about the fact that I had this thing that I didn't understand. Now, either they're going to accept it or they're not going to accept it. I don't care. But before, it did matter. I don't know if it was vanity or what. I can't really put my finger on it. I think the peer pressure and things like that are too much."

Unresolved Conflicts

As forthright as Mark wants to be about his LD, there are still some remaining areas of conflicting feelings and beliefs; incoherence within the self remains. For example, he says, "I don't want to back off. I don't want to back off and really ask for help. I like to think there's nothing I can't do, and so I don't want to ask for help. But sometimes I need to. But then I get scared."

Another area of remaining conflict is his belief, on the one hand, that he simply has to live with the LD, but on the other, that it's important to try to fix it. "I'm at the point where if I lose this job or move on, I'm buying my own computer. Then I won't have to write things down and take the chance of making an error. I'm not going to try to fix this problem." But as he continues to talk about future plans, he unconsciously shifts ground, saying, "I mean, I'd like to go back and get a little work on my spelling, because I didn't work on that when I had the opportunity in college."

Mark is both resigned to being "alien" and absolutely convinced he can "fix" his LD, which he says is "nothing." He knows he needs to understand his limitations, but in him is also an upbeat, cocky optimism, a sense that he is willing to—even *needs* to—prove he can take on any challenge. He is convinced that whatever he does, some essential social structures will have to be in place, owing to his learning disability and his unique way of thinking and learning. "I know I have to be with food-for-thought-type people. Otherwise I'll go nuts, because I'm like a chameleon. You put me in the wrong situation, with the mediocrity people who are not thinkers, I'll start to shrivel up. I'm like a raisin." He is also aware that his career must be coordinated with his strengths in social skills and also in analytical thinking. "That's where I could thrive, because my learning disability has caused me to concentrate on logistics all my life. Putting the whole puzzle together, the breaking down of everything, building it back up. I'm good at analysis and logistics. The more complex something is, the more simple it is for me. The more simple, the more complex. That's how it works with me. *That's a paradox.*"

Psychotherapeutic Commentary

Just as the singular term "dyslexia" actually refers to a multiplicity of conditions—disorders of decoding of written language, comprehension of written language, expressive speech, writing, auditory processing, comprehension of spoken language, etc.—the singular term "personality" should be understood to refer to the multiplicity of states and processes of self. It is the combination of temperament and training, nature and nurture, time of day and time of life, that makes us who we are at any given time. In psychotherapy sessions the states of personality of the two participants can be seen parading by one after another, if we look for them—sometimes interacting, sometimes following their own agendas. Indeed, this can be seen in any setting when one attempts to look beneath the surface at what is happening inside the people participating in the events. Thus, what goes on within and between persons—personality and relationship—is actually like a group process.

The study of personality has been hampered by the need for objectivity in psychological research. Reducing personality to what could be objectively studied, such as by tests composed of multiple choice questions, solves some research problems at the expense of removing the most interesting and important aspects of what one is trying to learn about. It is as if one were trying to study animals but could only count the number of feet they have. Since cows, elephants, wolves, and tigers all have four feet, one could reasonably conclude that they are the same.

Psychoanalytic therapists have been free to study personality without such constraints, and the best of them have done a great deal of good work. However, their findings are clouded by the subjectivity of the reporters and their need to either cast their findings in Freudian terminology or else invent a new terminology to express them, so that the turf wars within psychoanalysis, which are legendary, continue unabated.

The psychotherapeutic treatment of each client is in part a study of his personality. A great deal can be learned if we look simply, openly, and deeply, and try to keep our own subjectivity (as therapists) out of it as much as possible. One of the most satisfying aspects of psychotherapy for me is forming a partnership with my client in the study of his personality. This therapeutic alliance is inevitably gratifying and healing for the client. It results in bringing to conscious awareness previously unconscious processes and creates possibilities of choice in the client's emotional and behavioral life where previously little or none existed.

How can a therapist proceed with such an investigation, and how can she engage a learning disabled client like Mark in the process? Reading Mark's comments, one is impressed with his production of analogies and metaphors, which are both frequent and rich in quality. Since one of the most important tools in the study of personality is metaphor—indeed, personality itself operates in part on a metaphoric basis—we see here a way to connect with Mark and invite him to go on a psychotherapeutic journey of discovery and maturation of self.

Metaphor in Personality and Psychotherapy

The essence of metaphor is that one thing stands for, represents, or provides a similitude of another. *Merriam-Webster's Collegiate Dictionary, Tenth Edition* (1996) defines metaphor as "a figure of speech in which a word or phrase literally denoting one kind of object or idea is used in place of another to suggest a likeness or analogy between them (as in 'drowning in money')." Metaphor, usually encountered as a concept in language, is now becoming understood by cognitive scientists and psychotherapists as the basis of the way the mind recognizes situations, events, and processes. Different organizations of self cohere or are grouped around metaphors, and perception itself is largely a metaphoric process. Thus, metaphor is a basic form of thought and can occur in nonverbal as well as verbal thought.

Incidentally, this is one reason why stories (or at least some stories) are so attractive: They express as well as engage a basic function of mind. In the best stories, such as the story of the lion who saw his reflection in the water, words form images that stand for experiences that people have (Shah, 1998).[2] The fact that this tale comes from an ancient tradition of human development suggests that the emerging modern concept of the metaphoric operation of mind has been known to at least some people since ancient times. And stories can be of much use in mental healing within and outside of psychotherapy (Williams, 1998).

Psychoanalyst Arnold Modell discussed the metaphoric function of mind at a conference on Psychoanalysis, Neurobiology, and Therapeutic Change in Chicago in March, 1998. He considered metaphor not just a form of language, but also a form of operation of mind: "Metaphor is not just a figure of speech. Metaphor is a basic and primary element of thought, the process through which meaning is transferred to different domains, and thus transformed. Analogy is the first step, but metaphor is like a template by which we parse familiar experience onto [what is] unfamiliar."

Thus, Modell shows us how metaphoric thought enables us to move from situations and environments we know into those we don't. The essence of metaphor is that one thing stands for another. Since both verbal information and nonverbal perceptions can stand for, represent, or invoke other experiences, the metaphoric operation of mind can take place either way.

Modell discussed two types of cognitive metaphors: "frozen" metaphor and "fluid" metaphor. "Frozen" metaphors are "primitive and unambiguous." They can be caused by "intense emotional experiences," which act as "templates" that are then "involuntarily projected onto the current environment." "Fluid metaphors" are "ambiguous and involve the self in imaginative ways, leading to new ways of experiencing the world." "Frozen metaphors" are often at the basis of emotional illness, causing us to react to ordinary situations in the present as if they were traumatic situations from our past. "Fluid metaphors" are healthy and adaptive. This has crucial implications for understanding psychotherapy: "The transformation of frozen into fluid metaphors is what treatment is all about."

There is a clue here as to what is effective in psychoanalytically oriented psychotherapy. It isn't that the study of formative experiences reveals dark secrets about buried events and urges, the avoidance of which has determined our lives, as Freud and others supposed. Rather, the study of formative experiences discloses the patterns of interpretation—the metaphoric templates—we continue to use to make sense of what happened to us, even after their usefulness has passed. Thus, psychotherapy provides the opportunity to become aware of these old patterns and consciously adapt them to conditions of our lives today.

The abundant contradictions and lack of coherence in Mark's descriptions of himself become more comprehensible when looked at in terms of a self as a process involving multiple metaphors, some of the most important of which are essentially "frozen." When he says, "You can be and you can't be," he means, among other things, that you can exist as a competent person and an incompetent person simultaneously. This means that Mark can never experience himself as a competent person without simultaneously experiencing himself as impaired. That this is a conflict within his self or identity is clear by his minimizing of his problem ("Hey, I've got this problem. It's no big deal"), and exaggeratedly bragging about his abilities ("I can . . . do stuff you probably can't even think about"), while the clear import of his comments is that his learning disabilities have been of such magnitude in his life that they have largely determined the quality of it.

The experience of feeling as if he were lying "naked under the desk" has become a "frozen metaphor" for Mark, one which is evoked many times each day. As a child, he coped with it by "hiding," and he used several strategies to accomplish this, including not having a social life, cheating in school, and working twice as hard at schoolwork so that it would not only be correct in content but look correct in form. By the time of his interview with Carol, he was trying to be more authentically himself—trying not to "hide"—but he still feels "naked" about his learning disability. Psychologically, he doesn't appear to have much sense of self or perspective on who he really is, beyond the endless struggle to cope. Now that he is out of school, he seems to be rather compulsively trying to substitute competence for weakness in every life domain. So his identity seems still to be driven by frozen metaphors of painful failure that he is trying to cope with by establishing mastery.

From the interview data, it would appear that Mark is not dealing with these issues in psychotherapy or any other way. Instead he is trying to conquer his profound sense of alienation ("Like I come from another planet . . . I'm just as smart as them, but I'm not one of them") by becoming a master of various skills, but it won't work. Mark already knows that he's smart, but his achievements don't take away the feeling of always being on the edge of failure. In psychotherapy, Mark would be invited to explore how his formative experiences have come to determine the ways in which he sees himself and experiences his relationships. The combination of a deeper experience of self and a more objective perception of self would lead to the identification of oneself as fundamentally human, like everyone else, but with a personal, unique pattern of strengths and weaknesses. Thus, if psychotherapy were effective, it would help Mark both to be more comfortable within himself and to see himself as one among humanity instead of, as now, a man defined by his deficiencies, struggling to overcome them with skills.

Personal Constructs

Mark's conflicting, paradoxical feelings about, and perceptions of, himself show a number of ways in which he feels that he is either up or down about something: for example, "I'm proud of myself/I'm ashamed." These paradoxical positions recall George Kelly's idea of "personal constructs," in which personal issues are defined within the personality by their opposite poles, one of which the person tries to identify with and the other to reject (Kelly, 1963). Given these choices, it is easy to see why Mark would try to select the more positive side of the construct, the one that would result in his feeling better about himself. This may temporarily lead to more self-confidence, but it isn't likely to be very deeply rooted, since the self-deprecating side of the construct is always there, ready to be evoked by any experience of awkwardness or failure. No matter how proud of himself Mark tries to be, he can feel deeply ashamed of himself in a heartbeat, because each side of the construct is as attached to the other as are the two sides of a coin. Note that neither side of the construct passes the reality test: Mark is neither the superstar he strives to be nor the idiot he fears he is. Psychotherapy would try to replace this dichotomized experience of self with a more balanced sense of self, based on who Mark really is—sometimes better and sometimes worse, but never really superstar or idiot. Such a sense of self is more stable, liberated from the ups and downs of being on one side of the construct or the other. It provides a more secure platform, so to speak, from which to reach out into life to seek one's goals.

It looks like Mark is trying to increase his self-esteem by increasing his sense of mastery, but that won't really address the problem of his feeling of nakedness and his lack of a place of his own among humanity. In psychotherapy, he could look at the different ways in which his sense of self and world was frozen in painful early experiences and observe how readily those early experiences and perceptions are evoked by current situations.

In psychotherapy with persons with learning disabilities the role of literacy and, more broadly, the kinds of cognition underlying academic success in defining human adequacy are often addressed, either directly or as a subtext to therapeutic conversation. It isn't unusual for persons with learning disabilities to feel as if they are members of some sort of subhuman species compared with those who have no such problems in school. Yet there are real questions in both the scientific and artistic communities about the adequacy of school learning to express the full range of human nature and potential.

Literacy and Evolution

In 1977, Joseph Bogen, the neurosurgeon who conducted the "split-brain" surgery on severe epileptics that led to so much information about the characteristics of the two hemispheres, spoke in a symposium in Chicago organized by the Institute for the Study of Human Knowledge. He discussed research findings on the specialization of the two cerebral hemispheres in humans for different forms of information-processing (Bogen, 1969). During the question period after his talk, he was asked about the implications of the new knowledge about the human brain for literacy. His reply startled me and has provided food for thought ever since.

What he said was this: Every behavior associated with survival during human evolution has been adapted into the brain. By the time he or she reaches five years of age, every child (except the most severely disabled) learns to talk, to understand speech, to walk, and so on; that is, almost 100% of children learn to do these things, which have been acquired as biological characteristics through evolution. Reading, however, has not been necessary for biological survival; indeed, it has only been available to most people to learn for a few centuries. Therefore, there is no biological reason to expect that everyone should be able to read; 100% literacy would not make biological sense in the context of human evolution. Rather, one would expect that a characteristic such as literacy, which is useful but hasn't been selectively adapted through evolution, would be distributed in the population like any other characteristic that has some but not universal usefulness.[3]

Mark's learning disabilities extend beyond literacy, since his malapropisms are in oral speech, and he may have sequencing or other issues that remain undiagnosed. We leave him, in this chapter, fighting to overcome his deficits through sheer talent and force of will, without an impression of how he will find his way to a more harmonious personal and social existence. In psychotherapy—emotional healing through conversation within a particular kind of relationship—if it went well, Mark's metaphors would be acknowledged and made conscious, so they could become less "frozen," more "fluid," and his experience could open up to include more of the variety that life has to offer. Various parts of his personality would be verified, some enhanced, and all more usefully organized: each too true to be discarded, too incomplete to be running the show, and too dominated by obsolete perceptual metaphors to be able to respond to the opportunities and challenges of today and tomorrow.

CHAPTER 4

The Rebel without a Clue
LD, Adult Life, and Self-Esteem

*Over the phone, the disembodied voice spits out detailed direc-
tions to some destination, but the words slough off without
sticking, like arrows flung at an armored tank. What did they
say, what did I read, what do I do now? You see expectant
looks across the table, you are supposed to do something, say
something. Won't somebody give me a script to this drama
called life? Why does everybody know their lines except me?
. . . Like the James Dean movie, "Rebel without a Cause," just
call me Rebel without a Clue!*

—Jimmie Shreve

"I've been reading a few books lately on learning disabilities in
adults," remarks Kerry. "I've been learning some things about
myself that I didn't know. I've read about how things that happened
in your childhood are still unresolved and how people with LD will
probably need counseling. I've been reading about LD diagnosis in
order to get to know myself. And it's scary! Learning about yourself
is scary. But just knowing I'm not the only one with these problems
is helpful."

Kerry Turner has been reading about learning disabilities in her
role as leader of a local self-help support group for adults with
learning disabilities. Her active participation in this support group
is typical of her approach to life. Petite and energetic, with a cap of
dark curls and an elfin face, Kerry has been interested in learning
about LD for quite some time, not only to find out as much as possible about her own situation, but also to do what she can to educate

the public. Even in high school she was involved in a peer-counseling group for other students with LD. Reflecting on that time, she muses, "Senior year in high school was the first time that I *really* understood that I was learning disabled. My mom got me involved in a learning disabilities support group for teenagers. They taught me about LD and they took me out public speaking and that's how I learned about my own learning disability." In college she traveled to special high school "college nights" for students with disabilities and, along with official representatives of various colleges, spoke to high school students with disabilities about what it was like to be in college and how she coped with her LD.

Kerry graduated from college six years ago and has held several jobs in the social services field, though none for very long. She is currently a vocational rehabilitation specialist with a private social service agency, teaching vocational and adaptive skills to clients with various physical and mental disabilities. "My caseload is 18 at the moment. I supervise my clients, do staffings, write up my observations, do their payroll, and run sessions like how to get a job, grooming, hygiene, and the basic independent living skills."

From this brief portrait it would appear that Kerry is a successful young adult, on her way to a productive, fulfilling future. But as we get to know Kerry, a different picture will emerge, and ironically, many of the vocational skills that she teaches her clients at the rehabilitation center involve the very issues that she struggles with on a daily basis and that make her life so difficult. Although Kerry is intelligent and hardworking, her learning disability has had a major impact on her education and her career. She is in constant danger of losing her job not only because she annoys her supervisors and coworkers, but also because her learning disabilities affect the quality of her work. Her social life is unsatisfying, as are her relationships with her colleagues at the rehabilitation center.

"At work," says Kerry, "I do not fit in. I don't understand some of the things my coworkers are saying. I don't catch some of the things they are talking about. And they want to know about my personal life, but they won't tell me about theirs. Whenever I ask people to go out for lunch, it's like 'forget it,'" she sighs. "They end up going out to lunch with the other guys. I'm never invited." Kerry's self-esteem suffers frequently. She looks defeated, and at the same time a plaintive tone colors her voice. "I don't get it. What am I doing wrong? Whenever we lose a staff member, and it's maybe just two of us women there, and the woman's really nice, and I think maybe we're becoming close friends, all of a sudden some new female comes in, and I get thrown out and the two of them become real close. It's happened a couple of times to me already."

In addition to problems of fitting in socially, and in spite of having a job coach who intermittently provides guidance and advocacy, she is frequently in trouble with her boss. She is involved in one "crisis" after another, including claims for worker's compensation for injuries on the job, and is always on the brink of being let go. "Bonnie, my supervisor, says she doesn't want to work with me," Kerry says with more than a hint of anger in her voice. "She says I don't take responsibility and she's tired of covering for me. Which is not true. I'm working hard, getting so I know how to do the job. I'm treated very unfairly. I'm constantly being yelled at."

Thanks to her intelligence and persistence, Kerry has more than adequate "book learning" and has even gotten through college, but the transition to adulthood has been rocky and prolonged. While she lives independently with a roommate, she still receives considerable support—at the age of 27—from her family. Although most people associate learning disabilities with school, follow-up studies tell us that the underlying cognitive weaknesses do not disappear with graduation; for some people with LD, adulthood presents an even greater challenge than childhood. Because people like Kerry are competent in some ways but have difficulty with what ought to be relatively simple aspects of adult life, self-esteem becomes a complex issue. The purpose of this chapter is to explore the interconnections among LD, self-esteem, and the challenges of adult living.

Longitudinal research on learning disabled children indicates that as adults the majority do maintain jobs and can support themselves (Cruickshank, Morse, & Johns, 1980; Rogan & Hartman, 1976), particularly if they have had affluent and supportive families and adequate educational experiences (Abbott & Frank, 1975; Rawson, 1968; Rogan & Hartman, 1976; Silver & Hagin, 1985). Two studies have focused on people with LD who have led successful adult lives; these investigations have shed some light on the personal qualities linked to vocational success (Gerber & Reiff, 1994; Spekman, Goldberg, & Herman, 1992). Both found that the factors distinguishing successful from unsuccessful LD adults include self-awareness, acceptance of their learning disability, goal-directedness, persistence, and the ability to seek and accept help in ways that promote independence. However, some of them, Like Kerry, find themselves caught in a cycle of vocational difficulties and decreasing self-esteem.

Kerry has a variety of cognitive processing problems, including subtle but serious problems with oral language that were evident early in life. "I wasn't talking. I just pointed to things. I had speech therapy when I was around 3 years old all the way through fifth grade." Although articulation of words is no longer a problem, Kerry's auditory processing difficulties remain. She often misunderstands instructions at work or finds that what people say to her doesn't quite make sense, although it appears to be clear to everyone else. So she frequently misses important information or annoys people with frequent requests for clarification.

She also has difficulty expressing her thoughts, has problems with word choice and ordering ideas coherently, and often trips over grammatical constructions. "At work I get told I talk like an LD. I use the wrong word for the wrong thing, and I get corrected on that. I use the wrong tense, and I don't know I'm doing it. I always have problems. I know what I want to say; it's in my mind exactly and it does not come out right. Oh God, I did one today. I needed to speak to my doctor, so I was telling the nurse on the phone what time I could be reached if Dr. B called me. I said to her 'My lunch hour, where [sic] I could be reached, is from 12:30 to 12:15.' When in reality I meant 12:30 to 1:15, but I don't know, it comes out wrong. Or I might give instructions to a client and I might have left something out. I do better demonstrating something than I do verbalizing it."

These communication problems in turn have an enormous, though subtle, affective impact. Kerry's language difficulties are interpreted by others as signs of ignorance or poor education, and consequently she feels she is treated dismissively or not taken seriously. But she points out another, even more devastating consequence of language problems which therapists need to consider quite seriously in the context of establishing a therapeutic relationship. "I think the thing I would most like people to understand is that I live with a real fear all the time—fear of being misunderstood. I never know if what I say is what I intended to say, or whether I will completely understand what others say to me. Because of my disability I never know if I can trust what I hear or say, so that means I have a great need for security, for dependability in other people."

Unfortunately, precisely because of her learning disability she alienates the very people she needs to trust and have a dependable relationship with. "I know some of the things I do don't make it easy for other people. For example, when I keep asking questions for clarification, or I keep repeating and rephrasing what other people say, it's because I don't trust *myself,* but people interpret it to mean I don't trust *them.* So the very thing I need most, security and trust, is the hardest to gain." Thus, the impact of oral language problems goes far beyond an occasional misunderstanding and can affect basic aspects of the development of the self.

In addition, Kerry is easily confused by any communication that involves a discrepancy between verbal and nonverbal messages. She may not pick up on a sarcastic tone of voice and so takes the sarcastic comment literally, and as a result appears naive or slow-witted and is frequently laughed at. Similarly, she often does not realize when someone is teasing her, because although the words may seem implausible, they are spoken with a serious, truthful expression and tone of voice. Of course, she is a natural target for teasing since she annoys other people with her own verbal ineptitude, does not understand subtle verbal humor, and is quite vulnerable. "They tease me all the time," she sighs. "Sometimes I take things seriously, and they say, 'We're just teasing, Kerry! We're just joking with you! Take it as a joke!' I mean, it's like, I'm sorry! but so often I don't 'get it.'"

Her processing difficulties involve not only oral language but also visual perception. "Last week when I had my eyes checked at the doctor's office, the F on the chart kept closing. I kept saying either it's an F or a P. If you look at it long enough, it turns into the other one, and I'm watching it dance up and down. I could see the letters clearly; they weren't fuzzy, but my mind plays tricks with what I see. Or when I go through the doorway, I don't make it all the way through. Part of my body gets hooked to it. It's perceptual."

Kerry's oral language problems combine with these visual perception problems to make reading and spelling very difficult. In college she had accommodations for testing, including extended time and a proofreader to check for inadvertent errors attributable to her perceptual or language problems. "They would check that my answer sheet was correct, that I didn't skip a line. Or with my grammar and spelling, I would first tell them exactly what I wanted to write, then I had to go write it down, and then they would check and see if what I wrote was what I said, because you'll find out I'll write differently from what I say, and also the other way around."

Even today her reading problems persist. She reflects, "I do flip words when I read, or add things. I'll add a whole line or I'll add a word that is really on the line below or above. Also I have difficulty understanding what I read because I don't know what a lot of the words mean, or I get tangled up in complex sentences." Kerry still works regularly on her reading with a tutor, but she is plagued—like many adults with LD—by the inconsistency of her skills. "One day she'll have me read and she'll be thinking, 'Why is Kerry having tutoring? She reads so beautifully.' And the next time, she'll be saying, 'My God, what happened to her? I thought she knew how to read.' I guess it depends on the wording, it depends on the book, on what you're reading, and how that day is going for you. It's really weird."

These problems have predictable results at work, where she is deeply frustrated. "To this day I have reading problems at work. Even some of my clients correct me in my reading. Last week I was at a staffing and we had a new form to use. I can write the word *initiative*, but I couldn't read it on this new form. I was just humiliated. I know it on the old form and I know it in my own handwriting which was on the other side of the paper. But there on this new form, I could not read it. Why? Don't ask me!"

Communication with her supervisors has deteriorated far beyond the occasional misunderstandings caused by Kerry's learning disability, to the point where negative reports are being placed in her employment file. Unfortunately, she has little insight into the origin of her boss's anger and criticism, which seem incomprehensible and unjustified to her. While some adults with LD have long histories of unstable employment, social isolation, substance abuse, or psychiatric problems, Kerry is tenacious and manages to hang onto her job, but the struggle is constant, the problems unrelenting, the effort monumental. Loss of a job is threatening for anyone, but for a person with LD it is particularly difficult. Kerry has cognitive problems in many areas, so finding a job that is a good fit with her unique set of strengths and weaknesses will not be easy. "You know, if I had the skills to get a new job, maybe in another field, I'd do it. But it's not that easy. For me, getting fired and trying to find *any* job is something else again because I have a learning disability. I would have to learn a whole new field, get out of social service. A new job? I don't think so. I can't work and go to school at the same time like other people can."

This is not the first time that Kerry's career has been in jeopardy. In college, her goal of becoming a teacher was thwarted by her learning disability. Several faculty members had serious reservations about her ability to work productively in a classroom. But characteristically, Kerry disagrees. "I really did very good work. It's just that certain people couldn't see me teaching. Especially this one professor tore me apart for the whole semester. And the disabled student services office didn't do a damn thing to help me," she says petulantly. "I was told I wouldn't have any extra help if I student-teached [sic]. I wouldn't have someone to correct my grammar and spelling. They told me if I tried and failed, I would get no degree at all. They got me so upset that even the dean got involved to try and help calm me down. They talked me into doing this internship and called it a non-teaching degree, and so I ended up with a general studies degree."

But Kerry is not at all convinced that she wouldn't have been a good teacher. As she sees it, her job at the rehabilitation agency is mainly a teaching job. "Gosh, if you really think of it, all the stuff I do, I can handle the teaching! Look what I'm doing now! I am running groups and writing IHP's [Individualized Habilitation Plans]. And at college they're cutting me off, saying I don't know all that stuff. So you tell me! Of course, now it's hard because my boss is very much into this perfectionist writing and everything. But in reality, I should have been able to teach." Even though she had developed her reading and spelling skills to the point where, with appropriate accommodations, she was able to function at a college level, she is in many ways still unprepared for adult life, especially at work where her job requires well-developed communication and social skills. Though she reads eagerly about learning disabilities and understands quite a bit about her own cognitive problems on an intellectual level, she does not seem ready to face how significantly her problems affect her performance on the job.

Inevitably, Kerry's deepest pain comes from the fact that virtually no one understands how hard she struggles to keep from losing that ever-so-tenuous control over her life. The very fact that she does manage, even marginally, suggests to others that she must be as capable as they are, so that her efforts are met at best with lack of appreciation and support and at worst with criticism and rejection. Like many other LD adults, she is hanging by a twig. "I do get depressed. I have a lot of anxiety and stress on me, because I run into problems *every day of my life.* I'm nervous. I just can't go to bed and fall asleep. And because of the anxiety, it's like I've been losing my mind more and more these days. I know what I want to do, but I find myself in the wrong room. Or I'm going into the freezer, but I find I've gone into the refrigerator."

For many people with LD, adulthood allows them eventually to find a niche more comfortable than the constant torture of the schoolroom. Their social and emotional health improve greatly because they can take advantage of new opportunities and focus on making the most of their strengths, instead of being criticized continuously for their inability to read or spell. But for others, "a seeming inability to understand why life continues to be a struggle creates a tragic and self-perpetuating cycle of loneliness and despair" (Reiff & Gerber, 1994, p. 72). Kerry's story helps us to look more closely at the cognitive and emotional problems that interfere with adjustment to adult life and have an impact on self-esteem. Through her story we can begin to see the powerful ripple effect of LD on the domains of (1) social and interpersonal relations, i.e., *social issues,* (2) satisfying and successful employment, i.e., *vocational issues,* and (3) the day-to-day world of *daily living issues.*

Development of Social Skills

Social skills development is a complex process, and having a learning disability can interfere with this development in several tightly interwoven ways. When working with patients with LD, therapists may need to consider external, environmental factors that influence social skills development, i.e., the responses of others to the learning disabled person. It is also important to consider internal, emotional, and cognitive factors, i.e., the learning disability itself and the client's responses to it (Reiff & Gerber, 1994).

Environmental Factors

For some learning disabled individuals, in the words of Jean-Paul Sartre, "Hell is other people." The negative perceptions of other people limit the development of social skills because critical attitudes decrease opportunities to learn socially appropriate behaviors. These environmental limitations include

- the effect of the very label "learning disability,"
- rejection by normal peers, with in consequence,
- a restricted peer group consisting mainly of others with disabilities, as well as
- perceptions of social incompetence, which result in self-fulfilling prophecies (Reiff & Gerber, pp. 74–75).

Kerry has experienced many of these environmental limitations, particularly rejection by peers, which no doubt played a part in her delayed social development. Thinking back to her childhood, she reflects, "When I was growing up I always had problems. People who I became friends with became enemies. Or they played as though we were friends, and then teased me, and all that."

Emotional Factors

Just as these external factors affect acquisition of social skills, what Reiff and Gerber call "emotional baggage" can also have a marked negative impact. They list a number of possible negative emotions related to learning disabilities that can interfere with social development:

- feelings of frustration and exasperation at performance demands
- feelings of bitterness about treatment received in school
- feelings of incompetence and lowered self-worth
- feelings of being stupid, expressed in a spectrum of emotions ranging from anger to depression to challenge
- a "psychological backlash" in which those who think they must be stupid seek the company of "dummies" and "losers," which then undermines social relationships.

Undoubtedly, therapists who work with clients with learning disabilities could add many more negative emotions to this list. Addressing the unresolved emotional baggage carried from childhood will need to be a major focus in therapy with many adults with LD.

Kerry continues to experience feelings of frustration and exasperation about performance demands on the job and bitterness about treatment she has received. She also acknowledges feelings of social incompetence and lowered self-esteem. For example, she is afraid she will look stupid when she is in the company of other adults who are not disabled, and she is afraid she will be rejected because she has LD. "If I try to forget that I'm LD, things are better for me. If I remember I'm LD, it's harder. It's like, I'm holding my mouth with my finger in it [sic], and I won't say anything. Anything I do will seem LD-ish. When you're out in society with no other LD's, and the people are not at your level, then there's a problem. And that's where socialization becomes difficult."

Kerry is generally reluctant to get close to her friends, not only because she fears that she'll do something wrong that will destroy the relationship, but also to protect herself from anticipated rejection and separation. "I've let myself get closer with my friends who are also LD, but when I become close to somebody, then I get rejected, whether because they're busy, or they move away, or someone at work takes a maternity leave. I take that as a rejection, and it's hard for me to deal with the separation."

Cognitive Factors

Although environmental and emotional factors may account for the social skills problems faced by some adults with LD, they do not completely explain why social skills deficits are so pervasive. Thus we must consider a third factor, namely cognitive deficits. By their very nature specific problems in processing information can have a primary effect on social skills development, and for this reason they are especially important in the present context. Reif and Gerber (1994) list a small body of research that has identified various primary cognitive difficulties that directly affect social skills development. These include:

- the inability to make central inferences in social settings (Gerber, 1978)
- less sensitivity to others' thoughts and feelings (Garber, 1989)
- poor judgment of others' moods and attitudes (Lerner, 1993)
- doing or saying inappropriate things (Lerner, 1993)
- problems comprehending humor (Pickering, Pickering, & Buchanan, 1987)
- problems discriminating response requirements in social situations (Larson & Gerber, 1987).

Kerry exhibits a number of these difficulties: She says inappropriate things and has problems comprehending humor as well as sarcasm and teasing. She also frequently has difficulty judging others' moods and attitudes and knowing how to react in social situations. For example, in college during a peer tutoring session, Kerry failed to pick up on the other student's frustration before it boiled over and didn't know how to handle the situation once it did. "She started telling me that what we were reviewing was simple, and that I should have known this already. She started calling me 'dummy' and 'retard' and she started pointing her finger at me. She put it in my mouth! I told her to get my finger out of my mouth and she refused, so I kind of took my teeth, but I didn't bite down on her, I just kind of touched it. I mean, you don't put your hand in someone's mouth! And so she smashed me in my face. I had all the problems in the world."

Kerry's cognitive problems affect social development in other, less direct ways as well. For example, as a college student she found that self-imposed isolation was essential for studying, but this isolation provided few opportunities to develop appropriate adult-level social skills. "People who wanted to go out with me even on the weekends had to drag me away from my books because classes were so hard. I went out with my head in the book. When I lived off campus I hibernated in the library. I had to do it to stay out of the noise."[1]

In Kerry's case, then, environmental, emotional, and cognitive factors, all of which are related to her learning disability, have had a substantial cumulative effect. But this is not the whole story. Because Kerry is quite vulnerable emotionally she has become a scapegoat. Many of her problems are truly not her fault, at least initially, but a pattern of victimization and blaming developed early in life and has now become entrenched. To begin to understand this complex phenomenon we need to explore why she is so vulnerable. As her story unfolds, we see the dynamic interaction between primary emotional issues and learning disabilities.

Kerry's initial vulnerability can be explained, in part, in affective terms, since her mother died shortly after she was born. "When I wasn't even eight months old, my Mom died of cancer. Then my father remarried, but the marriage only lasted for I think a year. She had my little brother, Ryan, but they got divorced. I guess I was three. I was real close to my father, and he was wanting a mother for me, I guess, so he got married again when I was going into second grade. They had two kids from that marriage, so I have one half-brother and two half-sisters and that mother is still with me today." At the age of eight, Kerry remembers, she was still working through these issues of loss. She reflects, "I remember in third grade my teacher had me announce to everybody that my mommy died. I was finally getting to a point where it really hit me. I could admit to it." Dealing with death and divorce is certainly difficult for any child, and for Kerry the unstable family relationships, as well as the grief of loss, undoubtedly play a major role in her insecurity and vulnerability.

Fortunately, Kerry has a strong relationship with her current stepmother. "Even though I really wasn't her kid, just through marriage, she became my mother. She's the only mother I really know. And it took me a long time emotionally to accept her as my mother. She's not my mother who gave birth to me, but she is my mother. Adjusting was hard. So probably some of my emotional problems come from that."

Kerry's therapist would surely want to address issues of loss and grief at appropriate times during therapy, but the situation is even more complex because we also need to consider the developmental consequences of her learning disabilities. Early auditory processing and oral communication difficulties made the world an unpredictable, incomprehensible place for her. As a preschooler, her oral language problems and additional visual processing problems made it difficult for her to pick up social cues, participate easily in the social activities of young children, and learn such basic social skills as how to make friends. Now, as an adult, her frequent requests for repetition and clarification are incorrectly interpreted by others as signs of mistrust on her part, thus undermining interpersonal relationships and increasing her insecurity all the more.

As early as first and second grade, Kerry's difficulty making friends and her humiliating experiences with schoolwork made her the target of frequent teasing. "I used to get called names. Dummy . . . retard . . . frowny . . . smelly . . . that's all I can remember, but they used to call me a lot of names. Sticks and stones, you know, that kind of situation. Sometimes I would say that. But mostly I would cry, or fight them, or go tattle on people. I did different things. It was hard to ignore them. It was very easy for me to be picked on, teased on, be the scapegoat, because people caught on."

Kerry's early history of family instability and grief undoubtedly created within her immense insecurity and a predisposition to vulnerability that then led to the kind of defensive reactions that only encouraged more teasing. But her learning disabilities added immeasurably to this insecurity; in fact, for many children a learning disability is enough in and of itself to create the level of insecurity and vulnerability that Kerry exhibits. To a young child with LD, who is unable to make friends because of communication problems and unable to learn to read when it seems so easy for everyone else, the world is a bewildering, unpredictable, humiliating place. The teacher's impatience and the other children's laughter seem inexplicable when a child is trying hard to please and doing the best she can.

And things get even worse for Kerry. "In sixth grade, I even had somebody put a dog's leash on me. A dog's leash! I ran into the teacher's room with the dog leash still on. I first started getting in trouble for it, but finally I told the teacher that they put it on me and she really got mad. I got let go of it and these guys got into trouble for it. Matter of fact, these guys who did it, one of them was from special ed, so I got picked on that way too."

By the time Kerry entered high school, her learning disability and accompanying reading problems created many occasions for a continuing cycle of victimization and defensive reactions. "I remember in U.S. History class, we had to go around the room and read a paragraph each. OK, I did that, I did what we were supposed to. But then when the teacher the next day asked for volunteers everybody volunteered *me,* and started laughing. I cried." Kerry's eyes fill up with tears as she remembers the humiliation of that day. "I should have ran out [sic] but I didn't." For Kerry, learning disabilities combine with issues of loss and vulnerability to impede development of social skills.

Some people with LD have intact social skills but suffer greatly from having to cope with their disability. Others have more success dealing with their disability but have difficulty developing adequate social skills. Still others, like Kerry, may have significant difficulty in both areas. Reiff and Gerber conclude that "environments range from nurturing to destructive, with the potential to ameliorate or exacerbate inherent social difficulties. No matter what combination of circumstances has led to social/emotional problems, interpersonal failings in childhood may have deleterious consequences in adulthood" (1994, p. 75).

Development of Vocational Skills

People with learning disabilities encounter many roadblocks when they seek employment. During the hiring process, they are intimidated by written tests of basic skills and are faced with the dilemma of whether or not to disclose the fact of their learning disability. Keeping a job is even more of a challenge because employers typically have little understanding of LD. For example, a new employee with LD who is assigned to two weeks of job training may need assistance in reading training manuals or other large amounts of printed material, but job trainers often meet such requests with skepticism ("She's just lazy") or outright hostility ("I don't need this! He's going to be a liability right from the start"). Similarly, someone with memory or organization problems may find it helpful to come to work 15 minutes early in order to have a few quiet minutes to get ready for the day. However, such behavior is often misinterpreted as being aggressively competitive, or the employee may be criticized and penalized for trying to earn unauthorized overtime. Those who request specific accommodations often find that, although supervisors agree to them in principle, they often don't understand LD well enough to follow through effectively.

Even success and promotions are fraught with hazards. Successful employees with LD often find that the only reward for success is promotion to a different type of job, one which may not be appropriate given their particular set of cognitive strengths and weaknesses. Thus, there are many virtually unavoidable pitfalls in a system that is driven by market forces and has very little understanding of the needs or problems of those with disabilities. However, some problems on the job are created by the learning disability itself. Here again, Kerry's story is revealing.

Mismatch Between the Person and the Demands of the Job

In many cases, people with LD do not have a clear or realistic notion of their own processing strengths and weaknesses, and thus either overestimate or underestimate their ability to perform a particular job. In Kerry's case, her level of oral and written communication skills is not well matched with the demands of a job that requires appropriate communication between her and her disabled clients, her supervisors, and other social service agency personnel. "My boss will tear me apart, rewrite my whole staffing report. He'll put in words I might not even know. I mean, talk about being discouraged. He really discourages me tremendously."

Poor Relationships with
Supervisors and Coworkers

More job-related difficulties are probably caused by underlying problems with social skills than by academic deficiencies or vocational incompetence (Reiff & Gerber, 1994). Coworkers and supervisors are often willing to accommodate the learning disability of a person who is well-liked, but the opposite is rarely true. In Kerry's case, teasing and tattling still form the basis of many of her interactions at work. She relates how a coworker pulled a chair from underneath her. Then, ever the scapegoat, she reacted by tattling. "I went to Nancy, my supervisor, and told her what happened. But you know Nancy. Sarah and Nancy try to run the whole floor. They're good friends. And I'm left out all the time." Kerry concludes she is being discriminated against because of her disability. "The problem was that they learned I was LD, and they had problems dealing with me because they have 'LD' in the back of their minds." Clients with LD often need to understand their own behavior better and learn to separate social skills problems from accompanying emotional reactions.

Poor Job Performance Due to
Loss of Control and Confidence

It is hardly surprising that performance difficulty at work leads to an anxious feeling of loss of control over one's environment. In their study of successful adults with LD, Gerber and Reiff (1994) found that the need for control, here understood as the drive and ability to manage one's life, was the dominant issue in all their subjects' efforts to be successful. Less successful adults with LD often do not understand the nature of their learning disability or how it affects them at work. Some do not perceive the difficulties they are now having at work as being related to their previous problems in school. Consequently, they are utterly unprepared to deal with the difficulties they experience at work. Their vital sense of control slips away and is replaced by a cycle of loss of control, loss of self-esteem, and depression. (See the discussion of Stephen in Chapter 1.)

Difficulty with Accommodations, Advocacy, and Asking for Help

People with LD often have difficulty gaining control of their work because they are caught in the dilemma of how to function when self-esteem demands independence but the learning disability demands assistance. They still harbor great fear that they are stupid and believe that admitting any kind of weakness will only prove that fear to be true. They feel that asking for accommodations means not only revealing their disability (a secret they have been trying to hide for years) but also diminishing their independence. Of course not all people with LD need assistance at work. However, for those who do but don't receive it, control slips away or is impossible to establish. They may need to learn to reconceptualize the use of support not as an ego-diminishing crutch but rather as a means of efficient functioning, a way not to waste time struggling with things that are distracting and nonessential.

As if these emotional barriers to asking for help were not enough, pragmatic considerations are important as well. Realistically, there is no guarantee in most work settings that requests for accommodations will be received with appropriate understanding. More likely they will be met with outright rejection, incomprehension, or suspicion that the person is trying to get away with something.

Even if they have become comfortable with the notion of asking for and accepting assistance, many people with LD have difficulty knowing what accommodations to ask for. They may be unclear about the specific nature of their learning disability, and thus have difficulty predicting how the disability will affect them at work. Brown and Gerber (1994) provide a very useful discussion of accommodations in the workplace, indicating the types of assistance that are appropriate for specific types of LD (see also Brown, Gerber, & Dowdy, 1990).

Much of the frustration encountered by the learning disabled employee is caused by a system that is largely unaware of and unwilling to deal with the needs of the learning disabled. To be successful, adults must understand their learning disability well enough to seek out a job that does not put too much stress on their areas of weakness. However, when people with LD are not realistic about their own abilities and/or bring fear, anger, and mistrust with them to a workplace that is largely insensitive to their situation, the prognosis for a successful vocational outcome is not encouraging. Counselors can assist clients to understand how their imperfect social skills and/or emotional baggage undermine their ability to succeed on the job.

Development of Daily Living Skills

In addition to causing significant problems at work, LD makes everyday life much more difficult.[2] As Johnson and Blalock (1987) suggest, all learning disabilities interfere to some extent with daily living, independence, and social maturity. Even people with isolated reading or spelling problems may have some difficulty with daily living skills, for example, using alphabetized references such as phone books or encyclopedias. However, nonverbal learning disabilities typically have an even greater impact on daily life. Nonverbal processing problems involve early developmental deficits in visual-spatial and temporal abilities, as well as visual-motor coordination. According to Rourke (1989), such difficulties in turn affect hypothesis testing, organization, problem-solving, and adapting to novel situations.

The impact of both verbal and nonverbal deficits on skills of everyday living can be persistent and debilitating. Adults with LD may have problems writing and remembering addresses and phone numbers, taking public transportation, writing thank-you notes, signing personal checks, calculating tips and the price of sale items, doubling or reducing recipes, and using devices such as thermometers, gauges, and rulers. They may have difficulty setting alarm clocks, tying neckties, opening cardboard milk or juice cartons, folding paper in thirds to fit in an envelope, hanging pictures, putting things on clothes hangers, packing boxes, wrapping packages, and arranging books on a shelf. They may have problems coordinating color and style of clothing ensembles, reading maps, and scheduling appointments (Johnson & Blalock, 1987; Reiff & Gerber, 1994). Many with nonverbal LD have difficulty learning to drive. Problems with planning and problem-solving make it difficult to negotiate our complex social bureaucracy—the telephone company, the IRS, the social welfare and health care systems.[3]

Anxiety and fear accompany these daily difficulties. As Jimmie Shreve (1993), a civil engineer with LD, writes,

> Thoughts, words, names, pictures, sounds all swirl round in your head, randomly appearing and disappearing. You walk into a room, and then you cannot remember why you came in. Reading a book, your eyes scan the lines of black ants without comprehension. Your eyes drop to the bottom of the page like a lead weight sinking to the bottom of a lake. And you have no idea what you have just read. Over the phone, the disembodied voice spits out detailed directions to some destination, but the words slough off without sticking, like arrows flung at an armored tank. What did they say, what did I read, what do I do now? You see expectant looks across the table, you are supposed to do something, say something. Won't somebody give me a script to this drama called life? Why does everybody know their lines except me? . . . Like the James Dean movie, *Rebel without a Cause,* just call me "Rebel without a Clue!" (pp. 20–21)

Kerry agrees. "I don't get it. I'm working hard. I'm trying my best. But they don't see it. And it's even worse! My boss uses all this high-tech vocabulary. I get so frustrated. All these words!" Shreve dedicates his book to "all those that come after me who are just trying to be themselves and struggle to understand why the world won't cooperate" (p. 3). He goes on to discuss how even the simplest everyday event creates inordinate amounts of fear and anxiety.

> The presence of fear is never ending. When you are responding to a conversation in a zombie-like fashion with "neutral comments" of "I see," "OK," and so on, with the speaker's words tumbling through your head without comprehension to be immediately forgotten, the fear is that you will be caught. . . . There is the fear of being out of control. Of being pulled into a situation where your coping skills, learned through years of "faking it," will not be adequate to let you respond to the avalanche of sights and sounds and social innuendoes. There is the fear of being shunned. That those around you would not work

with you, play with you, be with you, if they knew that you were not "normal," that you cannot do it the way they do, have to do it another way. But the worst fear of all, the terrifying fear is that "they" are right. That when "they" say that you are lazy, stupid, or crazy they are correct. That when "they" say that "you can just do it" and that "you aren't trying hard enough," they have been right all along. (p. 21)

Likening himself to a square peg in a world of round holes, Shreve asks whether there are really any square holes out there and then answers his own question. "Yes, there are if you make them. To make a square hole that will fit your corners you have two choices. You can create your own hole, work for yourself under your own conditions. Or you can work at chipping away at a round hole to make it square, winning some as you break chunks off the circle's edge, losing some as a part of your square edges are chipped and damaged" (p. 437). "Working at creating a square hole can feel like the work of Sisyphus. It is exhausting to continually have to chip away at the circle, and painful when your own sides are chipped and damaged. And why, LD folks ask with increasing rage, am *I* forced to make square holes in the first place? After all, I am the one with the disability!" (p. 438).

But there is a third possibility that Shreve doesn't mention: In the course of trying to make square holes, the person with LD may simply get ground down. Those who are rubbed raw in the process of creating square holes often get caught in a downward spiral of loss of control, lowered self-esteem, and despair. When they seek treatment because the chipping and damaging are too painful, therapists and counselors can have a greater impact if they understand how people with LD have reached this state of affairs.

Psychotherapeutic Commentary

It is very difficult to establish and maintain a therapeutic alliance with a client in deep denial, but that is what Kerry's therapist would have to try to do. The therapeutic alliance is the relationship within which the therapist supports the client in her efforts to cope more effectively with the opportunities and challenges of her life. To cope more effectively the client must be motivated to become more realistic—at least in some ways—in her assessment of life and her relationship with it. But this is exactly what Kerry seems to want not to do. Instead, she seems determined to impose her own wishes about the kind of life she wants onto a situation that she may not really be able to succeed in.

Denial has its causes, its roots. Kerry may be one of these people with peaks of intelligence among valleys of learning disability. She may be struggling to find a way to express her intelligence, but if so, she may have chosen unwisely. She may be trying to make her parents proud of her and to avoid disappointing them. She may have come to see self-esteem as an end in itself rather than a means to an end. Kerry's denial may have various and intertwined roots, and it may take quite an extensive psychotherapeutic relationship to help her to acknowledge the realities of her life and take positive steps to put it on a more successful footing.

It appears that Kerry has chosen a career in which her most glaring disabilities are in precisely those areas that are required for success, disabilities for which her considerable strengths may not be sufficient compensation. If drive and determination alone were enough to succeed as a vocational rehabilitation counselor, Kerry certainly would succeed, for she has these attributes in abundance. But drive and determination by themselves aren't enough to make up for the lack of social perception and communication skills that are necessary to her job. Although she has worked hard to acquire information about learning disabilities, she hasn't yet learned that success in life is usually based on identifying the things that we're good enough at and doing one or more of them, and knowing what we're poor at and getting that out of the way on the job. If you can't sing on key, you probably won't make a living as a singer; you might do it as a hobby, but don't quit your day job. Kerry's public speaking skills and her ability to gather information about learning disabilities are of little use in a job that requires good interpersonal relationships and problem-solving skills, when she doesn't have those skills, and no amount of wishing and trying will create them for her.

Kerry seems to be in over her head in her job, and the prognosis looks pretty bleak unless she can find a niche in her agency where her skills can be used to good effect and her deficits minimized. She seems to be trying to hold onto a job for which she is not well enough qualified, despite some skills, and to prove that she can do as well as she wishes she could. She seems to be trying to make herself feel good about herself even though her self-esteem isn't based on real ability to fulfill her responsibilities. Some of her mistakes are serious, requiring her supervisor, and perhaps others, to do her work for her. Tension mounts as she receives frequent criticism, both professional and social. Her supervisor has started the paper trail that may result in her demotion or termination. No prospect of a brighter turn of events is apparent.

Because Kerry seems to be trying so hard to prove herself in a career whose requirements she seems, on the whole, to be unable to fulfill, her therapist may find her a challenging person to form a therapeutic alliance with. If the crucial question of whether she has the skills to succeed in her chosen field is raised by her therapist, Kerry may leave therapy so quickly that she will never really have been in it. However, if her therapist just agrees that she is being treated unfairly on her job, he may form an alliance with Kerry, but it won't be a therapeutic one.

The essence of a therapeutic alliance is that it supports the client while helping her to become more realistic. A few moments of calm, detached observation of her situation in life should be enough for Kerry to see that she's entered a career path where she's unlikely to succeed, and that she would be better off starting with her strengths and seeing where she could plug those in vocationally. This is, after all, nothing more than Kerry herself would probably advise one of her clients. But it may take many months of psychotherapy for her to overcome her denial enough to have those moments of self-observation. Much of the purpose of that psychotherapy would be, through the therapeutic alliance, to change the basis of her self-esteem.

If Kerry's self-esteem were based on a real desire to be successful in life, she would already be planning her escape. She would have recognized that obstacles to success in this field are probably greater than she can overcome and turned her attention to finding a job to which she could apply her drive, determination, and ability to go at something step-by-step, and in which she would not need a lot of skill in social perception or interpersonal communication. There are such jobs, but they tend not to be seen as "professional," high-status, white-collar jobs. It may be that Kerry has made proving herself in a "professional" job the bar she must get over to justify the self-esteem to which she appears to be rather precariously—but determinedly—clinging. When you are clinging to such fragile and ultimately unrealistic self-esteem, you are truly hanging by a twig.

If this is the case, then Kerry is making her self-esteem depend on her fulfilling an image of what she would like to be rather than being the person she really is. Such self-esteem is really false self-esteem, because it is not based on the person's real abilities and doesn't lead to success in her undertakings. Let us consider the difference between such false self-esteem and the healthy self-esteem that is based on real ability and leads to successful adaptation.

Real and False Self-Esteem

Merriam-Webster's Collegiate Dictionary (1996) defines self as: "The entire person of an individual," and esteem as: "the regard in which one is held; especially, high regard." The *Penguin Dictionary of Psychology* (Reber, 1995) defines self-esteem as: "The degree to which one values oneself . . . the degree of self-esteem (high or low) is usually specified." So self-esteem has to do with the feeling that one is uniquely valuable. But on what is that sense of value based?

The importance of good self-esteem has entered our psychological folklore: "He'll try anything; he has high self-esteem." "She's afraid to try anything; she has low self-esteem." Low self-esteem is used to justify everything from depression to delinquency, and parents, teachers, and therapists are adjured to cultivate high self-esteem in children. But we aren't told how, and the message often comes down to just trying to help kids feel good about themselves.

The truth is that there are two different kinds of self-esteem: real self-esteem and false self-esteem, or healthy and pathological self-esteem. Healthy self-esteem is based on self-confidence derived from mastery, the experience of having been able to do things. Healthy self-esteem is genuine and authentic, in the sense that the individual feels that she can do things that she really can do. Healthy self-esteem supports the person through trying times and supports further personal growth.

Pathological self-esteem is self-esteem as an end in itself. It is derived from others trying to make the child feel good about herself separate from what she has done to contribute to her own well-being or anyone else's. Pathological self-esteem is a fantasy because it is based on an imagination of what one is like and worth, not on what one has really been and done. Pathological self-esteem supports nothing, but has itself to be supported, and so drains energy from the person and those around her.

Stress and Self-Esteem

The relationship between stress and healthy self-esteem is key, in that a certain amount of stress is absolutely necessary for genuine self-esteem to develop. Hans Selye introduced this concept of stress, referring to it as an "adaptation syndrome" (Selye, 1952). He points out that stress is an inherently neutral idea:

> The term "stress" has been used so loosely and applied to so many areas that it is perhaps easiest to understand what stress is not. Contrary to widespread public opinion, stress is not synonymous with nervous depression, tension, fatigue or discouragement. The only way to characterize stress is to call it a nonspecific response of the body to any demand. . . . *You should not and cannot avoid stress,* because to eliminate it completely would be to destroy life itself. (Selye, 1977, p. 91)

Every living being needs a certain amount of stress to mature and develop properly. Too much stress can cause distress and damage, but so can too little. Think of a voluntary muscle, like the muscles in our legs that we use when we walk. Too much stress causes tissue damage, and if continued could lead to serious injury. But the muscle needs a certain amount of stress in order to function, and if it doesn't receive enough stress it will become weak and flaccid. The same is true of the human personality. Too much stress can overwhelm and cause breakdown, but too little results in failure to develop strength, resilience, self-reliance, and resourcefulness. Abraham Maslow (1968) said that we need to face and meet challenges in life in order to know that we are capable of meeting them. Many of the "peak" human beings whom Maslow studied had lived through very trying circumstances indeed. Psychotherapist Pat Williams, of the European Therapy Studies Institute,[4] speaking on emotional intelligence, actually advises her listeners to study "prison literature," the writings of people who have had to face and overcome tremendous hardships, such as being kidnaped and imprisoned in an underground cell, or having to cope with life after a stroke or dreadful illness left them terribly impaired (Williams, 1997).

Learning Disabilities and Stress

If stress plays a necessary role in the development of personality, what role does it play in the personality of a person with learning disabilities? As we have seen, persons with learning disabilities suffer enormous distress from the direct effects of the disabilities, as well as from how they are treated because of them. Stronger people, like Dominic (whom we will meet in the next chapter), may respond to stressors such as the contempt of the principal of his school by determining to overcome the effects of his disabilities and succeed in life. But even Dominic, for all his strength of personality, was terribly hurt in his emotional life by such treatment, and it is easy to see how persons of lesser strength might be even more traumatized. Clearly, it is very important to minimize such unnecessary suffering.

At the same time, Selye teaches us that insufficient stress hurts the healthy development of the organism. If this is so, what kinds of stressors should persons with learning disabilities experience in order to foster their healthy self-development? The answer is: whatever they can handle with their own resources and their support systems, and whatever is developmentally appropriate at each stage of life.

June Edson, who taught early childhood development at Goddard College and with whom I worked in the Goddard College Nursery Kindergarten, told a story that I've found very meaningful and have told again and again. She once visited a Native American family. As she and the parents sat chatting in the living room, a young child of three or four years tried unsuccessfully to turn the doorknob on a door to get into another room. June instinctively began to rise to open the door for the child, but, noticing that his parents didn't move, and not wanting to do anything improper in what was, to her, another culture, she remained seated. She and the child's parents sat and talked for twenty or thirty minutes while the child tried, patiently and persistently, to open the door—trying and failing, trying and failing. June was quite uncomfortable about this but didn't say anything, fearful of hurting the parents' feelings. Finally, the child succeeded, opened the door, and went into the next room. June reported that she then realized that the child had learned something that he never would have learned if someone had jumped up and opened the door for him. By not helping him, his parents were indirectly teaching him what he could do for himself.

Persons with learning disabilities have strengths, and their survival and success in life will be based in large part on their developing and applying their strengths. So, they should be encouraged to be as independent and responsible as possible and appropriate at each stage of their lives. Also, they should be presented with challenges in their areas of strength and in proportion to their strengths, so that they can develop a strong sense of self and self-confidence. One client, though severely dyslexic, was a talented outdoorswoman—a hiker, climber, kayaker, leader and teacher of outdoor experiences. Her self-confidence derived from her successes, not from her deficits, although she knew that she had to work on them and had to have help in order to do that.

I've often seen persons with severe learning disabilities in high school, college, or beyond, whose parents do their laundry, purchase their food, and prepare their meals, although they are perfectly capable of doing such things. The parents' attempts to be supportive actually become counterproductive, by removing appropriate sources of healthy stress from their adult children's lives.

Parental Overprotection and Pathological Self-Esteem

Concerned but overprotective parents often inadvertently inhibit the development of genuine self-esteem and support the development of false self-esteem in children with learning disabilities. They do this by "protecting" their children from experiencing genuine challenges and responsibilities in life at the level that they are able to manage at any particular time and by failing to encourage their children to strive to achieve more independence over time. They "protect" their children from such necessary stress because of the misguided idea that their children are already suffering so much because of their learning disabilities that they shouldn't have to suffer any more. Of course, the result of such well-meaning but counterproductive parenting is that their children do not develop their resourcefulness, responsibility, and resilience to the same degree that they would if they had been encouraged to apply themselves to appropriate tasks along the way.

Under these circumstances children cannot develop healthy self-esteem based on the experience of competence in meeting life's challenges. Instead, they often develop false self-esteem, based not on competence but on the perception that the people who love them want them to feel good about themselves. Feeling good about oneself becomes an end in itself, and this carries over into their choice of activities. They may do something—or not do something—because doing it makes them feel good about themselves or not doing it enables them to avoid unpleasant feelings about themselves, rather than because the thing is worth doing—or not doing—on its own merits.

Trapped in False Self-Esteem

Kerry doesn't seem able to think realistically about her job and her alternatives, because she seems to be trapped in a dilemma of false selfesteem. Although her situation is getting worse, her self-esteem depends on believing that she is doing well enough so that things will be all right. She may support her false position by telling herself that her situation is not as bad as it really is or that she is not responsible for her problems. She may blame others and feel like a complete victim. But she is trapped in a prison partly of her own making, unwilling to leave though the door is, in fact, unlocked.

The price of leaving her prison is the acknowledgment that she is who she is, not who she wants to be, and that her ways of connecting successfully with life have to be based on her strengths, not her wishes. Such a shift, from pursuing unrealistic wishes to focusing on goals that really can be accomplished, is a major goal of psychotherapy with clients in such a dilemma. A therapeutic question such as, "When did you decide that overcoming your weaknesses was more important than expressing your strengths?" might help Kerry focus on and engage with this issue.

The prejudice that a professional job is the only worthwhile expression of intelligence is deeply rooted in our supposedly classless society, and it causes a world of grief for some persons with learning disabilities. Laura Lehtinen Rogan, the founder of Cove School, once told me that she'd observed that the learning disabled children of blue-collar parents often had an easier time finding their way in life after school than did the children of white-collar parents, especially when the white-collar parents had been professionals for several generations and expected their children to follow in the family footsteps, despite learning disabilities that may have resulted in an elementary or junior high school reading level. In such cases, it seems to me, the parents' wishes for their children are really their wishes for themselves; it is unseemly that a child of *theirs* might work in a blue-collar or other nonprofessional job. Yet success in work depends on doing something you can, in fact, do. For persons with learning disabilities, that means doing something where one's strengths can be expressed to their best effect and one's weaknesses can be minimized.

In the process of realistically exploring her own vocational alternatives, Kerry might have a lot of mourning to do. She may need to mourn the loss of academic and career achievement and status that her learning disability—and her environment's response to that disability—have cost her. She may need to mourn for the little girl who, after losing her mother early, set her heart on gaining the approval of others and attaining a certain social status, a status her LD may prevent her from achieving. She may have to give those losses their due acknowledgment, and give mourning its due time, before she can turn her attention toward her future with a more realistic attitude.

If you were Kerry's psychotherapist, the initial challenge would be to make an empathic connection. A comment like "It seems that you're trying so hard to prove yourself" might help Kerry open the door to a discussion of her lifelong struggle to succeed in school and in her career. If this led to the formation of a therapeutic alliance between Kerry and yourself as her therapist, and if that alliance helped her to assess more objectively whether there was a niche in her agency where she could succeed or whether it would be wiser to find another kind of work, then therapy would be successful.

Unfortunately, as we leave Kerry, there seems to be no hint that she might begin to see herself and her life differently, or even enter psychotherapy looking for help. Yet things seem to be getting worse for her on the job, and it seems likely that, sooner or later, matters will come to a head. Some depressions are precipitated because people who have been living a lie for too long are finally overtaken by events.

. . . .

CHAPTER 5

The Worst Thing . . . and the Best
LD, ADD, and Addiction

After I got involved with AA, it took me a year to start to realize, "OK, now I'm cleaned out, now I've got some problems. What am I going to do with all these problems?" And my biggest problem was I couldn't read. The addiction was the worst thing that ever happened to me, but it was the best. It was the best because it opened my eyes and as time went on I was able to use the program with other problems that I had besides the addiction—my learning disability and my reactions to it.

—Dominic Markowski

Dominic Markowski is dyslexic. He has significant difficulty reading and spelling, but owns his own very successful construction business and now, in his mid-fifties, is well on his way to becoming a self-made millionaire. He has been recognized as a civic leader, recently receiving the Citizen-of-the-Year award in his small suburban community. Today, Dominic is never without his pocket-size electronic speller with a voice synthesizer. If he needs to read a business contract, he types in the words he doesn't know and the machine pronounces them. If he needs to know how to spell a word, he types in his best approximation and the machine offers a choice of correctly spelled words.

Dominic is able to cope fairly well with his learning disability, and his own life is running smoothly these days, but this was not always the case, as his recollections of drug abuse indicate. "Yeah, it's been 14 years. I go to meetings all the time. I go to AA. I went to Narcotics Anonymous, but there was no sobriety there. Half the guys would be there only for a year, if that, and I couldn't stay straight, so I went to AA and stuck to that. I don't ever want to go back to drugs again. I just lost my head. Before I got involved in drugs I had a drinking problem, but I was able to control the drinking to some extent. I actually stopped. I refused to drink for the longest time and then I got involved in drugs. I heard about marijuana back years ago when they were saying it was physically nonaddictive. That's how it started and it just escalated. I was broken in half. I had nothing. I didn't have *me* anymore. In my mind I was developing plans for how I was going to be a backpacker and live off the trains.

"The drug addiction was the *worst* thing that ever happened to me, but it was the *best*. It was the best because it opened my eyes and as time went on I was able to use the program with *other* problems that I had besides the addiction—my learning disability and my reactions to it. I can stop beating myself up much sooner than I ever have before, so I will not react and harm myself so badly if I do start on myself. I guess everybody has a journey to talk about. And their journey was just as pleasant and just as harsh as the person standing next to them, as they see it. And when I confess to that thought it's very healthy, because then I don't pick on myself."

Even now Dominic has a tendency to pick on himself. "Oh yeah, I do it because I think very little of myself. And I go through stages of worse times. It's like ocean waves. I go up and down. For the longest time I used to keep saying, 'I wish I was dead.' I wouldn't mean it. I was just saying that. Sometimes I wished I was, at the moment. I had suicide feelings that came in and out. Of course wanting to live and deal with life was stronger than the desire to just end it all. Hopefully I'll still say that in other moments in the future. Yeah, I hope for that."

As Dominic's case demonstrates, learning disabilities may underlie problems with substance abuse. The purpose of the chapter is to explore the nature of the connections between learning disabilities, attention deficits, and emotional or behavior disorders such as addiction. We will see how these connections are dynamic and bidirectional, such that cognitive processing problems lead to and exacerbate emotional problems, just as they in turn lead to and exacerbate learning problems.

The connections between emotional disorders and learning disabilities begin in childhood and often continue into adulthood, making people with LD vulnerable to emotional distress throughout the life span.[1] Often these emotional problems are not merely secondary reactions to school failure, but a direct result of cognitive processing difficulties (Schechter, 1974). These links have been documented clinically in a few studies, but the topic has not been pursued systematically in either the learning disabilities or psychology literature. Existing research suggests that adults with LD have problems with social adjustment, emotional lability, frustration, control of emotions and temper, depression, lack of motivation, and lack of self-confidence. They describe themselves as being moody, nervous, disorganized, and easily discouraged (Buchanan & Wolf, 1986; Hoffman et al., 1987).[2]

However, these studies document only the *existence* of a relationship and do not investigate its nature or direction. Orenstein (1992) recognizes that much work is needed to explicate the underlying mechanisms, since much of the learning disability literature overlooks the psychological ramifications of this problem, just as much of the psychoanalytic and other therapeutic literature overlooks the cognitive ramifications. Orenstein has "the eerie feeling of looking at two sides of the same coin: the disavowal of cognition from affect and vice versa" (p. 122). She further suggests that there is a strong psychoanalytic assumption among many therapists that lack of appropriate nurturing or developmental delays in emotional growth represent the primary problem, and that the weight of this assumption accounts for the lack of recognition that cognitive processing deficits can be a primary cause of emotional problems. This point of view doesn't match Dominic's experience or Orenstein's own qualitative research, in which her LD subjects state unequivocally their conviction that the underlying cause of their emotional difficulties is their innate and permanent cognitive deficits.

Reflecting on his earliest childhood years, Dominic says, "I failed first grade, and I remember trying to learn to read. I felt like I just couldn't pick it up. Everyone else was able to. When they had the alphabet up on the board. . . . I couldn't remember the whole alphabet properly for the longest time. I was dumb in that period of my thinking. Yet at the same time I knew I wasn't, because I was able to somewhat figure out the same things that other people could figure out or sometimes even better. So I wasn't totally dumb. I heard the word retarded as time went on, and I started to believe that I was partially retarded. It was very scary.

"When I was in third grade everybody would read a paragraph. When it came to my turn I just felt a lot of fear. My face felt like it was hot. I felt a terrible panic feeling when it was my turn to read, because I couldn't read it and everybody was going to notice this, and I didn't want everybody to know how terrible I was." Failure to learn to read diminished the assurance of recognition and acceptance by those who were important in his life and led to feelings of helplessness, shame, and humiliation (Westman, 1990). Thinking about those experiences, Dominic says, "Our biggest enemy is not our learning disability as I see it. It's us, ourselves. We destroy ourselves by setting ourselves up as lesser than we are. We are our worst enemy, not anyone else. Not because we're learning disabled. Our learning disability is just a small thing. The *reaction* is most important, the issue of getting this monkey off my back."

Dominic interprets his feelings of helplessness as immaturity. Acknowledging the close connection between immaturity and dependence, he goes on to say, "We'll react to things immaturely, because we haven't grown up in many ways." For example, even in adulthood, "people take over, and one minute we're happy that they take over and the next minute we're resentful. From day one while you're developing as a young person, you're already being treated differently and it's already being noticed that you have a difficulty, and so you feel lesser. And immediately you start setting up forms of protection, like letting people help you when you really don't need help, and it becomes a very difficult situation." Adults with LD often alternate between dependency and the rejection of dependency.

Though he always had trouble in school, Dominic's learning disability was not diagnosed until he was 38 years old. "After I got involved with AA, it took me a year to start to realize, 'OK, now I'm cleaned out, now I've got some problems. What am I going to do with all these problems?' And my biggest problem was I couldn't read, and maybe I was lazy." He resolved to do something about his inability to read as a way of combating his "laziness," and began working privately with a reading tutor. The tutor mentioned the possibility of dyslexia and encouraged him to get an evaluation. When he did, his intelligence was assessed as being in the high average range. Although he did not enjoy the testing, Dominic felt that it helped. "They talked about a mental block in my ability to pick up the skills of reading, and I said, 'Oh, thank you! I'm not responsible!' I thought I was, because I did goof off so many times! And not being so retarded!"

Dominic's diagnostic testing confirmed deficits in both auditory and visual short-term memory that made it difficult for him to learn to read. These deficits continue to affect him at work and in daily functioning. "I don't want to write things down, but I will. A friend of mine, a chemist [sic] teacher taught me to keep notes, how to keep records, like a diary, and how to use the diary. I write things down at work. If I give a customer a price, I write it down."

The testing also confirmed that Dominic has visual and auditory sequencing problems. In addition to having difficulty with sequential thinking and use of language, he has difficulty with the sequence of numbers and of sounds in words (he pronounces *irrelevant* as *irrevalent,* and even confuses it with *irreverent*). "But see, it isn't so horribly horrible, like *everything* I do is backwards. No, it isn't that way at all. That's the simple, nasty thing about it. It's very subtle." Dominic has learned that anxiety can make the effect of the learning disability worse. "I'll get going, you know, I'm running late, and I get uptight, or else I'm very tired, and these tendencies to reverse things pop out a little earlier, and they're a little worse. It's terrible to send my workmen to an address and reverse the numbers. And I'm better now because I slow down and I'll say it twice. Sometimes if I still doubt it, I'll repeat it again." As with most people with LD, his weaknesses are inconsistent, better on some days and worse on others. "There are what I call 'LD Days.' Things aren't connecting and if I start out a day like that I immediately say, 'Wait a minute. Let's slow down and let the day catch up to me.'"

The insight Dominic has gained from the evaluation has helped him be more aware of how the learning disability affects his life on a daily basis, but things were much more difficult for him back in school. He recalls having been retained once in first grade, and then again in junior high. "They held me back in seventh grade to prepare me for high school, so I could read better. But they really didn't teach me that much, at least I didn't feel that they did." Learning disabilities were not as widely known when Dominic was in grade school as they are today, and as is invariably the case with learning disabled individuals, standard remedial reading programs are rarely helpful, because they don't take into account the particular cognitive strengths and weaknesses of the individual.

And he still spent a lot of time trying to hide his difficulty with reading. "I started becoming compulsive over behavior patterns, joking around. It was part of my personality. I always was a class clown and I wished that I wasn't, but I just couldn't stop. I still am today. If I'm in an insecure position, I joke around a lot. I use it as a hide-out and that's a fact." Although Dominic is being really hard on himself, he recognizes that joking around is probably a less harmful coping mechanism than a lot of others. "Now that's true. I am better off with it than without it. Without it I would be really, uhhhh, cuckoo. I would have nowhere to get away. So it's good."

Even though he was held back in seventh grade, Dominic tried to maintain some self-respect in other ways. "The first job I had I was about 13. I was a paperboy. And I identified that this was good for me because otherwise I had too much free time and would do crazy things. I used to hang around with these guys and we were really good with a slingshot. And we had BB guns. We would get our winter clothes on and we would have war with BB guns. That was reckless! I used to do lots of crazy, reckless things. I remember jumping from one car to another car, door to door, doing like 60, 70 miles an hour, to prove that I could. It was nuts, absolutely nuts.

"When I first got married, before I got involved in drugs, I got involved in motocross. I went to a track one day and I saw these guys come off of a jump and I said, 'I've got to do that!' I had a drive to do these things, and before I knew it I was involved. I bought myself a good motorcycle, and I went out with a friend of mine and we went racing. He used to call me 'Bailout,' because I used to bail out when I lost it. It was the most exciting thing I ever did, but it was totally reckless."

Dominic recognizes a connection between his reckless behavior and his cognitive problems. "I had to concentrate when I practiced and then when I raced. I could only concentrate on one thing, because if I didn't, I would go bash. When I raced, things slowed down for me. I couldn't concentrate on all this stuff that was going on in my life. See, it was a hide-out. I was physically hyperkinetic. I would bounce from one thing to another when I was young, and I never stopped, you know? But when I got older, what happened was that the bouncing around slowed down, but my *mind* kept going."

Dominic has never been diagnosed as having ADD, but many signs are there, including a high activity level as a child, reckless behavior, distractibility, and difficulty sustaining attention. He sees his reckless behavior as a response to a perceived restlessness, and as he says, danger served to focus his concentration. Hallowell and Ratey (1994), in a highly relevant discussion, identify a particular type of ADD that they call "ADD with High-Risk Behaviors." They suggest that, although most people with ADD are easily bored, the adult with "high-stim ADD" particularly abhors boredom. This adult may seek stimulation through relatively safe activities or through riskier behaviors such as gambling, having dangerous romantic liaisons, making risky business deals, or getting involved in bungee-jumping, car-racing, or some other high-risk activity.

In addition, although Dominic is not physically hyperactive as an adult, his mind still races, and his particular set of ADD characteristics includes being especially sensitive to internal stimuli. He seems prone to what Levine (1998) refers to as free-flight distractibility, in which a single experience or thought triggers an extended chain of associations, which can be quite irrelevant to the topic at hand. Because of such distractibility, patients like Dominic might miss much of what a therapist is saying, not because of defensiveness, resistance, or some oedipal projection on the therapist, but just because of an inability to properly inhibit one's internal stimuli. Therapists may need to find ways to cue the patient to refocus attention.

Further, counselors should be aware that Dominic's attention problems are not an isolated disorder.[3] They are integrally related to his learning disability and directly connected to his emotional problems, which makes diagnostic identification more complex. Having an attention deficit probably *predisposes* one to other kinds of problems (both emotional and cognitive) and vice versa. As Levine puts it, the diagnostic challenge for the therapist is "not to isolate a single trait, but to ensure that we account for the multiple sources and complications often associated with these traits" (1989, p. 51).

Even though his days of truly reckless behavior are in the past, Dominic's attention problems still affect his daily functioning in many ways. For example, he has had a less than perfect driving record. "I've had accidents and I know why. It's because I'll look, but I'm paying attention to what's in my head, and I'll look and see no cars, and I'll pull out. I don't do that so much now because I say, 'OK. Today I'm going to slow down.' I used to let emotions and worry get in my way like a bumblebee in a car and forget where I'm at." Dominic uses the metaphor of the bee to represent his reaction to his learning disability, and we see clearly the close connection of attention problems and LD. As Dominic says, "Paying attention to a bumblebee plus the total insanity of the fear of a bumblebee can get you into a car accident and kill you."

Dominic's memories of his reckless behaviors distract him from the narrative line of his story, as is typical of people with ADD. "Where was I? Oh yeah, I was talking about high school. The first couple of years I was very scared. I didn't know how the hell I was going to get out of school. And I did nothing but joke it away, so I went to summer school every year." He not only blew off his first two years of high school but soon gained a reputation as a boy who planned pranks and practical jokes. "I would do things deliberately, I think, subconsciously deliberately. I would whip out a cigarette and smoke it right in the cafeteria, just to be a smartass. I had nothing against the teachers. It was the ability to act up or ditch and not get caught. One time we were in the cafeteria and the teacher who was the monitor would patrol the area. He would go out this door and in that door, and it would take, oh, maybe 10 seconds from the time he went out and then came in again. So I would look at my watch and time him exactly. I rolled an orange to make it really juicy, and I threw it at another kid and was sitting down and sleeping by the time the teacher came back in. It was just perfect timing! I felt ashamed at what I did. I wasn't proud of myself, but I *was* proud of myself to be able to establish that I could do it and not get caught." As with many adults with LD, at times Dominic has too much self-esteem, at other times too little.

Dysfunctional Compensatory Mechanisms

Dominic's need to play practical jokes highlights one pathway that connects learning disabilities with psychopathology, namely, inappropriate compensatory mechanisms. People with LD can compensate for weak areas of cognitive processing (e.g., weak memory) or for inadequate skills (e.g., poor reading skills) by substituting areas of stronger ability or by manipulating the environment to achieve a better fit with their particular set of cognitive strengths and weaknesses. While Kohut (1977, 1984) saw all compensatory strategies as healthy responses to an imperfect environment, in the case of the learning disabled individual it is useful to distinguish between those compensatory strategies that are indeed healthy adaptations and those that tend to become dysfunctional.

Healthy compensatory strategies are clever, pragmatic adaptations that enable a person to get around the obstacles created by the learning disability. People with LD use these techniques to compensate for a particular processing deficit, and they are usually things one *does* or ways one interacts *with the environment*. For instance, Dominic devised a map strategy for taking and giving directions and makes regular use of his pocket speller. The development and use of these healthy compensatory techniques are motivated by a desire to succeed in spite of deficits and are justifiably a source of pride for many learning disabled people.

The invention and use of compensatory techniques are often indications of high IQ. It is interesting that during their diagnostic testing Mary (Chapter 2) and Dominic both felt that standardized tests could never be a true measure of their intelligence and that the diagnostician was not aware that clues to their intelligence might lie in the compensatory techniques they had developed. "It was bothersome," Dominic says. "I knew she was going to see all the dumminess of me and she wasn't going to see my cleverness. It's impossible to see the cleverness on the tests." And Mary said of her first evaluation, "She told me I had a 100 IQ. Hundred is average! And I had done so many things! I taught preschool, taught religion on the Navaho reservation, raised six kids, ran the PTA, and did a great job! I didn't think she would *ever* be able to really understand that my coping skills are a sign of my intelligence."

A second, much different type of compensation consists in relatively general or global ways of behaving. Kaplan and Shachter (1991) point out that any disability, including LD, can become a core issue around which self-concept develops. They maintain that this core issue affects the coping patterns and the defenses that become part of the patient's adaptive style. In their clinical practice they are alert to the adaptive styles that have become dysfunctional and are interfering with normal adult pursuits. While the first sort of compensation (pragmatic adaptations) arises from feelings of inefficacy, the second sort is motivated by feelings of personal inadequacy and need (Orenstein, 1992). For example, having been singled out as different and rejected because he couldn't learn to read, Dominic adopted the role of clown in part to gain acceptance that he couldn't win by being a successful student. It also provided an outlet for his intelligence, which was thwarted in academic pursuits. And his success provided him with reassurance that he could do *something* better than the other children. "One time I'd gotten a bunch of guys—about twenty, thirty guys—and there was this one fellow who was like a guard in the parking lot. He wasn't very smart, and he was pretty nasty, kind of a smart aleck. So I had all these guys gather around, and I barked like a dog, and I slammed on the lockers. It sounded like this dog was killed and we locked it in the locker. The guard was frantic, but the guys were all crowded around, and he was convinced I was the killer of this dog. I would do things like this all the time." Even when he plays jokes, using his social intelligence—to use Gardner's (1985) term—in an antisocial way, he does it successfully.

However, this compensatory strategy soon became dysfunctional, and in retrospect Dominic regrets his shameful behavior. "Such stupidity! And it got me in trouble at school. I was in the principal's office all the time, and he didn't like me. He had no respect for me at all. I don't know how I dreamed these tricks up. Well, I had a great imagination. I was almost nuts. I used to think I was crazy because I did all those things. It was compulsive!" But Dominic was unable to use his intelligence to succeed academically, and so he channeled his ability in other directions. "There was nothing left for me," he says with anguish in his voice. "And I got noticed in this fashion. I wasn't getting awarded [sic] in the areas where I wasn't doing well in school. I always was a class clown, and I wished that I wasn't, but I just couldn't stop. It was part of my personality."

Such dysfunctional compensatory strategies ease the pain but allow no further growth (Orenstein, 1992). "One minute I didn't like myself, the next minute I loved myself. That's where I was. Earlier we were talking about that split feeling? That paradox? I had that! I still carry it today, and it can switch from one moment to the next, and I have to go into the bathroom, you know, go somewhere alone and say, 'Dominic, what are you doing to yourself?'"

Fortunately, in spite of this inappropriate coping mechanism, Dominic was able to rely on other personal resources, which included cleverness and strong will. He continues his story by reflecting, "I graduated in four years and summer school. I was really angry that they wouldn't give me that diploma in June. That hurt. But really it was a good kick in the ass. I knew it was me that blew it, nobody else. Anybody can go through high school in four years. What really irked me was I couldn't read anything. I understood it in class, but I couldn't read it. I never thought I ever possibly could make it through college. It was a total impossibility. My parents offered it to me, to let me go to college. But it was a total fear. I did not want to touch it. I was so glad to get out of school. And I could get my life together. And then the biggest fear was what the hell was I going to do with my life? I had no background like most kids did. I said to myself a thousand times, if I could only read I could go to the moon. Because I was not dumb. I wanted to be a scientist but it was impossible, you know."

In contrast to school, work provided an area where he could succeed. "Even before I graduated, I worked in a food store. I took it seriously. It was more than just putting in hours. One thing I liked about work was that I was an individual and I could hide out and not be the person that couldn't read. Not that I didn't have troubles, but I was cleverly able to hide my disability. I couldn't read the items on the shelves, and someone would say go get this or that, and I would get it by just identifying it by the picture, or what you see, or what they tell you. And I felt good when I did.

"Once I said to a friend of mine at the store, 'I'm going to become a millionaire.' The million dollars isn't worth anything. It was the drawing of the line between success and not success. It was such an immature way of being, and I know this especially today. But I couldn't help it. It was a way of showing that I had ability. People always told me I wasn't going to be a this and I wasn't going to be a that. I spent a lot of time in the principal's office and he said to me, 'You'll never make a gas station attendant.' He said, 'You'll probably never even be a garbage man.' And I said back to him, I said, 'Well, if I'm a gas station attendant then I'm going to own the gas station. And if I'm a garbage collector, I'm going to own the garbage company. And that's all there is to it.' You know, I'm going to make that goal! I'm going to be a millionaire. I hope to be. I'm well on my way. I don't horde my money. I mean I've got a $16,000 organ, so I don't horde my money. I've got a big TV. I've got the motorcycle. But I don't spend it unwisely, and I have been successful. My business is doing very well."

Dominic attributes his success to strong will. "After the food store, I started on my way trying different jobs. And about the fifth job down the line is the one I'm in today. I was working for a small construction company and when the owner retired he offered to let me buy it. It was a risk, but I took it. And the thing that made me successful was that damn sp . . . I was going to say 'spite.' No, it was that strong will. Back on those earlier jobs, I always promised myself that I would work at least a year and a half to give myself a chance, because I knew the first six months on any job I was going to be scared and would want to leave. I came home many times wanting to cry. I was weak. I wanted to procrastinate so bad. I was scared and I couldn't explain it to my wife. I wasn't getting along with her at that time. It was very scary, but I was successful because I just kept it up. That damn spite. But it wasn't spite; it was that strong will. It got me in trouble sometimes, but it's been my blessing in other ways."

Unresolved Feelings from Childhood

Here, Dominic has identified a second pathway connecting LD with emotional disorders. The "spite," which motivated him to stay for at least a year and a half in each job, was the same feeling that prompted him to tell his high school principal that he would own the gas station. His anger at being told more than once that he would never amount to anything is still unresolved.[4]

Reiff and Gerber (1994) point out that such anger was an extremely pervasive feeling in their sample of LD adults. The individuals in their study were angry about the treatment they had received at school and home (e.g., being teased, ridiculed, let down, or rejected), angry that they had been called stupid and lazy, or angry that adults' attitudes had limited their opportunities, particularly when told that they would never amount to much. "For many adults with learning disabilities, those feelings are more than mere memory; the feelings continue to play a part of adult experience, often tinting, sometimes staining, the landscape of their social and emotional lives" (p. 77).

Barton and Fuhrmann (1994) connect childhood wounds to unresolved grief. "Rage, anguish, guilt, sadness, betrayal, fear, jealousy—all of the feelings associated with grieving a major loss—are common to adults with learning disabilities." In their experience, many adults with learning disabilities have never mourned the loss of "what they cannot do that other people do easily, the loss of academic and personal self-esteem, the opportunities for the future that are out of reach" (p. 85).

After his declaration to the school principal about owning the gas station, Dominic continued to work at the grocery store while he searched for a job that could lead to a satisfying career. "I worked at the food store for a year and a half, until I got myself in trouble with one of these compulsive, stupid, behavior things one night. I started joking around, and we ended up having a food fight. Flour, sugar, hamburger meat—everything. We were locking the store and we were throwing things. We just had a war! The meat market guy saw the meat on the ceiling and that did it! We got fired!

"After I left there, I got this job in shipping and receiving in office supplies. I told them how poorly I read and they actually thought I was joking. It made me feel proud of myself because I really pulled the wool over their eyes. I had tricks of doing it, you know, all of these tricks that were lies. This one person wrote orders up and no one could read his writing, so I would use that for an excuse. I would look at an order and say, 'Oh, there's that George Barker again. I can't read his writing. Can you make this out? Damn person has writing like a doctor.' They didn't pick it up that I was learning disabled. But I didn't stay. I asked for a raise and for more responsibility, and they said I wasn't ready. So I decided to leave.

"Then I tried truck route sales with a bakery. It worked out fine. The only reason I quit was that I was trying to find a way to grow into something, and I wasn't satisfied that that was it. I had to make a decision. Either I would stay with being a driver, or else be involved in sales. If I was going to be a chicken, I would be a driver. If I wanted to push myself I would go into sales and deal with more anxieties and fears. And the fears I'm talking about aren't just everyday fears that other people feel. You just don't realize the intimidation of the fear of being found out. The fear that someone would just say, 'Well, he doesn't know how to read. He can't do this job, so fire him.' And I had feared that I was going to meet up with this kind of a hatchet person. On the one hand, they're right, you know? But I just wanted to do a good job and get ahead. Every job I had, I took it, and I cried, because I was so scared. I was overwhelmed with all this fear, thinking, 'How am I going to do it?' It was just terrible." The emotional turmoil Dominic experienced each time he took a new job was overwhelming, and the anxiety created by always blaming himself continues today.

Anxiety and Exhaustion

The constant experience of anxiety, of fear of failure or of being found out, and of exhaustion from overdoing it, constitutes a third pathway that connects LD with emotional disorders. It may lead one to search for a way to relax or escape, including self-medication. "That's true," Dominic says, with insight about his years of drug abuse. "I was exhausted. All I wanted to do was just relax. That's all I wanted to do, nothing more. Didn't want to get addicted. I didn't even want to get high. I didn't want to do it every day. I didn't want to do it at night. I was so stressed! Even when I was in grade school—it was back as early as that date—I would say to myself, 'Tonight's the night I'm going to get drunk and just relax. And later I started with drugs. I've been in the program for 14 years, and I know people who have been in it all the way through that period of time and they don't have a drinking problem anymore, but they're working to get away from the thinking problem that caused the anxiety to want to excape [sic] from it." Some people who find themselves in psychiatric hospitals or alcohol or drug rehabilitation programs and can't get clean may eventually discover that at the root of the problem is an undiagnosed learning disability or unresolved emotional issues that are related to it.

People with LD, especially those with good intelligence, work harder and longer to accomplish the same amount as other people. They have talents that allow them to succeed in some areas, but then, driven by the desire to be or at least appear normal, they conclude that with enough effort they can achieve as well as anyone. And many times they succeed, but the resulting success is accompanied by exhaustion, panic attacks, or psychosomatic symptoms. For example, Mark (Chapter 3) said, "I thought I was lazy. I still think that. I think that's what drives me. I always think I should eliminate all procrastination, from everything from the waxing of the car to the cleaning of the laundry, getting the work done at work. . . . But I tried that, and I almost killed myself. I mean my body was going; there was something wrong with me, chest pains, and so on."

But Dominic's story is not complete, and as we will now see, early family issues are also involved in his abuse of drugs and alcohol.

From the traditional psychodynamic perspective, children bring family or personal problems with them to school, which subsequently leads to classic difficulties with classroom discipline or academic progress. But the LD specialist often sees the reverse sort of connection, in which cognitively based learning problems have serious emotional consequences. Dominic's story is important because it illustrates a situation in which both sorts of causes are operating simultaneously and dynamically.

Dominic allows us to see the connection between LD issues and family dysfunction as he was growing up (his father was critical and distant, his mother an alcoholic), particularly as they related to issues of trust. "Well, you know, I never trusted my parents. I was scared that they'd find out that I was dumb, that I had that a reading problem. I was scared that they wouldn't want anything to do with me. Scared they'd find out I was retarded. I never trusted my parents' love for me. I never felt that my dad really loved me. I felt that he felt responsible for me, but he didn't love me. Actually, I trusted my mother. I would do anything for her, you know. But then I had to be careful, too, because she was a heavy drinker.

"One thing that was good for me. My mother was good to me. She always found good things to say about me. She never said bad things about me. My dad did. But my mother did the opposite. She really supported me as who I was. She gave me responsibility and made me feel proud of it. When she started working full-time—I think I was 11 or 12 years old—she had me clean the house and she paid me. Two bucks was big bucks back those days, and I really cleaned the house. I broke the house down into this section this week, and that section the next. I vacuumed the whole house up and I got the clothes ready and she made me feel proud that I did such a good job. And she bragged about it to other people.

"She made me feel good about myself when I did good things. And she didn't beat me up when I did anything bad. If I said anything nasty to my mom, she'd just slap me across the face. And I deserved it. She was a nice person. I wish she didn't die. She died because of alcohol. She was drunk and she went and took a bath that night and fell and hit her head and got scalded. It was horrible.

"But I didn't trust my dad. I didn't trust my brother. My brother was a weird person. He did creepy things. He's an alcoholic, too. He was an exhibitionist and he was picked up a couple times. He was called Charlie Chicken in high school. That was another reason I came on so strong." Dominic's voice takes on a new tone, suggesting a sudden insight into an additional motivation for his reckless behavior as an adolescent. "Charlie Chicken . . . yeah . . . I wasn't going to be a Charlie Chicken. That would hurt. That would hurt bad. God. So that was another goal. Besides my learning problems, I didn't want to be like Charlie Chicken.

"See, the reason why I didn't trust my dad was that anytime I ever did a little mischief he always told me he was going to send me away. And I couldn't believe it! He said he was going to send me away to boarding school. And it wasn't just every so often; it was *all . . . the . . . time.*" Dominic groans, intense pain evident in his voice and face. "And he called me dumb and stupid all the time. He didn't know what he . . . I know logically . . . I know this today, very logically, he did not know what kind of problem I had and how much it affected me when he said those words to me. He had no idea. But it really hurt, and I really kind of believed it. He was a hard-core German person, and he was a hard worker. He favored my brother. It was obvious he didn't like me.

"And then the day came when my brother really got in trouble that one time, and the police were there. My dad was crying and he told me what happened, and then he says, 'What hurts so bad is we loved him so much. We loved the both of you so much. You have no idea.' And I stood there and I was flabbergasted! I thought, 'Why didn't you tell me this before? How come you told me when I was 4 or 5 years old that I was too old to kiss you, Dad? Huh? It's cruel.' But I didn't mean to speak so angry about my father."

Learning disabled individuals grow up in dysfunctional families as frequently as other individuals, and it is the *interaction* of family issues and a learning disability that makes the LD person especially vulnerable to serious emotional difficulties. It would be easy to conclude that family issues were *sufficient reasons* for Dominic's substance abuse, and indeed Dominic may well have needed therapy even if he were not learning disabled. But a therapist who looks closely at the four reasons he gives for not trusting his father's love would see that they reveal important clues that point to a more complex situation.

- Love was never displayed. His father rejected his hugs and kisses.
- He was scared that his father would find out that he couldn't read.

- His father threatened to send him away to boarding school whenever he got into mischief.
- His father favored his brother. "It was obvious he didn't like me . . . [because] he called me dumb and stupid all the time."

It is telling that all except the first reason are directly related to school and his learning disability. Not only was he afraid that his father didn't like him because he was dumb, but he was also threatened with banishment whenever he got into mischief—which we have seen was a direct result of his attention deficit and a dysfunctional coping mechanism to deflect attention from his poor academic achievement. Negative self-concept and fears related to his learning disability disrupt the bonds of trust and color his perception that his brother was the favored son.

Later, Dominic's marriage was affected by the complex interrelationship among these unique needs and problems. He tells us, "When I married my wife she thought she was pregnant and I was just trying to be the right person, and I married her. There were a lot of problems. I did have love for her. But I was scared that she wasn't the person for me, because she had a personality in her that was very difficult to deal with. And she talked about being mistreated at home by her parents, so we had a terrible start." But Dominic did tell his wife before they got married about his difficulty with reading, though his learning disability had not yet been identified. "Oh, yes. I did talk about it. I cleared myself before we got married. I told her a number of months before we ever thought about marriage and before we had gotten involved that deeply, because I didn't want to come across as a fake."

Nevertheless, Dominic's story illustrates how a learning disability can directly affect the marriage partnership. "Every time I had to ask how to spell something, it affected me. She took care of the checkbook and wrote up all the checks. She took care of all the mail that came in and went out of the household. She was running the man's position as we understood it in those days—we're talking about 1962. And she was trying to go to school. She was under a lot of pressure, and before you knew it she was trying to tell me I couldn't hear. I kept saying I *could* hear. But I was saying 'What?' all the time, because I can't pay attention and remember what you're saying. It was part of my learning disability, but we didn't know it at the time. So we got ahold of a hearing aid person and he checked my hearing and he said, 'Your hearing is just fine.' And then I blamed her for the whole thing. I held that against her, that she thought there was something wrong with me."

As a result of the circumstances of their marriage, their sexual relationship was difficult from the beginning. "I still wonder if the sexual problem was because of the LD, because we had problems identifying the male and the female role in the marriage. Then because of my other insecurities I didn't think she loved me, and I overreacted because I didn't believe in myself. Also I don't know how to say it, if it's true or not, I don't know how much I loved her at that time. And all of these feelings just magnified. I thought, 'Did she get married because she thought she was put in a corner? Well, I was willing to work this out. But my wife, she started feeling littled [sic] that she was married to a dumbbell. It made me furious when she said that. She had no idea about the pills I was taking, no idea what clever game-playing I was doing behind her back."

Eventually, through AA and his evaluation for learning disabilities, Dominic was able to better understand his drug addiction and explain to his wife what had been going on. "It was really a nervous breakdown of not being able to deal with the feelings about the learning disability and all the complex activities going on in my life. The kids were getting older. I had this threatening feeling that I had to accomplish some way to support a family and find the right job where I could grow, but where my LD wouldn't get in the way, and where I wouldn't be found out. And it was very important to me that I could support her, not she's supporting me. And it did make her feel good to learn that I was just having a nervous breakdown. And it was true. I know this within myself. I didn't know how to deal with all these screwups in my life, and I was reacting off of all these things. It was a horrible guilt trip that I still walk today. I was just trying to find love. That's all I was looking for. She was a pretty tough cookie back in those days, almost nasty. She said some nasty things to me when we were first married. I forgive her. She is a different person today. She doesn't do that any longer. She really doesn't."

Though his current relationship with his wife is quite positive, other affective problems remain. Reflecting on the emotional lability that is part of the complex overlap between learning disabilities and emotional disorders, Dominic says, "I might be cross when I really shouldn't be. I might be overly blah and I really shouldn't be because something is really going on, you know? I need someone to point these things out—I guess we all need that. But I think an LD person needs that a lot. Fear or anger about the LD affects my judgments sometimes. We bounce all over the place emotionally. I think we're emotionally sick people from the episodes that we've gone through and we need to start understanding why we were picked on. I've gotta get off my tail sometimes, and my wife gets me to do that.

"So it's been a lot. In some ways, I don't trust her still today, and I don't like that. For example, I was going to have her read the changing of the address of the downtown office to me and it's been sitting there for four weeks. And I think, 'Oh, I'll wait until the right time comes to ask her, when I can approach her in a high spirit where there's no strain and she feels very sing-songy.' But things have been very busy, so I haven't done it. But see how I do this? I'm scared to ask her, because I don't want to have her feel that she's married to a dumb-dumb. I can forgive her logically for calling me names. But sometimes the way I react, I guess I haven't fully accepted it one hundred percent. I wish for that today. And I'll try to strive for that. I don't know why I haven't, honest to God. It's going to cost me some pain. I'll have to do it soon. We're going to have to retire some day, and the day I retire is the day I'm going to have to learn to live with this every day."

Psychotherapeutic Commentary

Dominic didn't need learning disabilities and attention deficit issues to have psychological problems. His alcoholic mother literally drank herself to death, his father was consistently distant, critical, and rejecting, and his brother never grew up. But he did have learning and attentional issues, and they are complex and diagnostically nuanced by his giftedness. His educational experience was abysmal; the collective blindness of his school to his gifts and problems culminated in the principal telling him that he'd never amount to anything. Dominic's psychotherapy would have to be broad enough to include awareness of learning disabilities, adult child of an alcoholic, substance abuse, gifted LD, and attention deficit disorder, as well as the family, personality, and identity issues that are the usual "grist for the mill" of psychotherapy.

Consider the complexity and interactive dynamics of his psychological issues. Dominic's dyslexia prevented him from learning how

to read along with his classmates in school, and his learning problems seem to go beyond that, too, as we will consider below. He has
to struggle to keep his attention where he wants it to be and is highly susceptible to distraction, especially from internal stimuli. His
gifts for social relationship and leadership have played a huge role
in his life and in the development of his personality, for better and
for worse. They were the basis of his troublesome behavior as a child
and adolescent, as well as for his eventual success as an adult. His
mother's alcoholism was progressive and fatal, which could not have
failed to have profoundly affected him, although he does no more
than relate the bare facts in his interview. But he became substance
dependent himself and is still in recovery. In his family, the severe
dysfunction culminating in the accidental self-inflicted death of a
parent was further polarized in response to the emergence of his
learning problems. Indeed, when his learning problems emerged,
it was in the context of family and educational environments that
made things worse when they should have been making things better. The challenge for Dominic's psychotherapist would be to establish a therapeutic alliance in which they could study the reciprocal
interactions among complex learning and attentional abilities and
disabilities, extreme family dysfunction, substance abuse, and the
traumatic impact of dysfunctional educational institutions.

Developmental Issues

The family and the school are the two main social institutions
charged with the cultivation of children's human nature; religion
sometimes is a third, but usually a distant one, and it didn't seem to
have played a large role in Dominic's early life. When we study his
childhood development, it is within these contexts.

Both parents appear to have been seriously emotionally ill. His
mother's alcoholism would eventually prove fatal. His father's emotional illness is less clear, but depression and personality disorder
seem to be evident in his apparently completely negative and rejecting attitude toward Dominic.

When Dominic entered school, as the child of these parents, he
soon found himself in another painful and confusing set of relationships with adults. He came to realize that, for some completely
incomprehensible reason, he couldn't keep up with his classmates
in reading, and his teachers treated him as if he were deliberately
slacking. As he struggled to adjust to the fact that something strange

was wrong with him (even though he didn't feel any different than he ever had), he also struggled to adjust to his teachers' judgment of him as personally responsible for his problems in school.

Now we can assume that this didn't make sense to Dominic, because he knew very well that he wasn't trying not to read. He wanted to learn to read like the other children could. He wasn't trying to oppose the teachers; he was trying to learn. But he couldn't learn to read, for some mysterious reason, and his teachers perceived him as opposing them. He cared about learning and about how his teachers saw him, but there was nothing he could do about it. His teachers perceived him as not caring. He tried as hard as he could, but nothing helped, and his teachers accused him of not trying.

Dominic's educational problems further exacerbated the dysfunction in his family, particularly his relationships with his parents and their relationship with each other. His father's indiscriminate criticism and his mother's indiscriminate support further polarized their already damaged relationship around the issue of their son's disability. This provided attitudinal role models that Dominic internalized. Indeed, the cycling within his personality between grandiosity and self-abnegation, apparent in his interview, may be partly anchored to role models he internalized from his parents, as well as partly emerging from the peaks and valleys, the gifts and learning disabilities, of his own cognitive profile. This is a subtlety that is important for the therapist of someone like Dominic to grasp, at least intuitively, because if you don't glean this about him, you can't really have much of a therapeutic relationship with him.

Clearly, Dominic is a rather bright and perceptive person, especially socially. He applies himself diligently and effectively to the solution of problems that are important to him. His success in business and social life, and even in recovery from drug addiction, is due to these qualities, which he must have also had to some extent as a child. Consider the impact on such a child of the recognition that he is unable to learn something that virtually all his peers, even the ones who are his inferiors in other important ways, are able to. The teachers are spending most of the class time teaching reading, something that he can't learn. He tries and tries, but nothing works. Is he really more stupid than all his peers? Some of the teachers and his father seem to think so. Should he believe them? When they tell him that he doesn't care and isn't trying, he knows that they're wrong. When they tell him that he can't read, he knows that they're right. How is he to make sense out of all this? What does it mean about him, about his peers and the adults in his life, and about his relationships with them? Why is his mother so supportive in all of this?

We all learn to use our strengths to cope with the challenges of life, and Dominic turned to his social skills to help him cope with his incomprehensible inability to learn what everyone else could. Although he couldn't learn how to read, he was able to make others laugh and entertain them, which is some sort of success. He was able to gain their attention and respect by being a clown. And he was determined to succeed somehow at school; he wasn't just going to be a silent, invisible, nonreading nobody. This determination, among other qualities, would eventually enable Dominic to earn more money than the principal who told him that he would never amount to anything (an irony that particularly appeals to me!).

Diagnostic Complexity: Not Just Dyslexia

If inability to read were Dominic's only problem, it would be serious enough, but it isn't. His description of himself indicates at least two additional deficits, both in the content of what he says and in the manner with which he says it. First, there is evidence of an attention deficit disorder, particularly an inability to inhibit internal stimuli. Second, there is evidence of a sequencing deficit in his manner of speaking, and perhaps, of thinking.

Attention Deficit Disorder. There is an analogy between focusing attention and moving the body. In order to make a movement, some muscles must extend while others contract. In order to attend, we must both focus on something and also inhibit our attentional focus from straying to other things. Current understanding of the brain suggests that the frontal parts of each cerebral hemisphere contribute to the maintenance of a focus of attention in different and complementary ways. The right hemisphere appears to be responsible for the general perceptual orientation to the situation, including the dynamic process of it, while the left hemisphere is able to focus on one element at a time and put them together into a meaningful sequence (Ornstein, 1997). The brain contains many pathways between the frontal lobes and the midbrain, some of which are excitatory (they turn attention "on") and some of which are inhibitory (they turn attention "off"). Although we can't measure it directly, it appears that, like any other cognitive function, attention seems to have a normal range within which most people fall, and extremes at both ends of the normal distribution into which some people fall. The people whose attention falls outside the normal range may be highly distractible (hyperattentive) or very difficult to distract (hypoattentive). The first type has to struggle to maintain an attentional focus, while the second wouldn't notice a hungry lion until it was about to eat him, so to speak.

People who are easily distractible may be distracted by stimuli that occur outside, in their external environment, or inside, within their internal environment, or both. That is, people with attention deficit problems may be externally or internally distractible. Dominic laments that he is frequently distracted from what he is doing by inner thoughts, images, and feelings, even when he's driving. He loses the focus on his current goal. He becomes preoccupied with some feeling or image that has to do with his relationship with something or someone. He has to work very hard to maintain an external focus. He has to try to resist the tendency to be overcome by his internal images and their associated feelings. Thus, it appears that Dominic may have an oversensitivity to internal impulses combined with a relative deficit in ability to maintain his attentional focus on a specific object or task. This inability to inhibit internal impulses and maintain external attentional focus may be a form of attention deficit disorder.

Speech and Sequencing. Next, when we look at Dominic's speech pattern, we see that there is a staccato, almost poetic quality about it. He speaks in bursts of meaning, giving lines that are not necessarily clearly sequentially connected so that we, listening, have to put the pieces together, fill in the gaps between statements. Any good English teacher would instantly recognize the lack of sequence in his speech. Orderly sequence of language and the maintenance of a stable attentional focus, in most adults, appear to be largely the job of the left hemisphere. When all these deficits are put together—severe deficit in decoding written language, deficit in maintaining attentional focus on specific events, and deficit in sequencing spoken language—what begins to emerge, tentatively, is a neuropsychological picture of some kind of deficit in frontal left hemisphere functioning, since all these functions are, in most adults, mediated primarily by mid to frontal parts of the left hemisphere.

Diagnostic Complexity: Cognitive Strengths

On the other hand, Dominic appears to have significant strengths in cognitive areas associated with the right hemisphere (Ornstein, 1997). He is able to understand situations that he is in quite well and is able to relate very effectively to other people; just discussing his experience, he makes an immediate and powerful emotional connection with the interviewer and even the reader. He thinks dynamically—interactively rather than incrementally—and appears to have strong social skills and to be a natural leader. He has already learned a great deal from life itself, but he needs help in putting it together, thinking it through, and understanding how to apply what he has learned. Furthermore, he has a definite ability to observe himself, associated with the right hemisphere, which enables him to have a measure of self-knowledge, and this is something that we can work with in psychotherapy.

Psychotherapy and Learning Disabilities

Arthur Deikman (1979) usefully indicates three broad areas of psychotherapeutic concern:

- self-defeating behaviors such as inner emotional and cognitive conflicts, fantasies, wishes, dependencies, etc.,
- the need for meaning, and
- the need for personal evolution connected with the evolution of others.

As psychotherapists working with clients, we ask such questions as:

- What are the inner conflicts, fantasies, unrealistic thinking, frustrated wishes, repetitive self-defeating patterns of behavior, etc., that the patient uses to tie up his energy and negate his growth toward becoming a healthier and more effective person?
- Is there an absence of meaning in the patient's life, or is a poor substitute derived through self-defeating means (for example, by always having to be in the victim role)?
- Is there an absence of personal growth and connectedness to the growth process in others?

When a client has a learning disability, our understanding of his problems can be extended if we ask how it affects him in each of these three areas. For example:

- How does his learning disability affect his problems in adapting to life realistically and effectively?
- How does his learning disability (and his adjustment or maladjustment to it) affect his sense of meaning or purpose in life?
- How does his learning disability (and his adjustment or maladjustment to it) affect his conscious development and connection with the conscious development of others?

Role of the Learning Disability in Understanding of Self

One of the goals of psychotherapy is (usually) to foster an improved understanding of oneself on the part of the client. Clients typically come to therapy feeling stuck in a situation, but the ways they perceive and define their situation and themselves are usually connected to and sometimes produce the inability to progress. The presence of learning disabilities almost invariably warps the developing sense of self of the child (see Chapter 8). Successful experiences of living can help to mitigate this warping and restore a healthier sense of oneself. When one is stuck on some aspect of the warp, psychotherapy may be necessary. Obviously, psychotherapy for a person with a learning disability that does not in some way include the effects of the learning disability on the self can hardly hope to be as effective as psychotherapy that does.

Including LD Issues in Psychotherapy

Sometimes people with learning disabilities try to avoid having to acknowledge them or think about managing them, but Dominic is not like this. Once these fundamentals are made part of the psychotherapeutic conversation—as they would be in treating Dominic—there are three issues that relate specifically to his learning disabilities that will need to be explored:

- What does Dominic understand about his learning disabilities? Does he need to expand his understanding of his learning disabilities in order to progress? For example, if Dominic's understanding of his learning disabilities is limited to dyslexia, he's trying to solve a problem without adequate information. His attentional and sequencing issues, as well as his gifts, need to be included in his self-knowledge.
- What methods is Dominic using to compensate for his learning disabilities and how are they working? Could he identify other

ways of compensating that might work more effectively, or give him more choices in different situations?

• Is Dominic advocating for himself when and where he needs to? Does he need to learn how to advocate for himself more effectively or in another part of his life? Sometimes people can avoid lots of problems simply by explaining something about themselves to others.

Note that these questions would not come up in psychotherapy if the client were not learning disabled. The amount of psychotherapy time required to address such questions depends on how much a person's learning disability has affected his life. Such questions may be less important, and take up less time, with a patient whose learning disability is less severe than Dominic's and has had less impact on the client's sense of self.

For example, I once worked with a client with a mild auditory processing deficit who had graduated from college on the strength of his excellent visual memory. He could literally remember pages of text as visual images and read the answers off them during exams, as long as he wasn't too anxious or intoxicated (he used intoxicants to manage his anxiety). He was afraid to take a professional training course that would support his career aspirations because of his painful experiences in high school and college. This was a major issue for a while in psychotherapy. Once he realized that he could use his visual memory skill to pass the exam, and that it wasn't a disaster if he didn't pass the first time, and after he had found better ways to manage his anxiety and stopped using intoxicants (another major issue in treatment), he was able to take and pass the course. Afterward, his learning disability became a relatively minor issue in his psychotherapy, which was primarily concerned with other issues impinging on his sense of self. By comparison, learning disability issues loom large in Dominic's personal story and sense of self.

Diagnostic Complexity: Differentiating
LD and Non-LD Issues

In psychotherapy, we would try to develop an alliance with Dominic while studying the role of his learning disabilities (and how others responded to them) in the development of his personality. We would also need to study the factors in his environment that would have powerfully affected Dominic whether he had a learning disability or not. For example, the responses of the principal and some of his teachers to his learning disability were traumatic for Dominic, and that is due to his learning disability and how the school responded to it. But his father's critical attitude would have been there anyway; Dominic's learning disability was just a convenient target and perhaps made a bad situation worse. His mother's alcoholism would have been there anyway. The possibility that Dominic may feel guilty for her drinking and, in some way, responsible for her death seems possible and worth exploring. Dominic would probably have had inner pain and sought to assuage it with intoxicants regardless of his learning disability, although that made things worse for him. Helping Dominic improve his understanding of himself means helping him to see himself not just as a person with a learning disability in a culture that provided shame instead of remediation, nor only as the child of a rejecting father and an alcoholic mother in a society that places great stress on relationships and families, but as both.

Diagnostic Complexity: Therapeutic Diagnosis

Diagnosis is always an important part of therapy. I'm referring not to formal diagnosis, in which a term is selected from the *Diagnostic and Statistical Manual*, but rather to diagnosis in a much more pragmatic, existential, and working sense—the understanding that the client and therapist share about the nature of the patient's problems. For example, a patient might be, according to the *DSM-IV* criteria, clinically depressed, but she and her therapist might better understand her emotional state in terms of her inability to resolve the impossible demands that she experienced within her family while growing up. Or we might imagine three other clients who are clinically depressed: One needs short-term therapy leading to the decision to make necessary life changes; one needs long-term therapy leading to fundamental personality changes; and one needs immediate medication more than anything else. The *DSM-IV* diagnosis alone gives us very limited information. As long as someone presenting for treatment isn't suicidal, we would do better to direct our attention to her story, her personal history, and how that is expressed now in her personality.

When a patient has a learning disability, the diagnosis of "learning disability" is as useful in some ways, and useless in others, as a diagnosis of clinical depression. It is, at best, a point of departure, telling us that something is wrong but not what. When a client has a learning disability, we need to discover his strengths and weaknesses as a learner, so we can understand how they have affected the development of his personality, see how they currently operate, and explore what he can do to make better use of his strengths and compensate for his weaknesses.

Dominic presents to us diagnosed as dyslexic, and it is clear to him, and to us, that his problem learning to read is central to his emotional problems. However, dyslexia does not adequately encompass Dominic's learning problems. Like many clients with learning disabilities, Dominic understands that his inability to consistently maintain an external attentional focus and his problems with organizing his schedule may be due in part to cognitive deficits and not to some sort of character defect. Such understanding can make a world of difference, both to Dominic and to his therapist. For Dominic, it can both explain many of his problems in the past and point the way to how he can better manage himself in the present and future, liberating his capacity to organize and manage himself more intelligently. For his psychotherapist, it can provide a "road map" to help organize and orient work with him based on the realities of his cognitive functioning rather than a misdiagnosis of personality problems that are really due to cognitive functioning. Clearing away the potential errors of confusing cognitive problems with personality ones sharpens the therapist's focus on Dominic's real personality, with its strengths and weaknesses.

Cognitive Factors in the Psychotherapeutic Relationship

We take it as given that how a person thinks and perceives will have a large influence in how he engages in relationships. Psychotherapists often don't take that thought a step further to see how a learning disabled client's cognitive processes will affect how he participates in the psychotherapeutic relationship. Especially important is the question of how a client's learning disabilities affect how he communicates to the therapist and how he processes the therapist's communications to him (recall Kerry's communication problems in Chapter 4).

Dominic thinks and speaks in a staccato, almost poetic way, with a relative lack of sequential coherence, but a certain depth of perception of the situation at hand. And he is prone to being distracted from internal thoughts and feelings by whatever he is doing. A therapist seeking to establish an effective working relationship with him will have to learn to understand Dominic's "language," at least to some extent, and will also have to speak to Dominic in a way that he will be able to receive. Making elegant theoretical interpretations with such a client will probably be of little use, for example. Rather, the therapist may have to speak in short bursts of condensed meaning, especially at first. Perhaps the therapist will gradually be able to try to string insights together into sequences that Dominic will be able to track, encouraging the development of his own relatively weak sequential thinking ability; but that will come later. By contrast, patients with nonverbal cognitive deficits, who often use language in a very concrete manner and are usually oblivious to most nuance and implication, need to be spoken to in a very concrete, highly explicit way. Therapists working with such patients may have to do a lot more talking than they are used to, and a lot more teaching by translating ordinary behavioral expectations into explicit speech (see the discussion of Hannah in Chapter 7).

In addition, Dominic's tendency to be distracted by internal stimuli is likely to show up in psychotherapy, and the therapist will have to decide what to do about it. A therapist who doesn't recognize Dominic's attentional issue may misinterpret such digressions as entirely defensive. A therapist who recognizes that they are primarily attentional can treat them as such, for example, by saying something like, "That may be an important issue, Dominic, but now we're talking about [whatever], so let's continue with that and remember to return to this other issue later." As Dominic's therapist one would have to be the "minder of the sequence of the conversation," as it were. This is not to suggest that such digressions would be entirely nondefensive in nature. Indeed, deciding to what extent they were attentional and to what extent they were defensive, and especially when they were defensive, would be a psychotherapeutic goal.

Here is an example of how not knowing a client's learning deficit undermined a therapist's effectiveness, and how knowing it improved it. A social worker referred a client to me for evaluation because she was concerned that she didn't seem to be making progress in psychotherapy, despite seeming to have the requisite insight and motivation for progress. She wondered whether there might be an attention deficit disorder contributing to this lack of progress. My evaluation did not show an attention deficit disorder; however, I found that the client had a deficit in auditory language processing (understanding spoken language). On the other hand, she excelled at visual language processing (reading). Once this became clear, it was a simple step to recommend that the client take notes during sessions and recap the important points at the end of each session. This improved her memory of what had been discussed during the session and gave her therapist a chance to check on whether the client had forgotten—or not heard—important matters. This also gave the client insight into her own learning strengths and weaknesses, which she was able to apply to other situations.

Note that it would have been easy for the social worker to make the interpretation that her client was resisting her interpretations or was in some subtle way trying to undermine her own progress. In the light of the client's inability to remember much of what was said to her regardless of what it was, and her much better ability to remember what she reads, we see that such interpretations would have been incorrect. One channel of linguistic input is simply working much better than another.

An important goal of psychotherapy for clients with learning disabilities is to better understand how their cognitive strengths and weaknesses affect them. Dominic's psychotherapist might try to help him see how his rapid social perceptions help him to understand many situations more quickly and deeply than others. This kind of perception helps him to act effectively in his business, for example. And, there may be ways in which Dominic's social perception can be refined and honed to become even deeper. For example, in business situations he seems to understand just what people want, but he does not do so well in personal ones. Wouldn't his ability to relate to others and his life as a whole be immeasurably deepened if he could recognize interpersonal issues in social or family situations as well as he does in business ones?

On the other hand, his relative deficit in sequential thinking may hinder his ability to understand certain issues in personal relationships, especially when tracking events over time is important. For example, his history with his wife certainly appears to have affected her attitude toward him, but he seems to have difficulty holding onto the image of a relationship that has progressed through a series of stages. Rather, he seems to have a condensed, intensely meaningful impression of how it feels now, without much relationship to what came before or how things might proceed from here. Clearly, if he and his wife could share a more positive narrative of their past history and future aspirations, the likelihood of their relationship improving would be substantially increased. This is another issue that could be addressed in psychotherapy. Once again, the therapist who understands Dominic's difficulty in understanding how his wife's experience with him over time might affect her feelings now will be in a position to help him to make necessary cognitive adjustments. But the therapist who misinterprets Dominic's problems, who thinks that this in-the-moment attitude is primarily defensive or an expression of unconscious hostility, will be banging all their heads—therapist's, client's, and wife's—against the wall.

Diagnostic Complexity: Substance Abuse and Learning Disabilities

Finally, Dominic's issues with intoxicants, which emerge from his early experience as the child of an alcoholic parent and his biological predisposition to addiction, are inextricably intertwined with the painful consequences of his history of learning disability. Addicts typically use intoxicants to anesthetize emotional pain; there's more to it than just that, but that is a big part. In psychotherapy, Dominic's emotional pain would come into clearer focus together with his choice to depend on intoxicants rather than to rely on his intelligence to assuage the pain. "Intelligence" is used here in the widest sense and includes emotional, social, and personal intelligence. While not measured on cognitive or personality tests, these abilities have provided the foundations of Dominic's success in life. Understanding that he undervalued these capabilities within himself for so long—partly because they were undervalued by the cultures of his family and school—may be necessary to bring his strengths into clear focus and make them more accessible to Dominic now.

CHAPTER 6

We Had You Tested and Nothing's Wrong

LD and the Challenge of Diagnosis

*The woman who tested me said nothing was wrong with me,
no problem, it was just emotional. And so my mother always
used that against me. She would say, "We had you tested and
nothing's wrong. I always knew you were just lazy. You don't
try hard enough." It was my fault and that was always what
it was.*

—Sonja Resnikov

Sonja begins her story on a dramatic note. "I was 14. And my parents were going to turn me out of the house. And someone said, 'Well, you can put her in the hospital.' So they did, and it was an awful experience. It was tragic. Getting blamed and yelled at for things I didn't do, by therapists included."

Sonja was placed in psychiatric treatment with a diagnosis of conduct disorder, as a result of being perceived as violent and potentially harmful to her mother. However, treatment was not successful and she was discharged after a month. "Some people are worse than when they go in, and that was the case with me, because it meant having to stand up and lie and claim that I physically abused my mother in order to look as though I made some progress in treatment. That didn't help at all. I learned more about negative things and drugs by going in there. I was labeled as this violent person, which is sad, because I'm not a violent person at all."

Now, at the age of 24, Sonja Resnikov is about to graduate from college. She is no longer an out-of-control teenager, but the ten years since her hospitalization have been a struggle, and there are still many serious issues that need to be resolved. Her soft voice with its Virginia lilt contrasts dramatically with the harsh story she has to tell.

At home, before being hospitalized, Sonja's perception is that her parents neglected her. "Maybe my mother would buy food for everyone else and wouldn't buy it for me. Or she wouldn't pick me up when I needed a ride. She wasn't listening to me and just basically ignored me. Then I would react, but it was more like little tiffs we would get into, that *she* would call battery. Like she would put her hand in my face and I'd be like, 'Get away,' you know? I would be just so angry. And I was blamed for everything. I was the black sheep. The bad seed. And I got labeled as a violent kid. I was brutally abused verbally, and mostly emotionally, and physically too, but not as much as maybe you have heard of it happening to other people. There was no sexual abuse or anything, but we would get into arguments and that was a nightmare."

When hospitalization proved unsuccessful, the conflict escalated at home. "There was no support. They were throwing me out, and I had no place to stay and I had no control. And my mom would call the police and try to have me arrested. One time I think I put mustard on the couch because I was so angry. I forget what it was. And she tried to have me arrested for property damage. And the police said, 'Well, we can't arrest her for that, lady.' But finally one day we did end up at the police station, and she had me arrested for battery."

Sonja remembers that experience vividly. "You had police calling you a little bitch and saying that they didn't want their kids to ever grow up like you. You have no say if you're a kid. You're saying, 'I didn't *do* this,' and then you get these cocky adults who just totally believe your parents. And if you don't have your family on your side, you don't have anything. There are people who tell me I didn't have it as bad as some, but for me it was real depression, and inner turmoil, and emotional abuse that I still struggle with today."

After she was arrested and had served some time in a juvenile detention facility—she had just turned 15—Sonja's parents placed her in a group home. "I remember I was at this group home, and there were eight to ten people to a home. It was awful. School was just always very difficult for me. I remember it was summer and I was taking a history class. We were taking a test, and I knew that I had no idea what was going on. And the teacher was talking and I was thinking, 'This is insane. I'm not grasping *any* of this.' I was about to get my credits, my grades, and I felt this was just really useless, because I'm not understanding any of this, and I'm not going to pass, and I'm not going to succeed in this. And it wasn't my attitude either, because I really did try. I wasn't going to make it, and that was a big part of the reason. Also I couldn't stand the place, so I ran away." Although Sonja could have mentioned any number of problems she had at the group home, she zeroes in on school because to her it was the source of all her difficulties.

Although no one understood it at the time, Sonja is learning disabled, and this undiagnosed disability (in the areas of attention and spatial organization) and the resulting school failure contributed substantially to her feelings of desperation, which found their expression in the drastic action of running away. Such behavior masked the LD, and it is this incomplete diagnosis that makes Sonja's story especially important. The purpose of this chapter is to explore the challenges of diagnosis, the consequences of misdiagnosis, and the contributions of diagnosis to treatment.

Sonja continues to feel, quite strongly, that the accusations of violence were exaggerated. From her perspective, what is most salient is her own frustration and sense of being rejected and misunderstood, but from her parents' perspective Sonja seemed quite threatening, especially to her mother. It is quite possible that she mishandled her frustration. Even today she is not completely in touch with her own anger. But it does not really matter whose perceptions are more accurate. The fact is, Sonja was *perceived* by adults as being of potential harm to others and unmanageable at home, and by this stage in her life cognitive and affective problems were interacting in complex ways. The important point here is that the arguments and violence served to hide other issues that were never diagnosed or dealt with.

Reflecting on that time in her life, Sonja says, "Well, I wasn't *really* homeless, because I was in all these institutions. But I was," she says as she shakes her head sadly. "I have to say that I *felt* homeless." She had been in the group home for a year, attending the local high school (her junior year), when she ran away, but her parents refused to let her come back to her own home. "A counselor, some crazy counselor, had told them to lock me out. I ran to a friend's house, and then I called my mom. I begged her to let me stay with my grandma for a little bit, so I could get my stuff, and she said OK, so I was very relieved. But otherwise, no, she would never let me come home or do anything like that.

"So they let me go to the police and become a ward of the state. I went through foster care waiting for placement, and then I was in temporary shelters for a year. I was lucky because I had a roof over my head and I didn't live on the street, but I was just tossed around. And it was the most terrible experience. The most scary nightmare of a child who has no control over her life. And it affects you for the rest of your life. I've gotten over a lot of it, but it really has marked me for life."

Now, about to graduate from college, Sonja has made enormous progress both psychologically and educationally, pulling herself back from the edge of the chasm, though not without enormous cost, including an ulcer. Her behavior is no longer out of control, but whereas her adolescent acting out indicated hope for something better, now her anger has turned to resignation and so she is constantly fighting depression. What is her anger about? "Anger about people not listening, not understanding, and anger about my whole life!" But she also feels helpless to change things, so anger is a defense against powerlessness. Ultimately, "that anger just turns to depression. You're frustrated, and you get sad about it, but there's nothing you can do."

Sonja's spatial and attention deficits have not disappeared. They affect, for example, her ability to learn various forms of recreation and physical exercise. She recalls a recent incident in her recreational ballet class, which on the surface may seem fairly inconsequential, but which for her embodies and symbolizes her learning experiences since childhood, and which evokes all of the pain of so many of her attempts to learn over the years. Her ballet teacher was giving her some corrections, Sonja explains. "Well, my turnout was wrong; it was improper or something. She started yelling at me saying, 'You're not so-and-so, whoever, you know, some famous dancer. Don't put your leg that way,' and she gives an exaggerated shrug and says, 'What next?' It was very humiliating. When I go to ballet class, it's just for fun. I can understand that she wants me to do the right thing, but yelling at me's not going to help me. I was being really picked on. She just lost it! But that's nothing new."

Issues of spatiality plague her. When the other dancers go left, she goes right. The frequent public humiliation has led to shame and demoralization. "It seems like so many people do this to me. I have always had to put up with a lot of badgering and getting yelled at, and I always had to blame it on myself." And she wonders with more than a hint of despair, "Do I need an LD specialist to help me with *everything* I undertake?" She knows that in a sense the answer to her question is yes—her difficulties do affect every aspect of her life; there is no hiding from them. But in spite of continued disappointment and rejection, Sonja has an integrity and tenacious persistence that have served her well. "It gets frustrating to the point that I'm determined I won't quit! I have a right to learn! I just don't want her to make a big spectacle of it."

Sonja's parents probably could see early on that she was not going to fit in. Of course, all parents worry about their children and are concerned that they won't fit in with the expectations of the world. But some parents of children with learning disabilities try too hard to "make" them fit. Then the resulting situation, what we might call a "Procrustean bed syndrome," produces a cycle of overcorrection, loss of patience, and blaming the child, which may then give rise to oppositional/defiant disorder or to conduct disorder and overshadow the underlying attention deficit or learning disability.[1]

Although her parents were unaware of it, Sonja's inability to "fit in" was a direct result of her difficulties with spatial orientation and, to an even greater extent, problems with attention. Even as a preschooler, attention difficulties caused behaviors that were interpreted as "naughty." "When I was little I used to wander around a lot. One day I felt like going out, and I left the house. I just walked around the neighborhood and wandered into people's backyards. My family was in a panic. All my brothers and sisters were looking for me. They finally found me, but I was always wandering off, and that was considered bad. Looking back, I really don't know why I did it.

"Another time I was at my aunt's house, and I had gone to the grocery store with my sister. I had some bread, and then after we left the store my sister informed me that it wasn't paid for. Well, I didn't know that; I wouldn't steal on purpose. When we got back, she told my aunt. So I took the bread, and I ran—I don't know why I did this—I ran outside into the alley, and my uncle was chasing me, and I was just running around the alley with the bread saying, 'My name is Macaroni.'" Sonja's memories suggest problems with impulsivity and possibly hyperactivity rather than anger or defiance. "It wasn't as if I stole the bread. You know, I do a lot of things and don't know why I do them."

Impulsive behavior soon resulted in a major family crisis. "I didn't want to go to bed and I didn't want to brush my teeth either, so I hid under the bed while Mom was busy with the other kids. They couldn't find me and they were afraid I'd run away again. So they called the cops. I could see the shiny black shoes, and all of a sudden my sister looks down underneath the bed and goes, 'There she is!'" Sonja had no awareness of hyperactivity or impulsivity as a child even though her story suggests it may have been present. "I guess I thought that being fidgety was normal."

In spite of her difficulties, however, Sonja's first years in school were not difficult. "My mom helped me and it went all right. I wanted to get my work done. I didn't *want* to get in trouble. I was always a goody-two-shoes in school." Although later on Sonja's acting-out behavior became part of a cycle of reaction to her parents' discipline, she feels it originally occurred "because I was vying for my mom's attention." (Sonja was the youngest of six.)

But just a short while later, she began having problems both in and out of school. "Yeah, I did feel that I had problems. But they were just ignored. And my parents simply said, 'You don't try hard enough. Just try harder.' And that was it. I didn't try hard enough. I even had trouble playing with friends. My friend would say, 'OK, we're going to play school, so let's do some math problems,' and we'd have our little chalkboard, and my girlfriend would put the problems on the board, and there'd be two of us doing the problems, and mine would be totally wrong. My girlfriend would say something like, 'This is totally wrong! I just can't believe this, being with you jerks,' and she would be right. I'd just feel completely stupid. She would get really angry and mad with me, and I'd feel just really dumb because I couldn't do it."

Then problems at school increased. "Math was always the worst. I remember I had a math teacher who was telling me to do a problem on the board, and I couldn't get it right. He threw the chalk across the room, and threw the eraser down, and his face got all red, and he was yelling at me and screaming my name. There was nothing I could do, and I knew that." Just as in the ballet class, Sonja's teacher simply reached a point where he was so frustrated that he lost his patience.

Sonja had to endure constant reproaches from her family as well. "Yelling at me because I didn't try hard enough—that was a big thing with the family. My parents would say, 'Well, you don't have a C average, so you can't do any extra things.' Trying to do extracurriculars and things that I liked and not being allowed to do them because of my poor grades was a big part of my life."

In high school, nonverbal spatial problems continued to plague her. "I remember I had this band teacher. I was doing a marching routine, and I wasn't going the right way, or something. I remember the look he gave me. It's the same look that this gymnastics teacher would give me, a look that says, "What is *wrong* with you?" That's the worst feeling, when you have somebody who you think likes you and then they look at you with this look of disappointment or disgust, like you're some kind of idiot. It's the worst feeling in the world, because it's letting someone down. It's just an awful feeling of being rejected and feeling like you're nothing."

It was during her early high school years when family relationships worsened dramatically. "When I was younger they weren't really physically abusive, but I would say that my dad was physically abusive when I got older. He would hit me with a belt and stuff, or just grab me by my hair. One time I broke a plate because I was in a fight with my mom, and he came in and started pulling my hair, and pushing me to the floor and trying to make me pick the plate up.

"I spent a lot of time in the bathroom hiding, because he was physically very strong, and he *really* scared me. My brothers were very physical, and my sisters as well, and I felt like they had nothing to do except to make my life hell. Sometimes I would stay in the bathtub all night, because that was the only door that locked. I was scared to death, doing nothing for hours on end until he or my brothers or sisters went downstairs, because if I opened the door, I would really get punched around."

It was at this point that Sonja became a ward of the state. She lived in temporary shelters for nearly a year, and she recalls, "There was no education. You just sat there, you watched movies, you watched TV. You might do some grammar school, baby stuff, but that's all. That was my senior year. It was awful." Then, having graduated from high school and finally living in what she considered to be a fairly good, stable group home situation, Sonja was able to consider future plans. In spite of her dreadful experiences in school, she recognized the importance of education and attended a local community college. With her characteristic persistence and determination, lots of tutoring, and the advantage of only having to take one or two courses at a time, Sonja was able to pass her courses, getting straight C's.

Sonja also tried working, but unfortunately, her attention and spatial problems simply resurfaced in a new context. "I tried working at Kentucky Fried Chicken, but I couldn't grasp it. Someone would give me an order and I had to fill it. But I couldn't listen to the order and get it right. I left things out or put the wrong things in the bag. I worked there two days and I quit. I wasn't that I didn't try. I just knew I couldn't do it." She tried several other part-time jobs with the same results.

Then a dispute with a staff member led to her being discharged from the group home. "After I got kicked out, I was too old for another placement, and I didn't have anywhere to go." With some financial support from her dad she transferred to the local state college. But taking a full load at a four-year institution was much more difficult. "I wasn't getting the grades. I was really scared that I wouldn't be able to make it." By sheer chance this university had a support program for learning disabled students, and when she heard about it, she referred herself for testing. Not surprisingly, she was so restless and agitated that she could not work for longer than a few minutes and was unable to complete even a short test. Case notes from those testing sessions reveal that it was extremely difficult for her to express herself, as she impulsively tried to say everything at once. The clinician immediately referred her for a psychological evaluation for possible ADD. Perhaps because of her extreme anxiety as well as her attention problems, Sonja did not understand that the diagnosis was inconclusive because the testing could not be completed, nor that the clinician, suspecting ADD, was referring her for more appropriate testing. Instead, Sonja interpreted the evaluation results as follows: "They said I didn't qualify as being LD. They said I was going through the tests too fast, and that I wasn't paying attention. They thought I wasn't being serious, like I was just kind of going through the motions. But I did the best

I could. They said that I was too hyperactive and I didn't concentrate enough. And I thought, 'Well, whatever. Everyone's got a different horror story about me. This is just me, and it's hopeless forever.'"

By this time, depression had become her immediate concern. "I felt like I had to be hospitalized, OK? And you *know* I didn't want to do that. But I felt like I needed constant care. That's being honest with myself. I would sit there and just stare at my books. I was sleeping all day. I went to class and I slept. I was like, 'Please, somebody help me. Something's going on here and I can't control it and it's scaring me.' I couldn't get out of bed. I didn't have any motivation. I didn't know what to do because I couldn't live my life!" Sonja then sought help at the university counseling center. "I was on probation, and I was just terrified. What if my dad took the financial support away? I was scared of being homeless again. I was so depressed, but too scared to do nothing. So I went to the crisis counseling center, and that really helped me." The therapist prescribed a trial of Ritalin so that she could concentrate in class and suggested a complete psychological evaluation. His referral to Diane, a psychiatric social worker, eventually proved to be the turning point in Sonja's story.

Sonja was extremely leery of psychological testing because a previous evaluation had been traumatic and yielded no satisfactory explanation for her learning problems. "When I was 15, before I was placed in the psychiatric hospital, my parents took me to have an evaluation." Sonja doesn't remember any testing specifically for LD, only a general psychological evaluation. But nevertheless, "The woman who tested me said nothing was wrong with me, no problem, it was just emotional. And so my mother always used that against me. She would say, 'We had you tested and nothing's wrong. I always knew you were just lazy. You don't try hard enough.' It was my fault and that was *always* what it was. My mom never said I was stupid, but she gave me that impression. My brothers and sisters were always smarter than me. I was the dumb one."

Alternative Interpretations of Behavior

In spite of her misgivings and with Diane's encouragement, Sonja followed through on the referral from the university counseling center for additional psychological testing, which specified that the purpose of the evaluation was an assessment for (1) depression, (2) passive-aggressive personality disorder, and (3) adult attention deficit disorder. Before continuing with Sonja's story, it is worth taking a detailed look at the results of this second psychological evaluation. In most respects the diagnosis was not wrong, but something important was missed. Although no mention was made of learning disabilities in the referral or the subsequent evaluation, a number of clues are apparent when we examine the report carefully from a learning disabilities perspective. Sonja understood the results of the testing as follows: "Basically, they said it was all emotional. That was it. It was so frustrating." The summary of the psychological report bears her out, concluding with the follow diagnosis:

Axis I   Dysthymia

Axis III   Ulcer

Axis IV   Psychosocial stressors: poor school performance, financial problems, and changing residence—severity level 3, moderate

Axis V   Overall GAF scale 52—moderate difficulty functioning

Passive-aggressive personality disorder was ruled out. ADD was also ruled out with the simple statement that "measures of attention on these tests indicate that she is not suffering from this disorder." Apparently ADD was ruled out entirely on the basis of her WAIS-R performance, since the report states merely that "the distractibility factor is not significant."[2] The report summarizes the findings as follows:

> In synthesis, Sonja knows she has limited resources and unlimited needs. During this testing, she partitioned her energy reservoir to complete all tests. She was economical, affectively guarded, and withdrawn. She is afraid to think, to feel, to let go of her defensive stands, to engage in intellectual and social activities because she is afraid of losing control of her emotions of love and grief, of looking inside of herself and finding a confused person wasting away and of being rejected as her family rejected her early in life. Protection and constriction rather than production and creativity constitute her goals.

If we consider alternative interpretations of behavior, however, there are tantalizing observations scattered throughout narrative portion of the report that hint at ADD as well as a learning disability. Some of the more revealing comments in the report are as follows:

- *Punctuality.* "Sonja was three hours late to our second appointment." [*Examiner's Interpretation: none offered*]
- *Impulsivity.* "Her approach to tasks was sparing and disengaged, or impulsive and careless. She interrupted the examiner, and gave quick answers to difficult items, racing through the subtests, spending the least amount of energy in doing so. . . . Sonja is impulsive and negligent[3] in processing information, so some of her responses are formulated before the stimulus field is fully mediated." [*Examiner's Interpretation: "Sonja stated repeatedly that testing made her feel 'nervous.' . . . by answering the items impulsively, Sonja eliminated the source of her 'nervousness.'"*]
- *Organization.* "Sonja's planning ability and visual organization are poor. She did not take time to understand the whole stimuli [sic] presented. Sonja learns through trial and error, a more exhausting and frustrating learning experience." [*Examiner's Interpretation: ". . . by being careless, she could justify any possible mistakes she had made."*]
- *School Performance.* "Sonja has not benefited from her educational experience as much as one might expect, given her intellectual ability." [*Examiner's Interpretation: "It appears that anxiety may have interfered with her ability to learn. This hypothesis is made because her performance subtests which are responsive to anxiety are relatively lower than the verbal subtests."*]
- *Rate of Learning.* "Her grades constitute her biggest source of stress. She feels unable to understand concepts quickly." [*Examiner's Interpretation: None offered directly, but a bit later the report states: "Sonja has a limited reservoir intellectually." (Note that this interpretation conflicts with the statement above about intellectual ability.)*]

These interpretations are no doubt correct in that Sonja's ability to learn, her impulsivity in responding, and her interrupting the clinician were surely affected in no small measure by anxiety. But given her long history of school difficulties, we need to ask whether something else is going on, and whether this particular constellation of clinical observations is open to additional interpretations. A second look, through the lens of learning disabilities, yields the following alternative interpretations of the five points mentioned above:

- *Punctuality.* Sonja's lateness is linked to a larger problem with time management, as is typical in many cases of ADD (Kelly & Ramundo, 1993; Levine, 1998; Nadeau, 1993). Hallowell and Ratey (1994) note, "Of the people who consult with me for problems related to ADD, probably about a half are either late for their first appointment or miss it altogether. I have come to expect it. It comes with the territory" (p. 7).

- *Impulsivity.* Impulsivity, which Sonja exhibited by interrupting, racing through tests, etc., is often a hallmark of attention deficit disorder (*DSM-IV,* p. 84) and has been recognized as a common characteristic of ADD in adults (Hallowell & Ratey, 1994; Johnson & Blalock, 1987; Kelly & Ramundo, 1993; Nadeau, 1995).

- *Organization.* Sonja's poor planning ability, poor visual organization, and trial-and-error learning can be interpreted in a number of ways, e.g., as symptoms of inattention and/or distractibility (Levine, 1998) or difficulty with executive functions (Barkley, 1996; Westman, 1990). In Sonja's case the evaluator's observation of poor visual organization on IQ and projective tests lends itself to still another LD-related interpretation, i.e., that she had serious visual-spatial processing difficulties.

- *School Performance.* Sonja's examiner may have noted that anxiety contributed to poor school performance, but the converse interpretation is equally plausible. A third, even more likely interpretation is that by the time Sonja reached college-age the relationship was bi-directional. In any event, the inability to profit from one's education to an extent commensurate with one's intellectual ability is a hallmark of LD; a discrepancy between intellectual potential and actual performance is one of the central criteria in the definition of learning disabilities (*DSM-IV,* p. 46).

- *Rate of Learning.* Although Sonja's difficulty grasping concepts or learning anything quickly seemed to the examiner to be a result of limited intellectual ability or of anxiety, it could also be the result of problems with attention and distractibility (see Barkley, 1996). Hallowell, who is a psychotherapist with ADD himself, says of the time when he was diagnosed, "At last there was a term to explain . . . the rage I felt and the times I broke pencils and threw them around the room when I didn't immediately grasp a concept in grade school" (1994, p. x).

Thus, the clinical picture can be quite complex, because behaviors that are symptomatic of cognitive disorders often resemble those of affective disorders and vice versa. Adults with LD may exhibit some of the same behaviors observed in people with depression, mania, anxiety disorders, and a wide variety of personality disorders. Processing problems of perception or memory can resemble emotional blocks or dissociative states. People with receptive and/or expressive oral language problems, as well as those with nonverbal social perception problems, may have become loners, feeling socially inadequate and inhibited, with many behaviors resembling those of avoidant personality disorder. The poorly defined sense of self, unstable interpersonal relationships, and sensitivity to rejection that are typical of borderline personality disorder may also be the direct result of learning disabilities. Alternative interpretations of other behaviors are also possible. Restlessness, poor eye contact, or unclear expression of one's thoughts can be direct, primary results of a cognitive processing problem. Recurrent somatic complaints, substance abuse, or aggressive or grandiose behavior may be secondary reactions to living for years with LD. Hooper and Olley (1996) provide a very useful discussion of the comorbidity of psychological conditions and learning disabilities.

The characteristics of ADD—inattention, impulsivity, distractibility, hyperactivity, mood instability, intolerance of frustration or boredom, and need for intense stimulation—also lead to behaviors that frequently resemble a variety of psychopathologies. Lack of eye contact is not necessarily a sign of defensiveness. A patient's disorganized or associative thinking, tangential responses, and tendency to stray from the topic may need to be understood as attention deficits.

Hallowell and Ratey (1994) point out that ADD shares several traits with clinical depression, including susceptibility to dysphoric mood, sleep disturbances, superficial level of interest in activities, poor concentration, and poor self-image. Conduct disorders share aggressive, acting-out behaviors with ADD. The violence of adults who have been diagnosed with antisocial personality disorder may *not* be due "to a defect in their conscience or to psychosis or to some morbid familial conflict, but to the frustration intolerance and impulsivity of ADD" (p. 190). The person with ADD who interrupts, ignores personal space, and is inattentive to others may appear to have many behaviors of narcissistic personality disorder, i.e., selfishness, inconsiderateness, and immaturity. It is easy to mistake the disorganization, forgetting, lateness, and inattention associated with ADD for passive-aggressive personality disorder. Hallowell and Ratey also point out that people frequently experience ADD as chronic anxiety and compulsive worrying, which therapists may confuse with generalized anxiety disorder.

Tzelepis, Schubiner, and Warbasse (1995) provide a very useful guide to the differential diagnosis of ADD and psychopathology in adults. They suggest that ADD should be considered part of all psychiatric evaluations for adults and that a comprehensive evaluation will assess interpersonal, occupational, and education functioning as well as psychopathology. Tzelepis et al. point out that the symptoms of ADD are nonspecific and assert that it is extremely important to establish "both a differential diagnosis of other illnesses, which can mimic ADHD symptoms (i.e., is something else going on?), and the existence of comorbid conditions, which are often associated with ADHD (i.e., what else is going on?)" (p. 36). They review depression, bipolar disorder, anxiety disorders, substance abuse, antisocial disorders, schizophrenia, and several personality disorders, indicating how these disorders can either mimic or coexist with ADD. For each condition they show how a longitudinal perspective on the individual's development and careful attention to the negative outcomes of the untreated disorder can be helpful in establishing primacy or comorbidity.

Indicators of Learning Disabilities

Cognizant of the complexity of the diagnostic picture, Kaplan and Schachter (1991, p. 200) offer the following list of indicators of learning disability, which highlights the kinds of psychological symptoms that therapists are typically attuned to and that can be red flags for a possible learning disability. They suggest that when any of the following behaviors exist along with apparently adequate intelligence, child-rearing, and reality-testing, a learning disability may well be present.

- Significant discrepancies between apparent intellectual ability and school and/or work performance.
- Significant poverty of social judgment in intelligent adults from apparently normal families.
- Cognitive distortions and distorted perceptions of life events in the face of good intelligence, reasonable rearing, and adequate reality testing.
- Specific avoidance of selected tasks incongruent with apparent ability in other areas.
- Hatred of reading when intelligence is adequate.
- Problematic school history without evidence of poor intellectual ability or rearing.
- Impulsivity, explosiveness, poor frustration tolerance, and concentration problems in an adult with good intelligence and reasonable rearing. This may include a pattern of frequent job changes and difficulty relating to authority.
- Poor self-esteem and confused self-concept, particularly in school and work performance.
- A pervasive sense of badness, particularly in childhood recollections, despite good intelligence and reasonable rearing. The focus may be on "effort withheld"—an active posture in the face of repeated experiences of failure.
- Feelings of intellectual inferiority despite adequate educational test performance. Client may focus on diminished competitive endeavors and withdrawal of intellectual curiosity.
- Impaired interpersonal relationships as a result of a damaged or confused sense of self and revolving around concerns related to how others perceive his or her social and work performance.
- Gender-identity confusion supported by clumsiness, poor athletic ability, awkward moments, or inappropriate social responses.

With an awareness of the various combinations of behaviors and life patterns typical of LD, a therapist may notice many "red flags" during a standard clinical appraisal.[4] A checklist of such indicators can be found in Appendix I. When several of these indicators appear together, they constitute enough of a clinical picture to alert the therapist to suspect learning disabilities and/or ADD and to conduct, or refer for, further assessment. However, as Hallowell and Ratey (1994) suggest, the standard way of taking a history is often highly structured, not allowing clients a chance to discuss their concerns or chief complaints. They suggest starting an interview with a question that invites the person to say whatever he or she thinks matters. Often what matters most to people with LD is their sense of having been misunderstood and their fear of being deemed lazy, crazy, or stupid.

These gold nuggets of information may surface in different ways. They may come from clients' accounts of times when their spouses, supervisors, or parents accused them of being shiftless, immature, or impulsive. They may come from the patients themselves, who are berating themselves for not trying hard enough, for being irresponsible, stupid, or just a loser. Whatever the particular configuration, this information is always worth pursuing. *Why* are clients perceived as unmotivated, as not being able to get their act together, as having unrealized potential? Therapists who pursue this question will almost inevitably find a history of difficulty in learning at school and a continuing struggle to learn vocational, social, or other adaptive skills as an adult.

Johnson (1987) cautions that providing their history can be extremely painful for patients with LD because doing so may evoke old memories, unhappy days in school, or repeated problems at work. Even so, she points out that reviewing their history provides them with a unique opportunity to discuss their problems. With this in mind, she suggests that it may be necessary to allow as much as two hours for the history in order to give the adults ample time to air their concerns. Since clients with LD rarely have had the opportunity of speaking with someone who truly recognizes their problems, when therapists provide this opening, the experience is so emotionally charged that a veritable fountain of feelings and experiences often pours forth. While counselors will need to contain and channel this flow, it is important at the same time not to underestimate the power of this outpouring in terms of establishing a therapeutic alliance. To cut it off too hastily will remind clients of all the other people who callously dismissed their valiant but futile attempts to explain themselves. It will leave them thinking once again, "But you don't understand!"

Returning to Sonja's story, we can't help but be struck by her resilience even in the face of the discouraging results of the psychological evaluation. She continued to work with Diane, the psychiatric social worker, who helped her considerably. "I was able to build up a relationship with her. She really listened to what I was saying. And she believed what I was saying, that I wasn't making it up. I felt that she was in my corner and she was there to help. You can kind of tell when somebody knows what they're doing and is giving you good advice. She understood what my needs were, and we faced those issues and we settled them. One day at a time. We settled things one issue and one day at a time. What are we doing right now? OK, now we'll do this. You can feel whether your life is changing or not. It might take some time to see that, but eventually if you listen to yourself you can figure it out. I really trusted her." Diane urged Sonja to consider various options and eventually she returned to the university LD program to complete the testing there. These results proved to be most helpful, finally allowing Sonja and those who worked with her to grasp the complex interaction of her various cognitive and emotional problems. Though therapists need not be experts in diagnostic assessment of learning disabilities, they will find it very useful to have an overview of the components of a good assessment and a good diagnostic report, if only to find appropriate referral sources for patients.

Appropriate Assessment of LD

An appropriate assessment for learning disabilities contains a wide range of assessment techniques and will address the following areas:

- *Assessment of Cognitive Functioning.* A battery of standardized tests—of intelligence, memory, etc.—can be quite helpful, as long as one does not assume that standardized tests can reveal all there is to know about a client. Such tests can yield substantial information, but no published test or test battery (including the popular Woodcock-Johnson Psychoeducational Battery [WJ-R] or combination of the Wechsler Adult Intelligence Scale [WAIS] and the Wechsler Individualized Achievement Test [WIAT]) can provide a thorough diagnosis of LD.

    A report of test results should describe the subject's cognitive strengths and weaknesses in terms of specific verbal, nonverbal, and memory functions. Difficulties with attention, while not directly measurable, often (though not always) reveal themselves in cognitive testing and should be noticed and described.

- *Assessment of Academic, Social, and Vocational Functioning.* A battery of tests typically includes an assessment of basic skills: oral language, reading, spelling, written composition, and math. Reading assessment is further divided into tests of decoding (figuring out what the words say) and comprehension. For adults, an informal assessment of relevant social, vocational, and daily living skills should also be included. An important part of the assessment is a careful analysis of the client's performance errors, which then forms the basis of a description of the problems.

A good report of the test results will provide more than a simple listing of test scores. An important purpose of the assessment is to interpret and describe weaknesses in academic, social, and vocational skills in light of difficulties of cognitive functioning. For example, since attention and memory play a large part in reading comprehension, a person with attention problems, like Sonja, could be expected to have difficulty understanding and remembering what she reads.

- *Assessment of Personality and Emotional Functioning.* An assessment of personality may or may not be included in an evaluation for learning disabilities. Such an assessment can be especially valuable if psychological tests are viewed from multiple perspectives.[5] A report of the test results should indicate ways in which cognitive, academic, vocational, and emotional problems may interact.

- *Identification of Strengths.* In addition to understanding a person's weaknesses, a therapist who suspects a learning disability will certainly want to understand the client's *strengths*. A search for strengths in interviews, case histories, and observations, as well as in formal tests, is vital not only as an additional clue to learning disability (people with LD typically have areas of real strength as well as areas of weakness) but also as a way of eventually helping the patient to compensate and to keep the learning disability in perspective. A good diagnostic report will give indications of cognitive strengths (e.g., good overall intelligence, oral language, thinking skills, artistic or athletic skills, or specific processes such as memory), personal strengths (e.g., persistence, level of resiliency, sense of humor), and interpersonal strengths (e.g., ability to engage others who can provide appropriate support).

Since one purpose of an LD evaluation is the confirmation or disconfirmation of a suspected learning disability, some discussion of a specific diagnosis or label is inevitable.[6] However, by far the most important purpose of the evaluation is to provide enough information so that the client—along with appropriate support personnel—can understand the nature of the problem and plan for the future.

Fortunately for Sonja, the LD assessment alleviated much anxiety. "I was just so relieved when I was diagnosed with a learning disability." A combination of medication for the depression and attention problems, counseling, and LD remediation has enabled her to recover her equilibrium to the extent that she is now about to graduate from college and is poised, albeit precariously, for adult life. "When I think of the many, many people I needed to convince that there was something wrong besides emotional problems. And in the meantime people are saying to you, 'You've already been tested; you're nuts; there's nothing wrong with you.'"

Psychotherapeutic Commentary

Sometimes in our work as psychotherapists we have to undo or counter the damage that our clients have suffered at the hands of other psychotherapists or mental health professionals. Although it is sometimes assumed that mental health care must be either helpful or neutral, this is by no means always the case. Iain Chalmers, Director of the United Kingdom Cochrane Centre, which studies the efficacy (or inefficacy) of health care interventions, is quoted in an interview as saying, "All professionals need to recognize that, with the best of intentions, they can nevertheless do harm, and they need to take steps to try and reduce that possibility" (Winn & Tyrell, 1999).

Sonja's history of misdiagnosis and mistreatment breaks one's heart because of her needless suffering as a child, shatters the belief that education and mental health care have reached a consistently high level in our culture, and yet leaves one in awe at the strength of character and sheer perseverance that have eventually carried her to the brink of a successful life of her own. Eventually, she was correctly diagnosed and presumably treated by the same system that had failed her repeatedly earlier in her life. Maybe this is an example of how the thing that got you into trouble can get you out again.

I can't help thinking that so much of Sonja's suffering was unnecessary. Her hyperactivity wasn't subtle, so missing it for so many years was not because she had some sort of difficult-to-diagnose condition that only an expert might be expected to recognize.

Her learning issues may have been more subtle, but she was evaluated twice, as well as receiving specialized mental health care through the social service system, and both her attentional and learning issues remained unidentified. Sonja's family was also badly served by the education and mental health institutions of the culture. Notwithstanding the dysfunction within the family, Sonja's mother did refer her daughter for evaluation, and was told that there was nothing cognitively wrong with her. Seeing evaluations and case histories like Sonja's—and her case can be multiplied by hundreds if not thousands—I often end up feeling that some children from developed countries might as well be in a country so undeveloped that it is without schools, mental health care, or social service systems. At least the people in such countries realize that they are missing these things. Here we have institutions called "schools" that are supposed to educate, a "mental health" profession that is supposed to diagnose and treat clinical problems, and "social service systems" that are supposed to provide rehabilitation to those in dire need. Children go through these systems and are presumed to have received education, evaluation, treatment, and rehabilitation, but things aren't always what they seem.

The truth is that the social institutions that were supposed to educate and care for Sonja let her down massively and repeatedly. This is a central theme of the story of her life, and somehow she will have to come to terms with it. For a client like Sonja, coming to terms with her history and adjusting to the realities of her life may require her to develop a more balanced and realistic perspective on the institutions of the culture in which she grew up. Sometimes maturation requires that we recognize that we have been victimized, without feeling like victims.

There is a Sufi saying, "The value of the dwelling is in the dweller" (Shah, 1986). If no one is inside them who is perceptive and understanding, of what value were the schools and social service agencies that were supposedly there to help Sonja? If no one is inside them who is perceptive and understanding, they are of no use at all. They are worse than nothing, for they provide an illusion of education and care instead of an acknowledgment of their lack. Sonja's family and teachers could hold her entirely responsible for her educational and behavior problems, secure in the knowledge that there was nothing wrong with Sonja that a change in her attitude wouldn't cure.

For years, Sonja was not evaluated at all. That is squarely the fault of the school system, which should have had people on staff who would have recognized that Sonja was cognitively impaired, worked with her to determine the nature and extent of her deficits, treated her attentional and personal problems, and remediated her educational ones. When she was finally tested, the evaluator made the typical mistake of concluding that Sonja's problems were due to emotional and personality issues rather than to a mixture of cognitive and personality ones. The problem of diagnosticians finding what they expect to find is an old one, deeply entrenched in the mentality of training itself. To the evaluator who said that Sonja had a "limited reservoir intellectually," one is tempted to retort, "*You* have a limited reservoir of competence!"

As I write this, I'm completing the evaluation of a second grader whose teachers see her as having learning problems and whose school psychologist thought she wasn't worth testing because she was just slow. My evaluation shows that she is, in fact, quite bright, but that her learning style is such that she needs frequent recaps. Her parents will solve the problem by informing her teachers of her needs and transferring her to another school if the teachers don't respond. Left to the school's authority, she would presumably have fallen farther and farther behind. The school psychologist, whose very job exists to prevent this kind of problem, instead ends up contributing to it. He thinks that she's "slow," but in fact he's asleep on the job.

When Sonja was referred by her college mental health center for testing, the evaluator thought that she had given Sonja "measures of attention" that proved that she had no problem with attention. In fact, there are no measures of attention as such, period. Maybe someday we'll develop them, but when we do they won't be paper and pencil tests but rather something more like PET scans or functional MRIs of the operation of parts of the brain we've learned to associate with attention while the individual is doing tasks requiring certain kinds of attention.

Short of that, attention can't be observed directly, so one always has to infer it from a subject's behavior. We obtain behavioral samples involving attention from cognitive tests, careful clinical interviews, classroom or workplace observations, careful case histories, and the reports of people such as parents, supervisors, teachers, etc.[7] Thus, the diagnosis of attention deficit disorder is always a clinical judgment (see Chapter 8). ADD doesn't show up on a test like a tumor on a CAT scan. The diagnostic impressions and recommendations of a psychological evaluation are essentially a judgment—hopefully an enlightened, professional one. Like any judgment, they are only as good as the information, perception, and knowledge of the person who makes them.

In Sonja's case, the evaluator's own report contains information that disconfirms the findings. Alas, this doesn't help Sonja, but perhaps her story can prevent others from having to suffer this kind of mismanagement. Sonja exemplifies the individual whose educational and social problems are both cognitive and personal in origin. For understanding, advising, teaching, and treating such people, the importance of an evaluation that encompasses and differentiates (as far as can reasonably be done) both cognitive and personality/emotional problems is paramount. After all, how can teachers teach, advisers advise, parents understand, or psychotherapists treat a person like Sonja without knowing in at least a general way that:

- both her attention and her cognition are seriously impaired in some ways,
- her personality and emotional functioning are seriously impaired in some ways, and
- there is a reciprocal interaction between the two forms of impairment such that each exacerbates the other, although
- Sonja appears to have the cognitive and personal resources to understand and cope with her history and impairments, provided she is helped to understand them and develop a sense of self that puts her real needs and abilities first.

To her credit, and notwithstanding her other mistakes in parenting Sonja, her mother did bring her in for evaluation. We can only speculate about what the effect of a more accurate evaluation at that time might have been. As it was, the professional confirmation of Sonja's mother's belief that her daughter's problems were based on willful misbehavior intensified her misguided attempts to correct Sonja's misunderstood problems through inappropriate discipline.

It may be that the mother's belief in her daughter's willful misbehavior was based on fear. Parents of ADD/LD children are often

ADD/LD themselves, and they sometimes impose a fierce discipline on their children in a misguided attempt to force their problem behavior out of them.

One irony—in a case full of irony—is that, for a child like Sonja, correct parental discipline must emphasize helping her to settle down and refocus. Time-outs for infractions of clearly specified rules, followed by quiet conversation and discipline based on withholding privileges, all delivered with as calm and firm an attitude as can be mustered under the circumstances, are far more suited to helping the child get the best out of herself than verbal or physical attacks, which cause overstimulation and consequent impairment of the very qualities of corrective thought, perception, and feeling that constructive behavioral self-monitoring and change require. In general, hyperactive kids (and adults!) need to settle down and refocus when they become overstimulated, not become further overstimulated.

While we can't know for certain without an adequate evaluation, Sonja certainly seems to have been the kind of child who could have benefited from medication for ADD. This alone could have resulted in substantial improvements in her abilities to succeed in school and avoid trouble in relationships. As her story ends, Sonja has been correctly diagnosed and medicated at last, and it is making an important difference for her.

Any psychotherapist working with Sonja thus has to take into account the effects not only of her learning, attentional, and emotional disorders on her present functioning, but also of the severely dysfunctional nature of her family, school, and foster home environments and experiences. Like an anthropologist, Sonja's psychotherapist will have to understand Sonja's formative environment in terms of its impact on her development. And Sonja may have to become something of an anthropologist of her own life and society, too. The psychotherapist conveys this attitude to the patient by how he frames questions, investigates situations, makes comments and interpretations—in a word, by his attitude. His attitude will also convey to her a message about what her own attitude toward all this might be.

The issue of therapist attitude is a complex one, because the therapist's feelings obviously change as the patient, with therapist empathically in tow, re-experiences the various traumas of her life. As therapists we find ourselves angry at her tormentors, sorry for her suffering, and awed by the enormity of the challenges posed by merely functioning as a successful independent person. And such changes are a necessary part of the empathic bond of psychotherapy. But if we leave Sonja there we will not have seen her through to the development of an attitude that will enable her to move ahead in her own life as an adult.

That attitude is based on self-acceptance, acknowledging strengths as well as weaknesses, and on acceptance of responsibility for getting on with one's life despite how one has been mistreated and hurt by others. To do this, Sonja must recognize that those who were supposed to be responsible and to know better were themselves the victims of impaired training and personal development, and were too short of love and personal courage to rise to the occasion.

Some Therapeutic Questions

As Sonja's therapist, I would have in mind some questions as I consider how to approach her treatment:

- What is the nature of her learning disability and attention disorder?
- How does it affect her education and the rest of her life?
- How much do I need to know about her disability?
- How much does she need to know about it in order to understand herself sufficiently and to compensate for these problems in her life?
- How much *does* she know about it?
- How might these problems interfere with her ability to participate in a psychotherapeutic relationship?
- How should I change my method of working with Sonja to minimize the disruption of her learning and attention issues on our relationship?
- Are there ways Sonja can become aware of this interference?
- What are Sonja's strengths, and is she aware of them?
- How can these strengths become engaged in support of Sonja's therapeutic growth?
- How can I help Sonja acknowledge the damage that has been done to her while encouraging the development of her healthy self-confidence and without encouraging her to feel like a victim?

- How can I help Sonja to develop a balanced perspective toward education and mental health that will acknowledge both the damage that can be done by inept practitioners and the vital role that education and mental health services can have in supporting her real growth?

It is remarkable and worth thinking about that Sonja's psychiatric social worker, Diane, was able to support and help Sonja, step by step, to overcome the effects of the inept evaluations she received and eventually to find her way to a correct diagnosis and medical treatment. This illustrates the power of a good therapeutic relationship to support the emerging health within a client's personality, even in the face of serious educational and psychological misjudgment.

CHAPTER 7

I've Been Seeking Information All My Whole Life

LD and Multidisciplinary Intervention

I would give anything right now to understand what caused my problem. Maybe I'll never know, but I've been seeking information all my whole life. I need an understanding if I'm in a particular situation where I've messed up. How could I explain myself to somebody else if I don't understand why this happened? And I keep thinking its my fault. I messed up and I created this monster. I'm always being made to feel that I created my own problem.

—Hannah Kaplan

"I haven't been out of therapy for more than five years at a time since I was 16," remarks Hannah Kaplan, "and I've noticed that you reach plateaus where you can stop, but then other crises happen where you've got to go back again." For the last several years, these "other crises" have typically involved her interpersonal relationships at work, where her poor social skills annoy and anger her coworkers with frustrating and bewildering regularity. "You've got to have social skills when you work with three or four people in a small room (Hannah is a switchboard operator in a medium-sized company) and you interact for eight hours a day," says Hannah matter-of-factly. "There's no way to hide a problem when somebody works that close with you. Sooner or later you're going to do something that's going to throw them for a loop."

Crises and plateaus are not the only considerations behind Hannah's frequent stopping and returning to therapy over the years.

She has often found the outcome less than satisfactory. Speaking of many counselors and therapists she has known, Hannah says, "Most of them are . . . Well, just spill your guts when you're unhappy during a crisis, and that's fine and good. But these crises are going to keep recurring if you don't learn to understand where the basic problem is, where the LD is messing you up. But most therapists will be totally oblivious to why this is happening. And I think most of us who are LD float around from therapist to therapist our whole lives, because the average therapist doesn't understand about us."

Hannah's current sessions have turned out to be very helpful, however, so she is beginning to understand the nonverbal difficulties that have plagued her interpersonal relationships for so long. "I guess I always try to hide and act normal to everybody, but when something comes up I can't handle, they think, 'Well, gee, you should be able to handle it.' We're normal in some ways and abnormal in others. That throws people for a loop. They can't handle that. They would rather deal with a person who is totally unintelligent than deal with a person who in their eyes should know better because she's intelligent. They don't realize that perception and intelligence are not the same thing. They think you should be able to perceive if you have the brains to do it."

In spite of high average intelligence, Hannah's social skills problems frequently land her in trouble. For instance, she relates, "Scott, one of the technicians, is working on the telephone equipment and I'm asking questions. He always gets annoyed with me, and I know by the tone of his voice to back off with him because he gets very defensive. Whenever I ask a question, people think I'm questioning them. My supervisor says, 'Well, Scott knows how to do his job. That's an affront, an attack on him.' I'm not questioning Scott's job or his ability. But *I have no idea why he's acting this way.*"

But Hannah, a slight, wiry woman and a widow for many years, is a spunky survivor, and not even a highly complex combination of disabilities has diminished her energy, sense of humor, or desire to find a way to solve her social problems. Hannah's case is complicated by vision problems. "I have a neurological condition called nystagmus, which is involuntary eye movements." She attributes her characteristic lack of eye contact to the nystagmus, saying that she finds it difficult to focus her eyes on people's faces.

Since Hannah has been in therapy for many years, her story is particularly interesting in light of the main purpose of this chapter, which is to suggest guidelines for therapeutic intervention, particularly how to adapt goals and techniques to meet the patient's needs. A second purpose is to highlight the need for a multidisciplinary approach to therapy.

Hannah was diagnosed with a nonverbal learning disability only about three years ago, but her parents became concerned when she was very young. "The first time I was tested was when I was about three. They took me to a local hospital." Notations from her earliest medical records indicate that developmental milestones were delayed (she walked at 20 months and was not yet talking in sentences at three years) and social development was also slow (she did not play with other children and kept to herself a lot). These delays, together with the congenital nystagmus, seemed to the evaluating physician to warrant a diagnosis of mental retardation.

This devastating—and profoundly incorrect—diagnosis was a blow to her family and continued to have long-lasting emotional effects. "My parents only told me about this diagnosis at a much later date; I think I was about 16. I remember on the day they told me, I was talking with my grandma and she told me that my mother came home with me from the doctor and said that she didn't know what to do because the doctor wanted to put me away. My grandmother went to my defense and said, 'She's ours, we love her, she lives with us.' But I can't help but feel psychologically angry at the doctor who even would think that," says Hannah, her voice full of emotion. "I mean, I'm only three at the time. Why so quick to put people away? If I met him on the street, I'd really unload all my anger. I think I really would."

Since then, Hannah has been evaluated many times, and as an adult she has actively sought these assessments, always looking for some kind of explanation for her behavior that makes sense to her. But even though Hannah continued to seek help and information, the results of the evaluations were often equivocal, and their interpretation was always made more complicated by her nystagmus and mild difficulty with visual acuity (best correction 20/80 in both eyes). Historically, learning disabilities have often been misinterpreted as sensory or emotional problems. Many people with LD search for years for an explanation for their problems, and find that a diagnosis of sensory or emotional difficulties may be a partial explanation, but it is essentially unsatisfying in a way that they cannot explain. *Something else is going on.* And it is this "something else" that they legitimately persist in trying to identify. For several years, Hannah was determined to learn all she could about nonverbal learning disabilities.

Nonverbal learning disabilities (NLD) have been studied extensively by Byron Rourke (1989) and, although nonverbal perception problems were identified fairly early (Johnson & Myklebust, 1967; Strauss & Lehtinen, 1947), it is Rourke who has brought the concept of NLD to the attention of LD professionals.[1]

Nonverbal LD

Hannah's diagnosis is even more complex than her current therapist originally thought (as we will see in Jay's therapeutic commentary). But when the nonverbal learning disability diagnosis was made, the available information in her case history seemed to fit fairly well with Rourke's model. Early motor milestones were delayed, but instead of being mentally retarded she may well have suffered, as one report put it, "from sensory-motor integration difficulties which resulted in slow development in some specific neuromuscular functions." The magnitude of the contribution of her vision problems to these early developmental delays can't be determined, but in all probability some combination of sensory and neurological difficulties affected her ability to process nonverbal information both perceptually and conceptually from a very early age.

Casey, Rourke, and Picard (1991) discuss a number of features that characterize the NLD syndrome in children, some of which are highlighted here as they apply to Hannah's case.

- *Bilateral psychomotor coordination deficiencies, often more marked on the left side of the body.* We know from early medical records that Hannah's motor milestones were delayed, both walking and speaking. And of her situation today Hannah says, "I've always felt like a klutz. I'm not a good runner. I move quickly. I'm full of energy. But I'm not the most graceful person! Or if you're talking about sports, in grammar school, I got benched a lot because they wouldn't want me for a team. It's not that I didn't understand the rules, I could have argued baseball rules with anybody. But don't ask me to play the game. Hitting a ball would be a fluke."

- *Outstanding deficiencies in visual-spatial-organizational abilities.* Although we have little information about her early functioning, Hannah reports she has difficulty making practical visual-spatial judgments. "With leftovers I'd rather use a bigger bowl and leave some room at the top. But my mother is always saying, 'We can put it in a smaller bowl and save room in the fridge.' When I'm cooking, I'm always confused about what size pot I am going to use on the stove, so it doesn't boil over. I also have problems paying attention to fine visual details. I could miss dust or hair when I'm cleaning." But from what Hannah tells us, these are not primarily problems of visual acuity. "I see things right away if they're pointed out to me. But otherwise I may be oblivious. A hair is a very fine detail."

- *Marked deficits in nonverbal problem-solving, concept formation, hypothesis testing, and the capacity to benefit from positive and negative informational feedback in novel or otherwise complex situations.* This group of characteristics goes to the heart of Hannah's difficulties, as she has marked impairment in practical hypothesis-testing and problem-solving. But we must be precise here. She is quite capable of analyzing and discussing her social problems logically *after the fact*. But the ability to automatically size up a situation and make quick and accurate intuitive judgments is deficient. For example, at work she has difficulty quickly assessing the nature of a caller's problem. "It's getting a handle on the problem that's hard. Sometimes I have to ask more questions to find out what the person wants. And if I go by the rule, just two questions and then you have to refer the call, they'll be on my case for referring too many calls. Somehow, the other operators know why people are calling and can handle it in two questions. Somehow they have perceived it and I haven't."

  Hannah is also often unable to profit from feedback, since she has little intuitive feel for the dynamics of interpersonal situations. She can understand the logic of the feedback she gets from her boss ("you're being defensive") and can even explain it clearly it to someone else, but she doesn't profit from it in any practical sense and thus repeats her mistakes if the situation changes even slightly.

- *Extreme difficulty in adapting to novel and otherwise complex situations. An overreliance on prosaic, rote (and, in consequence, inappro-*

priate) behaviors in such situations. Here again we touch the heart of Hannah's difficulties. Complex social situations mystify her in daily life as well as at work, so she relies on rote formulas. "My family was invited to a wedding reception. I was talking to the sister of the bride, and a guy walks over, maybe my age. And the sister did the proper thing and introduced us. And then they went on talking to each other, and knowing that I have social problems, I wasn't going to mix in the conversation. So I decided I was going to be a listener. I wind up having to do that a lot. I think to myself, 'If I don't say anything, the *silence is golden routine* will work.' So I kept on listening, and my mother calls me over. And she says to me, 'Come away from them and let them be.' Nobody *told* me, 'It's private.' Nobody shooed me away. Sometimes people say 'This is private,' which I've learned is really a polite way of saying they don't want me. But this didn't even happen. I didn't pick it up, and I felt very depressed by that."

In addition, Hannah says with much feeling in her voice, "I am a creature of habit. Habit creates comfort for me. It creates predictability. It creates structure." Change is particularly hard for her to deal with. "I have trouble discerning when a change has taken place, so it catches me by surprise. And it used to be written in my reviews at work. 'She does not adapt well to changing situations. She doesn't accept change.' But I tell them, 'I adapt well to change if you *tell* me. If you don't *tell* me, how do I know change has occurred?'"

- *Much verbosity of a repetitive, straightforward, rote nature. Content disorder of language characterized by very poor psycholinguistic pragmatics. Reliance on language as a principal means for social relating, information gathering, and relief from anxiety.* In this feature on Rourke's list of NLD deficits, he highlights problems with *nonverbal* aspects of communication. In the following unedited excerpt, Hannah tells us of some of her communication problems, and at the same time inadvertently illustrates her repetitiveness as she provides some insight into her difficulties with the pragmatic use of language. "I don't always anticipate people's reactions. I don't always. I don't usually realize that what I'm saying is going to bring forth a negative response in the other person. And sometimes if the other person doesn't verbalize it clearly, I may not know that I even did. That I really actually did something to them unless they tell me, 'Hey, you said x, y, z.' If they don't tell me,

'Hey, you hurt this person' or 'You angered this person,' I won't necessarily know. I have trouble communicating with others, both ways. I have to check out that I understand what they're saying, and also I have a hard time making myself clear to somebody else. Not only may I not *perceive* the impact I've made on the other person, but at the same time I don't realize that I'm even doing something that's going to impact on them in a negative way."

- *Significant deficits in social perception, social judgment, and social interaction skills. A marked tendency toward social withdrawal and even isolation as age increases.* This last feature on Rourke's list of NLD characteristics is the net result of the other features, and is perhaps the most central and debilitating aspect of nonverbal learning disabilities in adults. Characterizing her difficulty with social perception, Hannah says, "Sometimes people give me a look and I think, 'You've got a look on your face, but I can't tell you what it is.'" Hannah's response to her problems is, understandably, withdrawal. "I think over the years I've avoided social situations. I'm very, very scared. For example, when I first came to the company, I wouldn't eat with anybody unless they approached my table. I've had problems in the past because I don't always know if I am too close and so I didn't want to invade anybody's space. I have to live in a guarded way. It's like you can't ever let down your guard or you're going to mess up."

Nevertheless, Hannah compensates to some degree for her inability to pick up visual social cues with an intuitive, natural ability to sense subtle tones of voice. In some cases this strong auditory skill makes her even more effective than the other operators. For example, she says, "I can sense a subtlety in the tone of voice if a person is trying to get past me to complain. The other operators say, 'You're always right. How do you know that?'"

Summing up the cumulative emotional effects of these several features of nonverbal learning disabilities, Rourke, Del Dotto, Rourke, and Casey (1990) make a convincing case for a strong relationship between nonverbal LD and emotional problems. They find that in their subjects with nonverbal learning disabilities, excessive anxiety, depression, and forms of internalized emotional disturbance increase significantly with age.

Hannah's social problems, which began as a preschooler (early medical records indicated that she did not play with other children), increased in adolescence. "I had no friends at all in high school. The other kids wouldn't want me at their table at lunch. The only thing I could pick up on was that they didn't like me. And I was easy to tease. There were these guys on my school bus that would ask me questions and then laugh at my answers. And I couldn't understand what I was doing that was weird or why they'd want to laugh at the responses I made. I was also easy to fool, because I went by outward appearances, by whether kids acted nice on the surface. But then one girl told me, 'Listening to people talk nice to your face doesn't mean that's what they do behind your back.'" Well, eventually I decided, 'Screw the social part, I'm here to get grades. I managed to override my feelings and get the grades and put it out of my mind. And I already was working part-time too, so I had some place to be. I didn't want to be home being bored. I didn't want to be fighting with my parents."

Dynamic Interaction of Cognitive and Emotional Problems

Although many of Hannah's problems can be directly attributed to cognitive deficits, these were not the only source of her emotional difficulties. Baffled by her strange social behavior, Hannah's father was highly critical, whereas her mother grew more protective. "Well, if it was something that I did or said, my mother would have taken me aside and told me I wasn't picking up on the clues people were giving out. But my father was quick to get up and take action. If he didn't like what I said, he'd tell me flat out in front of everybody. My mother would quietly tell me. My father wasn't so diplomatic about it. If I inadvertently said something that insulted him or angered him, he would have definitely retaliated at that moment. He would have started yelling. No question."

Her relationship with her siblings also was colored by her disabilities. "My older brother felt cheated that he had to go to the Chicago schools, which he felt were inferior. He was really resentful and he told me to my face. He picked me up at my girlfriend's house one day and he said, "You know, we'd be living in the suburbs, if it weren't for you having to go to a school in the city.'

"So finally we were going to move, and my mother looked at houses in Chicago. She looked in the nearby suburbs. I knew she wanted to move to Skokie. Some friends of hers tried to talk her into Skokie many years ago, and the only reason she didn't go for it was because of me. She even said that if it weren't for me she would have jumped at the opportunity, because there was a very good buy on a house that she would have taken. I felt like I stood in the way. So based on that and what my brother said, I sat down with my mom and I said, 'Let's move to Skokie.' My mother felt that the suburban schools would be too advanced for me and I would actually fall apart. She said, 'How are you going to make out in the schools there?' I said, 'I'll do it. I'm not going to see you not have what you want just because of me.' And I start crying and carrying on. I was very upset. I begged and pleaded for us to move to Skokie."

Given these circumstances, counselors and therapists can easily see how Hannah was even more vulnerable than most children to rejection and narcissistic injury. Because of both academic and social failure, she was constantly made aware that she just wasn't as good as her brothers and sisters. In addition, her cognitive problems directly interfered with interpersonal communication, since she was unable to explain her behavior, repair misunderstandings, or profit from her family's feedback. Not surprisingly, she was and is most distressed about being treated harshly by her father and being unable to live up to his expectations. "When I was doing poorly in school, my mother said, 'Well, you're 16. You could drop out of school.' But I said, 'No.' My father is Mr. Education. Unh uh. I don't think so. Knowing the type of person he is, I couldn't do that. I was feeling guilt for all that I was putting my parents through."

As a result of this narcissistic wounding, Hannah has a great deal of anger toward people who criticize. Nor is she unique in this respect. Painfully aware of their own failures, adults with LD have lived through a lifetime of name calling, teasing, put-downs, criticism, and rejection and are filled with unresolved anger at being treated in this way. Their deficits create more and more disappointment in their parents and stimulate the withdrawal of whatever nurturance they might have had. As Orenstein (1992) puts it, "The neurocognitive deficit usually goes along with a lack of human support to deal with such a deficit" (p.133). Thus there are very few people with LD who haven't been narcissistically wounded at least to some degree and who are not vulnerable to some form of personality problem.

A stabilizing force several years after high school was Hannah's marriage—arranged by a yenta—to Jacob. Although the marriage was difficult at times due to periods of illness and extreme stress, generally Hannah was able to find acceptance in the relationship and gained insight about her problems by discussing them with Jacob. "Oh yeah. I always told him things. He didn't always understand things, but he wasn't negative. In fact, he was a very sensitive person. I really miss him. I wish I could have him back. He's been gone almost nine years. It was hard to lose him, but when I married him I already knew that he was severely diabetic." When Jacob was alive and Hannah ran into a social problem, "I would consult him. I would say, 'Jacob, last night at so-and-so's house, what did you make of the situation?' And Jacob would tell me, 'Oh, they didn't like you.' Or, 'They were laughing at you.' See that's the thing. I didn't always know."

Even her husband's insights were not enough and the wounds of childhood were deep, so Hannah has sought help in many places. In those early years, however, it is not surprising that her very first encounter with the helping professions was not of her choosing. As her social problems increased, she came to the attention of high school counselors. "I was called in by the social worker and she told me I had to see a psychiatrist. I don't like changes that catch me off guard and unannounced. And I was 16. Don't tell *me* anything! Also, I didn't want to admit my visual problem [the nystagmus]."

"At first I was very negative in therapy. I didn't want to admit I had vision problems, until I said to the psychiatrist, Dr. Blackwell, 'OK, OK, I've got a visual problem, I admit it.' That was the first step. [Of course no one knew about her other disabilities then.] Mostly I would talk about the other kids at school, and he thought I was blaming them for my problems. But that was all part of my denial, just like my denial of my visual problems, so I didn't feel like I gained any territory in the first year and a half I went to him.

"But I went back again when I was 22. I was still living at home, and my father and I fought constantly. And I was starting to have problems at my job. Also I'd been reading a couple of books that had just been published on brain-damaged children. One of them was called *Something's Wrong with my Child,* which I loaned to my mother. When she read about social perception problems, she said, 'That's what you've got.' She knew it. So anyway, I'd done my homework and understood the problem a little bit. I was able to go back to Dr. Blackwell with things that I'd learned. I felt that I would get a lot of movement that way."

Hannah spent another two years with him, and then left after feeling again that she had reached a plateau. But she found a new therapist a few years later. "I liked Dr. Singleton. I liked him because he seemed to understand the problem. He was the one who said he thought I had sensorimotor integration problems and had LD when I was very young. But he never specifically mentioned nonverbal problems. Dr. Singleton shared things with me, too. From each of my therapists I learned something else. But sometimes progress seems to drop off. Dr. Singleton felt that I would do better with somebody else, so I went to see a woman that he recommended. I liked her, but I felt that she didn't know much about my problems." The pattern we see with Hannah is common among patients with learning disabilities: because one or more of the sources of her social behavior problems were not recognized and dealt with, whatever initial success she achieved in therapy could not be sustained. Often the LD patient seeks treatment, gains a measure of relief from the immediate crisis, but quickly reaches a plateau and either stops therapy or is referred elsewhere.

Successful Therapy

Successful therapy is possible, however. And although it involves broadening one's perspective as well as broadening the scope of therapy itself, it need not require intensive retraining. It begins with the willingness to embrace multiple and interrelated causes of the client's problems. In Hannah's case, sensory and emotional difficulties not only interact with each other but also mask her nonverbal problems. For example, one of her progress reports concluded, "The client seems to perceive things differently from others, with a tendency, when under stress, toward bending reality to make it more compatible with her own needs." Although Hannah may well "bend reality" in some ways, this is not the only source of her nonverbal misperceptions. Her underlying cognitive problems have merged with compatible emotional defenses to make it even more likely that she will continue to miss important social cues.

Hannah found her current therapist (Jay) as a result of a crisis in which she walked in on a staff meeting, not realizing that the birthday party that was scheduled immediately afterward had not yet begun. She was so shaken by this particular incident that she frantically sought assistance. Working with Jay has been a revelation for Hannah, particularly because he has been able to validate her problems. This point is important enough to warrant additional emphasis. Validation of the experience of being learning disabled is vital for a number of reasons.

First, the therapist can help patients find ways to understand their own disabilities and to explain themselves to others. Hannah says, "Dr. Einhorn can immediately depict and explain what's happening with me." About the crisis at work Hannah says, "He helped me analyze what was happening, that I didn't pick up on the cues that there was still a meeting going on. Then when I went back to my boss, I was able to explain and she understood." Second, patients with LD may never have had anyone from whom they could really obtain the comfort that comes from genuine understanding. Hannah says, "My boss said to me, 'How could you *not* know the difference?' meaning, 'How could you do such a *stupid* thing.' And she kept going on and on at me and I just started crying. I was horrified that somebody could be so angry with me. And when I told Dr. Einhorn, he immediately realized what I was talking about. I immediately needed that comfort." Third, people with LD yearn for respect for their intelligence, for what they have accomplished, and for the effort they have expended. The therapist's ability to validate the patient's experience contributes immeasurably to their sense that the therapist respects them.

Hallowell and Ratey underscore the importance of validating the learning disability: "The feeling within you of being understood can heal more wounds than any medication. . . . With time, and with work, your therapist and you can build, syllable by syllable, image by image, a sense of being known, and *sometimes known for the first time*" (1994, p. 226, italics added). Therapists who interpret learning disabilities solely from an emotional perspective will be perceived as being "just like my parents," "just like all my teachers," "just like my wife/husband," and will have a difficult time establishing the trust that is the foundation of a productive therapeutic relationship.

Successful therapy, then, begins with two overarching considerations: willingness to embrace multiple interrelated causes of emotional problems and ability to validate the experience of the LD client. Other, more specific considerations are equally important for successful therapy. We turn to these now.

Therapeutic Goals for Adults with LD

Therapeutic goals for clients with learning disabilities must be broader than those for clients with emotional disorders only. Clients with LD, just like their nondisabled counterparts, most often seek therapy to relieve the pain accompanying a variety of emotional crises associated with marriage, divorce, or child-rearing; social, educational, or vocational failure; or with the course of personal growth and development (Barton & Fuhrmann, 1994). Alleviation of emotional pain resulting from these crises and resolution of the client's problems are undoubtedly the goals foremost in the minds of most therapists. In addition, however, therapists will usually need to assist the client in understanding, accepting, and adjusting to the learning disability.[2] The rest of the remarks in this section amplify these additional considerations, since they are not typically considered a part of psychotherapy.

Ginsberg, Gerber, and Reiff (1994) suggest that many, perhaps most, who have successfully adjusted to their learning disability have engaged in a process of "reframing," i.e., reconceptualizing the past, restructuring their lives in the present, and anticipating the future within the context of their learning disability. They identify four stages of this reframing process: recognizing the learning disability, attaining a degree of acceptance, understanding the disability and all its implications, and taking action aimed at improvement. Let us consider each in turn.

Recognition

If the learning disability has been recently diagnosed, the process of recognition is usually accompanied by a feeling of euphoria and a reduction of guilt and self-blame. But soon clients experience depression or anger, as they begin to review their past experiences and attempt to integrate this new knowledge into their lives. Clients often need help dealing with the realization that confronting their learning disability will be a painful experience.

Clients whose learning disability was diagnosed in childhood may find it more difficult to face up to their disability than those who have recently gone through the assessment process. Often LD adults want to believe that they have outgrown or overcome their learning disability. In spite of *knowing* about their learning disability, they are still emotionally unprepared to deal with its impact in their daily lives. However, the crisis that led them to therapy may have been precipitated by a new and unsettling configuration of LD problems. Clients will need to consider their learning disability in the light of the emotional crisis that led them to therapy and then discover how it is still affecting them.

Acceptance

Once clients begin to recognize the emotional and practical impact of their learning disability, therapy can work toward acceptance, which usually involves grief for the loss of the client's "normal self." Barton and Fuhrmann (1994) caution therapists that many adults with learning disabilities have never mourned their losses (see Kerry in Chapter 4). "Although unresolved grief is virtually never the presenting problem of adults with learning disabilities, it is almost always not too far beneath the surface and needs to be recognized for the power it contains and the barrier it erects to further growth" (p. 85).

Acceptance involves understanding and dealing not only with emotions that result from external sources such as unfair treatment by parents and teachers, but also with emotions that result from the internal tension of the learning disability. Hannah must deal with the anger that is generated internally as one part of her (the intelligent, analytic, successful part) becomes more and more aggravated with the other part (the dumb, socially inept, failing part). Helping LD clients to understand and live more comfortably with this conflict constitutes an essential part of therapy.

Understanding

Ginsberg and colleagues' (1994) third stage of reframing involves acquiring a deeper understanding one's cognitive deficits and how they impact academic, vocational, and social aspects of life. As Barton and Fuhrmann (1994) suggest, it is *never* safe to assume that adult clients fully understand their learning disability. As children they may have been given oversimplified or incorrect explanations, and it is not easy to tell just what or how much they heard or were prepared to absorb. Furthermore, the same cognitive weakness can have a different impact at various developmental stages. Often at each developmental stage or critical life event (first job, marriage, empty nest), acceptance and understanding must be gained anew, and grieving and readjustment must be facilitated. Since diagnostic testing may be many years out of date, a reassessment can be quite valuable to both client and counselor.

Understanding one's strengths is at least as important as understanding the weaknesses. Although clues to a client's strengths should be available from a good diagnostic assessment, this information is not always emphasized in evaluations, so a search for strengths may well need to be a focus of therapy. Clients with LD have often been forced to concentrate on their weaknesses for so many years that they need extensive help discovering and owning those strengths.

Taking Action

Clients with LD must move forward, accepting responsibility for change with a certain degree of energy and tough-mindedness. It is at this point that a partnership between patient and therapist is most effective. Taking a more active role than is typical in many types of treatment, the therapist can work together with the patient to solve practical problems, remove barriers to stability, and set and achieve realistic goals.

Generally, goal-setting provokes very high levels of anxiety in LD clients, because many years of experience have taught them that goals are invitations to failure. It is often more helpful to lead clients to think in terms of "open-ended possibilities," which can be revised as they make progress and become gradually more familiar and comfortable with their unique sets of cognitive strengths and weaknesses.

Typically, clients with LD make better progress in therapy when it is accompanied both by progress in solving the practical problems of their lives and also by skills instruction in deficient areas (e.g., academic, social, vocational). Sometimes therapeutic intervention may be the first opportunity for a client to deal with painful memories of school and emotional resistance surrounding remedial instruction. Moving forward is often difficult, because expectations about pride and perfection, as well as dependence and independence, will need to change, and as Orenstein (1992) points out, this sort of change creates its own grief.

Interdisciplinary Approach to Therapy

Along with broader goals comes a corresponding increase in the challenges of treatment. In most cases, effective therapy must be interdisciplinary. Counselors and therapists may need to take on many additional roles, including those of

- an educator who teaches about learning disabilities and their effect on life skills;
- a mediator of feedback from the environment;
- a coach who provides assistance in solving life's problems and meeting life's challenges;
- an advocate who assists the client in obtaining appropriate accommodations; and
- a teacher who addresses academic, social, or vocational skills.

Some counselors and therapists feel it is more realistic to work in tandem with other professionals to address all the needs of clients with LD. Then, however, therapists must assume still another role, i.e., that of case manager. Though they are capable in many ways, people with LD often have difficulty negotiating the world of fragmented medical, social, and remedial services. A multidisciplinary practice that includes several professionals who can easily consult with one another may be the optimum arrangement.

Individualizing Therapy

While it is not necessary to make radical changes in one's approach, therapists can accommodate the cognitive strengths and weaknesses of the patient and thereby increase the likelihood of a successful outcome. Oral language problems, attention and organization problems, and nonverbal/social problems can interfere substantially with the process and outcome of therapy. Modifications to accommodate clients with these types of learning disabilities are addressed below.

Oral Language Problems

It is probably safe to say that most therapists have good oral language skills, if only because that is the regular medium of therapy. When the client does not share these skills, language is simultaneously the most important avenue for the communication of thoughts and feelings and an obstacle to doing so.

Disorders of language can be subtle and involve problems of either understanding others or expressing oneself. Difficulties may range from problems with grammar and word endings, to vocabulary and word-finding problems, to problems with knowing how to use language appropriately or effectively. While there is a rich tradition, especially but not exclusively from the psychoanalytic perspective, of interpreting oral language difficulties as indicators of psychopathology, therapists must be open to the possibility that these problems are manifestations not of the unconscious but rather of oral language processing deficits.

If the client has difficulty with the rate at which language is understood, therapists can slow their speech and repeat frequently. For those who have difficulty understanding complex words and sentences, therapists need to simplify their vocabulary, being very careful to define words and verify that the client has understood them, never taking comprehension for granted. The complexity and length of sentences should be decreased, as well as the complexity or number of ideas discussed at one time. Under these conditions not as much will be covered in a single session, but the alternative is confusion and even slower progress. Assuming that reading is not a serious problem, writing out a list of key ideas can be helpful. Therapists may want to use visual mapping, sometimes called "concept mapping," i.e., drawing charts and diagrams and illustrating points with sketches or visual analogies on newsprint or a whiteboard.

Since clients may also have problems with expressive language, the therapist should expect confusing malapropisms, vague language, tangled syntax, unfinished sentences, and tangential responses. Frequently, such clients have difficulty finding the exact word they want to use (dysnomia). Barton and Fuhrmann (1994) note that some appreciate it when therapists assist them by providing the right word, while others resent it. Frequent clarification and periodic comprehension checks are a necessary part of such therapy, and techniques such as mirroring what the client has said can be quite useful. Remember Kerry's point in Chapter 4 that she is unable to trust her communication abilities and feels much more secure when she uses redundant modes of expression. Therapists can encourage clients to prepare for a session by making written or tape-recorded notes and lists of questions and to bring in concept maps, diagrams, and simple sketches.

People with language problems often have difficulty with auditory memory, that is, remembering what they hear. Such memory lapses *may* be unconscious defenses or dissociations, but they may also be evidence of oral language difficulties. Clients with auditory memory problems may have considerable difficulty recalling conversations from previous therapy sessions, and so have difficulty picking up the thread a week later. They may not even remember points covered earlier in a single session. If these problems interfere with treatment, therapists can reserve a few minutes at the beginning and end of each session to review previous material and, just as important, provide continuity by discussing the focus of the next session. Clients can tape-record or take notes during the session; if therapists feel that taping is disruptive, they may want to give the client a short list or diagram covering the major points of the session. Homework can also be helpful in stimulating the client's memory between sessions.

It is worth noting that some clients with poor language ability have an excellent nonverbal social sense and an uncanny ability to "read" people. Therapists should be particularly careful to monitor themselves for inadvertent nonverbal messages when working with such clients.

Attention and Organization Problems

Therapists may need to make allowances to accommodate the client's attention span. The typical session may be too long, causing the client to get off track more easily. Frequent breaks, instead of being distractions, may help clients stay on topic. Fidgeting and distractibility may be signs of tension and anxiety, but commonly they indicate excessive motor activity. Therapists may wish to remove visually distracting objects from the office. However, many distractible clients actually concentrate more easily when they have some small, noiseless object to manipulate, or when they can stand or pace.

Hallowell and Ratey (1994) suggest that therapists play a more active role than usual in determining the structure and focus of therapy for clients with ADD, since external structure is often vital for them. They may get therapy started by asking a direct question and be more directive overall to help such clients stay on topic. Hallowell and Ratey make a crucial point in this regard: Although many therapists encourage free association as a way of letting go of conscious control and uncovering what lies beneath the surface, with ADD adults this techniques can easily backfire, "leaving both the client and therapist lost in a meaningless maze made of distractions and incomplete thoughts and images" (p. 228).

Nonverbal and Social Problems

Individuals with nonverbal and social perception problems typically compensate by relying primarily on fairly well developed verbal skills, generally a better match with the techniques typically used in therapy. Nevertheless, the poor practical problem-solving and lack of intuitive interpersonal skills that characterize nonverbal learning disabilities pose significant challenges for the therapist. The client may appear to have generally flat affect, and to be slow to warm up, indifferent, or rude. Normal methods of putting clients at ease, establishing rapport, or fostering the therapeutic alliance may seem to be ineffective, because the client does not notice or has difficulty interpreting the therapist's facial expressions, gestures, or body language. Clients may have poor eye contact and unusual or immature ways of expressing affect, or they may not follow the "rules" of appropriate personal space. Like Hannah, clients with poor visual skills often have a hyperdeveloped sensitivity to tone of voice and other prosodic cues. Thus, therapists in these situations need to pay careful attention to monitoring their voices, particularly for inadvertent messages of impatience or tension.

When visual and nonverbal problems predominate, treatment will need to be highly and explicitly verbal. Therapists should not assume that implicit messages are being perceived. They will find that much verbal repetition is necessary and that clients seem to be very slow to catch on to practical concepts. Therapists play the roles of interpreters of the social world, coaches for the development of more appropriate behaviors, and partners in the search for solutions to practical problems.

Increasing the Length of Therapy

Counselors may find that the pace of treatment is slower than with other clients because the learning disability tends to slow sessions down. Not as much is accomplished because of the need to get back on track, pause for clarification, or revisit issues periodically. A pro-longed relationship is advantageous, because it makes it easier to weigh the relative effects in any given situation of the client's learning disability and the emotional problems and then decide on the appropriate focus of treatment. For example, to what extent is a client's dependent behavior a manifestation of her personality disorder and to what extent is it the realistic dependence of a person who needs to have someone interpret and mediate for her? Answering such questions takes time and experience with the client. HMOs and other organizations that limit treatment to a predetermined number of sessions may not be appropriate for the client with learning disabilities, and alternative referrals should be investigated at the outset.

Reconceptualizing Resistance to Change

Therapists will often discover that, even though an LD client has accepted responsibility for change, progress is slow. Lack of change may result from the client's failure to understand his or her cognitive strengths and weaknesses. For example, to individuals with LD, the prospect of a job change is daunting. What looks like resistance is actually not knowing how to go about finding a job that is a good match with their abilities and disabilities or even what such a job might look like.

Cognitive rigidity may also interfere with change. With some LD clients, cognitive rigidity can legitimately be interpreted as a defense or as denial, but with others, it results directly from cognitive processing weaknesses. Because certain avenues of processing are blocked, people with LD may have fewer mental pathways for cognitive activities and thus fewer means for envisioning, planning for, or accomplishing change. Because skills are often limited as well, clients have more difficulty finding realistic practical alternatives. People with nonverbal LD are unable to accept change because of their difficulties with hypothesis-testing and problem-solving, as well as their general difficulty dealing with novelty. In addition, since difficulty with social skills is at the heart of nonverbal LD, change in interpersonal interactions will be a significant challenge.

Affectively charged issues, such as fear of failure, are also connected to resistance to change, but for clients with LD this fear is even more powerful than usual, because taking risks often means intense humiliation. Additionally, many people with LD fear that learning new skills could cost them the coping strategies they have struggled to develop.

People with LD are often quite "resistant" to feedback, but for legitimate reasons. LD clients typically perceive feedback as unjustified criticism, since they have heard nothing but reproach and disapproval from family, teachers, peers, coworkers, or supervisors. Further, experience has taught them that feedback has rarely been helpful (e.g., "Just try harder" has not been productive). Moreover, ingrained negative self-attributions lead them to reinterpret even useful feedback as evidence that confirms their belief that they are inadequate. ("What you're *really* saying is I'm dumb because I can't figure this out myself.") For all these reasons, therapists must consider how to present feedback, how to balance positive and negative feedback, and how to establish the level of trust that will ensure that the feedback is "heard."

In the following section, Jay provides his insights into therapy with people who are learning disabled and specifically with Hannah, who has been his patient for several years. "Dr. Einhorn is someone to work these things out with," Hannah says. "He is my best resource." In spite of the slow pace of her own therapy, Hannah has made measurable progress, though often only in very tiny increments. She has made the most progress through cognitive insights into how she exacerbates her own difficulties at work. After several years of therapy with Jay, she is still acquiring this understanding and hanging on, if only by a twig.

In spite of many setbacks, Hannah has retained her spunk and can laugh at some of her problems. For example, she says, "One time I had my son with me while I was visiting a friend. He said something, and my girlfriend said, 'Tommy, don't you lie to me! I know when you're lying whether your mother knows or not.' It was always a little difficult to figure out whether my child was lying because I don't pick up facial expressions. And I said, 'Sandy, he doesn't hem and haw, his voice doesn't sound like he's hunting for answers, he has a convincing tone in his voice. Are you sure he's lying?' She said, 'I know by the look in his eye he's lying.' And you know what? Sure enough, she got him to tell the truth. He fooled me. He had a poker voice!"

Psychotherapeutic Commentary

Hannah, whom I treated for several years, has a complex, difficult-to-diagnose disability. When she was an infant, a pediatrician told her mother that Hannah would likely end up in an institution and advised her to send her there early to spare everyone pain. As an adult, Hannah was diagnosed by a psychologist as not learning disabled at all. She received special education services throughout her years as a student because of her visual nystagmus, not her learning disabilities. Nystagmus causes her eyes to move back and forth very quickly, resulting in impaired vision. When she received services from the state department of vocational services, it was to provide a visual magnifier to help her see at work.

Hannah initially presented, in early middle age, with a history of severe social problems. She was always in conflict with someone at work about something, and she was quite depressed. Clearly, Hannah had some sort of nonverbal learning disability impairing her social perception. Although psychological testing done several years before had been interpreted as within normal limits, I thought that this was a mistaken diagnostic impression and that there was evidence of a nonverbal learning disability. Week after week, Hannah described new situations in which her conduct had provoked reproach or scorn at work because she either hadn't noticed or had completely misinterpreted what was going on between people. Fortunately, her supervisor seemed to understand that her difficulties in social perception were unintentional. She was willing to take time with Hannah to explain some of her mistakes. This supervisor was usually a supportive coach, but she got angry at Hannah when her gaffes involved people outside of her department, potentially making the supervisor look bad. As a result of Hannah's intense dedication to her job and her supervisor's coaching, she has consistently achieved perfect attendance records at work—for ten years at the time of writing. I believe that it is a record unmatched within her midsized company.

It would have been easy to misdiagnose Hannah as suffering from some sort of displaced aggression, to see her as directing her anger away from her parents, where it might presumably have formed in her early development, and targeting it at her peers and herself instead. But she was not expressing displaced aggression or defensiveness through her social behavior, not alienating people through deliberate or even unconsciously intended self-defeating choices. For her, to do so would have required the ability to accurately perceive how others were feeling and what they were doing in social interactions, which is precisely what Hannah could not do. The diagnosis of a social perception deficit based on a nonverbal learning disability put the focus where it belonged, on Hannah's problems understanding interpersonal interactions.

One day, Hannah arrived for her session with a batch of "Far Side" cartoons that had been clipped from newspapers and posted on an office bulletin board by her coworkers. "Can you tell me what's funny about these," she asked, "because I don't understand what people see in them." If you think it's easy to explain Gary Larson's humor to someone who has no understanding of nuance and needs to have everything explicitly stated, just try it sometime. It's one of the more difficult linguistic tasks I've ever tried.

The diagnosis of a social perception disorder didn't explain why the disorder was so severe, as severe as any I had seen, even though her test scores indicated only a mild nonverbal deficit. The most useful diagnosis is the one that explains a patient's symptoms both specifically and comprehensively, and I hadn't gotten there yet with Hannah.

Another persistent diagnostic problem involved a constellation of personality variables. Hannah felt persistently sorry for herself and had a great deal of underlying anger, which was unacknowledged when she began treatment and remained so for a long time. Cognitively, she persistently saw herself as victimized, which was often true, but her version of what was happening often failed to include her role. Attitudinally, she developed an "us-them" perspective, in which persons with learning disabilities were pitted against the rest of the world, which treated them with loathing and contempt. While there is some truth in this, Hannah took it to an oversimplified extreme. She also oversimplified learning disabilities, assuming that her deficits and experiences were the same as those of all other persons with learning disabilities. It was as if she couldn't recognize ways in which other people's mental processes might be different from her own.

Hannah presented her perspectives and attitudes in long, monotonous monologues, delivered with persistent, low-key intensity. If I interrupted her, even after ten or fifteen minutes, to respond to a point she had made, suggest another way of looking at things, or just to try to turn the monologue into a conversation, it was nearly impossible for Hannah to stop and listen to what I was saying. It often seemed that she was able to listen to what I said only when it was in reply to a question she had asked. Her conversation was like a train, stopping at stations but not in between. She tended to repeat the same subject or theme over and over again, persever-ating in a way that seemed quite necessary to her and was certainly boring to others. She would go on and on, even filling up an entire individual session, if I didn't intervene, and exhausting the patience of other adults with learning disabilities in a therapeutic support group that she later joined. Helping her to monitor and modify her perseverative monologuing became an important therapeutic goal. But this behavior is not typical of persons with nonverbal learning disabilities.

It was hard to interrupt Hannah's monologuing, for both of us. She just couldn't monitor her own talking, couldn't observe herself and make accommodations based on observation and feedback. I had to describe what she was doing to her in detail and help her to consider how such behavior might cause others to see her. It felt strange to interpret these most basic perceptions to another adult—things that we take for granted but that Hannah obviously couldn't comprehend. It was analogous to the way in which an occupational therapist might instruct a brain-injured adult in each step of feed-ing oneself. Even after Hannah accepted my description of what she was doing, she couldn't apply it to herself as she talked, couldn't use it to monitor herself. Eventually, unable to find anything else that worked and throwing subtlety to the wind, I began to simply insist, from time to time, that Hannah stop herself in midstream, stop right now, stop talking and listen. Sometimes substantial parts of ses-sions were spent just in helping Hannah stop monologuing and just listen to something in reply. It was very hard work, for both of us— hard for me as a therapist because it was so unusual for me and because I had to be so explicit and patient with her, hard for Han-nah because she seemed to have no way of changing course once she was thinking down a track; she was truly a train without brakes.

Gradually, over years, Hannah learned to stop talking when asked, but it was very hard for her. Even then, she continued men-tally perseverating on her theme, so that, although she had stopped talking, she couldn't listen to what was being said to her. In her mind, she was still monologuing, and she would often return to her monologue after I had stopped talking, as if nothing I had said had registered with her. I could see her working, hard, trying not to continue her line of talking/thinking, just trying to be quiet while I spoke. Finally, after years of individual and group treatment, she was able to stop and relax when explicitly advised to, but at best she could only partly place herself in a receptive state of mind to listen to the contribution of others. At the time of this writing, although she has made a great deal of progress and sometimes can stop talking and listen, at other times she can only stop talking after a while and can't listen.

It was obvious that Hannah's diagnosis was incomplete. Nonverbal learning disability and depression just didn't cover it. I wondered whether she might have some sort of personality disorder, especially a narcissistic type, since that might explain her apparently constant self-preoccupation, her overconcern with her own performance, and lack of awareness of others' views. But other aspects of narcissistic personality didn't fit. The grandiosity, overestimation of importance of self, and need for admiration that characterize narcissistic personality disorder according to the *DSM-IV* weren't present. She was always bothered by her mistakes and felt angry and helpless that she hadn't seen what she should have seen in a social situation. Rather than crave admiration for her accomplishments, she wished she could achieve more. This was no narcissist. In fact, I came to see Hannah as having achieved a great deal despite her disability, and I have told her that I regard her as one of my own role models for tenacity and personal courage in the face of adversity. And it's true.

So we still needed a comprehensive diagnosis that would encompass Hannah's social perception disorder (and the fact that it was far greater than it should be given her relatively mild nonverbal learning disability as indicated by testing), rigid thinking style, and nearly complete lack of empathy. Empathy is the "feeling for" another person, knowing how someone feels based on what we pick up, glean, or intuit. It is to be distinguished from sympathy, which is estimating how someone might be feeling based on what one has observed of his or her circumstances. Empathy is primarily a perceptual and intuitive process, while sympathy is mainly a logical one.

As far as I could tell, Hannah had little if any empathy; indeed, this was the source of many of her innocent social gaffes. Nevertheless, Hannah was quite sympathetic. When a coworker miscarried, for example, Hannah imagined that she must feel very sad and felt quite sorry for her. This was based on Hannah's logical deduction of how she would feel under those circumstances. Similarly, whenever a relative, friend (Hannah actually had several long-term friends, all with disabilities of various types), group member, or coworker was in noticeably painful or trying circumstances, Hannah would feel sorry for the person based on her deduction of how the situation would affect him and her estimate of how she would feel under those circumstances. She held firmly to her view, even when it was wrong. Hannah has taught me much about the difference between sympathy and empathy, for she is both quite sympathetic and quite unempathic, and nothing I've ever said to her about empathy has made sense to her.

While I was trying to resolve these diagnostic inconsistencies about Hannah, I attended a symposium on high-functioning autism and Asperger's disorder. This was an eye-opener for me, which eventually led to my diagnosing Hannah as high-functioning autistic.

Marian Sigman and Lisa Kapps describe the key elements of autism in their book, *Children with Autism: A Developmental Perspective* (1997). In 1943, Leo Kanner, a child psychiatrist living in the United States, published a paper describing a malady he called "infantile autism," the primary feature of which was an innate inability to form the usual affective contact with people. These children also tended to engage in repetitive behavior, made compulsive efforts to preserve order, and had a "desire for sameness," for things to always be stable and predictable. They had great difficulty adapting to change.

The next year, Hans Asperger, a pediatrician living in Germany, described a set of symptoms, later called Asperger's syndrome and now referred to as Asperger's disorder, quite similar to Kanner's. Like Kanner, Asperger identified a core social impairment in the children he studied. They had poor eye contact, limited empathy, impaired nonverbal communication, pedantic and monotonic speech, intense absorption in circumscribed topics like the weather, and marked resistance to change. Unlike Kanner's children, however, Asperger's did not have significant delays in language or cognitive development, aside from social cognition.

High-functioning autism and Asperger's disorder are clearly related. There is controversy about where to draw the line between them, causing some heated exchanges between presenters at the symposium I attended. But it was clear that this might be the diagnosis that would clarify the nature of Hannah's disorder by accounting for every one of her significant symptoms.

To investigate this further, I wanted to speak with Hannah's mother about her development. After obtaining Hannah's permission (eagerly given, since Hannah is always interested in any research or evaluation that might shed light on the nature of her problems), I arranged an interview with her mother, now in her seventies. She described a developmental history that confirmed the diagnosis of childhood autism. Hannah had not spoken until she was four years of age, then began to speak in complete sentences. She rocked compulsively as a child, flapped her arms as autistic children often do, and had great difficulty with change both as a child and as an adult. Of course, Hannah's mother knew it already: "I always thought she might be autistic," she told me.

So much for my brilliant diagnostic acumen.

Once Hannah's diagnosis was clearly established as within the autistic spectrum and most likely high-functioning autism, her life's story instantly made sense, and her treatment could proceed from a solid conceptual basis. She was not responsible for her social mistakes, although she did have to learn how to minimize and mitigate them as much as possible. Her tendency to perseverate and monologue, too, could be seen as rooted in her biology—to be minimized and mitigated, but not treated as symptoms of a primary emotional or personality disorder. By directly addressing these behaviors as symptoms of autism, treatment became easier: "Hannah, you're monologuing again." "Oh, OK."

On the job, Hannah became a more effective advocate for herself. "It's difficult for me to learn new tasks," she'd say. "I have to learn slowly and one step at a time."

Hannah had already made substantial progress as we muddled through the issues of her life together over a period of several years. The diagnosis of high-functioning autism supported continuing improvement. Her anger abated—not disappeared, but substantially decreased—as she was able to accept the circumstances of her life in a way that made sense to her. Her depression lifted substantially as well. At the time of writing, she is honeymooning with her new husband (who is blind) by going bowling with the league for visually impaired persons to which they both belong.

CHAPTER 8

Psychotherapy of Two Invisible Sources of Distress
A Framework for Therapy

by Jay Einhorn

There Is More Light Here
Someone saw Nasrudin searching for something on the ground.

"What have you lost, Mulla?" he asked.

"My key," said the Mulla. So they both went down on their knees and looked for it.

After a time the other man said, "Where exactly did you drop it?"

"In my own house."

"Then why are you looking here?"

"There is more light here than inside my own house."

—Idries Shah

As psychotherapists, we are always treating something or someone invisible: the self or personality of our patients or clients.[1] While their distress may be evident in emotional suffering or destructive behavior, the source of that distress is concealed within the mind of the person. Psychiatrists treat the symptoms directly, with medications that alter brain chemistry. Behavioral therapists work with behavior directly, with such strategies as systematic desensitization. Psychotherapists, by contrast, are primarily interested in how their patient's distress came about and what it means in the context of the patient's personality or sense of self, which in turn is seen not in isolation but within the context of his interpersonal history. Psychotherapists and therapeutically oriented counselors try to help their clients change their underlying way of being in order to become emotionally healthier and able to live more successful and satisfying lives. And that underlying way of being, for better or worse, is invisible.

As psychotherapists we do, of course, focus on our patients' emotional distress and destructive behavior—which are visible—but we do so to help them become more aware of their emotional and behavioral patterns, better able to understand them in the context of their personal histories, and so to change them (Deikman, 1982). Even such useful methods of treatment as relaxation training, while directly targeting emotional distress and disordered behavior, are intended to help patients develop their capacities for self-monitoring and personal choice. Such capacities are, by definition, invisible; they can only be experienced by the patient. Thus, both the source of psychological distress and its treatment take place in the invisible realm of the patient's experience, where no video camera or biofeedback monitor yet developed—or perhaps ever to be developed—can directly record what is happening.

Clients with Learning Disabilities

Psychotherapists treating clients with learning disabilities are working with two invisible sources of distress: their cognitive functioning and their personality. Indeed, persons with learning disabilities have often formed significant parts of their personalities around their learning disabilities. Understanding the nature of the learning disability and the role it has played in the development of the patient's personality is so important that failure to discern the learning disability may limit or undermine the effectiveness of psychotherapy.

It is remarkable that psychotherapy has worked for so long "in the dark" about learning disabilities. Psychotherapy has selectively focused on one aspect of the problem of human emotional and behavioral dysfunction—the personality—while neglecting the role of how we fundamentally think, communicate, and learn. It is as if there were a presumptive "standard working model" of the fundamentals of thinking, communicating, and learning, assumed to be present in every patient. And yet such a notion, if it were applied to personality rather than cognition, would be instantly rejected by all therapists.

At its best, psychotherapy has established the tradition of in-depth understanding of personality in the diagnosis and treatment of persons with emotional and behavioral disorders. Similarly, clinical education, at its best, has established the tradition of in-depth understanding of the individual learning patterns of persons with learning disabilities. It is time to combine the two traditions.

The Role of Cognition in the Development of the Self

Psychotherapists see personality problems as interruptions or malformations in development. We are thought to have personality problems in the present because something hurt us earlier in our development; that traumatic insult is assumed to have stopped or altered our normal development. The death of a parent, physical or emotional invasion or abandonment by a parent, birth of a sibling, divorce or remarriage of one's parents, abrupt dislocation, highly conflicted relationships with peers—all are examples of events that can have a profound emotional impact on a developing child.

Learning disabilities have a profound impact on the developing personality or self of a child. The development of cognition is intimately connected with the development of the sense of self within the child, and especially of self-esteem. A brief overview of the role of cognition in the development of the self may be helpful. It is useful (although an oversimplification) to visualize development as evolving through stages:

- *Conception to Birth.* The neonate's development is governed by its genetic code and modified by the fetal environment. Maternal nutrition and exposure to toxins can affect fetal development, as can such factors as maternal emotional state and other more subtle environmental influences.

- *Birth through about Two Years.* Children are busily establishing the fundamentals of learning in their first two years or so. Important areas include:
  - Constructing a stable sensory-perceptual world, learning to "make sense" of sensory input.

- Acquiring basic perceptual-motor control, including learning to crawl, walk, run, eat, toilet, and speak at least rudimentarily. Speech is a very complicated perceptual-motor process.
- Acquiring the beginnings of a passive vocabulary, also called receptive language, learning to recognize words.
- Acquiring the beginnings of social or interpersonal learning, learning what to expect from others, how to interpret their behavior and communication signals, learning how to behave toward them so as to increase gratification and control over how one is responded to by others.
- Beginning to develop a sense of self, as a person to whom others respond and the one to whom things belong (Deikman, 1976).

- *About Two Years through about Five Years.* The child consolidates and expands learning in all domains, building a foundation to meet his needs within his environment in a fully effective way at an age-appropriate level. This includes:
  - Completing a stable and reliable construction of reality, which orients a child to his environment.
  - Completing the acquisition of receptive and expressive language.
  - Completing the acquisition of motor control.
  - Completing the acquisition of social knowledge and interpersonal skills.
  - Elaborating a sense of self.

- *About Kindergarten through about Fifth Grade.* The child enters formal academic schooling, which takes her beyond family and neighborhood. This contact with new cultures, which she must at the least cope with and at best conquer, places new demands on, and offers new opportunities to, the developing child. By the completion of the fifth grade, the child without a learning disability will:
  - Learn to read, including decoding and comprehension, at approximate grade level.
  - Learn mathematics, including concepts and calculation, at approximate grade level.
  - Learn self-management
    - Emotionally,
    - Socially, and

- ○ Productively (schoolwork, homework, school projects, including planning and time management).
- Develop a repertoire of relationship skills that are effective with both adults and peers, both within and beyond her immediate family and neighborhood.
- Continue to elaborate a sense of self based on the inclusion and exclusion of impressions about what one is like and not like. A healthy sense of self supports a sense of internal and interpersonal security and flexibility, orients one toward competence and achievement in one's activities, and supports the ability to make personally correct choices.

- *About Sixth Grade through about Eighth Grade.* During this time, the child is beginning to enter puberty, and thus adulthood, in an intense and rapidly changing social environment. The child:
  - Consolidates his elementary academic skills and begins to apply them to increasingly demanding and complex academic projects, or experiences impairment in the acquisition, consolidation, and/or extension of elementary academic skills. A general trend differentiating elementary and junior high school development is that elementary education, like pre-elementary learning, largely utilizes learning through imitation, "absorption," and trial, error, and repeat trial learning of skills, while junior high school development places more emphasis on disciplined practice to acquire skills, critical thinking to evaluate information, and objective use of academic materials to acquire information about subjects.
  - Confronts increasingly intense choices of self-determination in emotion, behavior, and self-management, including:
    - ○ Attitudes toward males, females, teachers, parents, siblings, work, sexual behavior, local and national identity, social classes or groups, intoxicants, etc.
    - ○ Disidentification with parents and identification with peers (Cohen & Balikov, 1974).
  - Elaborates a sense of self that supports feelings of relatedness to, and separation from, all of the groups with which one is in contact, and through a changing set of configurations of self.

- *High School: In a Child, Out an "Adult."* All the trends in junior high intensify and culminate in a person who, upon graduation, will be regarded in most ways as an adult citizen who must make vitally important decisions about his or her own life and may be expected to become partially to completely financially independent.

Thus, the child's maturation includes continuous social, cognitive, and self development from precursors established before birth. There is no social perception or expression, no "self" or self-awareness, no understanding of others or communication, no relationship, without cognition.

Anatomically, the cognitive processes essential to learning are functionally localized on the cerebral cortex, the surface of the cerebrum, which is itself the top level of the brain. The cerebrum sits above and around the limbic system, which is a group of structures in the middle of the brain associated with important functions of self-regulation, such as memory, emotion, and appetites. The limbic system itself sits above and around the central core of the brain, which arises out of the spinal cord and is responsible for such basic life support as the operation of the cardiovascular and gastrointestinal systems.[2]

Most of the cerebrum is specialized for sensory interpretation and movement; for example, we "see" with the very back part of our brain, and can become "brain blind" from injuries there. But approximately the front third, the neocortex, is specialized for the kinds of thought and perception we regard as particularly human. The left frontal and prefrontal areas are specialized (in most adults) for sequential, one-step-at-a-time, focused cognition. This is the kind of activity that underlies much communication by language, in which each letter within each word, and each word within each sentence, must be in the correct sequence if the communication is to make sense. It is also the kind of cognition that brings our attention to a point of focus on anything. The right frontal and prefrontal areas are specialized (in most adults) for relational, all-together-at-once cognition. This is the kind of cognition that is necessary for understanding social situations, in which much of the information about what is expected of one, and others, is implicit and nonverbal rather than explicit and verbal. The right hemisphere is also important for proprioception, that is, the perception of the person's internal environment (Ornstein, 1997).

Cognitive defects may occur in any of the processes underlying perception, thought, learning, and communication. A partial list is given below. As you read it, consider how impairment in any of these cognitive functions, or any combination of them, might affect the development of any person through the approximate developmental niches described above. Cognitive deficits may occur in these (and other) functions:

- Receptive auditory language (understanding speech)
- Expressive spoken language (speech)
- Reading decoding (sounding out words)
- Reading comprehension (understanding written language)
- Expressive written language, content (writing what you think)
- Expressive written language, spelling, and/or rules (grammar, punctuation, capitalization)
- Mathematical concepts (knowing what operation is called for)
- Mathematical calculation (doing the operation correctly)
- Information organization (putting it together, prioritizing)
- Pattern perception
- Interpersonal/social perception
- Ability to attend to a particular matter and maintain that focus
- Ability to inhibit attention from potential distractions
- Ability to attend to a situation, identifying and maintaining prioritized role(s) and goal(s)
- Ability to inhibit perceptions and impulses that distract from or disrupt the maintenance of such orienting and prioritizing attention
- Ability to adjust one's mental set to accommodate incoming information
- Ability to learn new information at an optimal speed and to store and recall it in memory

Clearly, any disruption or deficit in normal cognitive development will have an impact on the educational, social, and personal development of the child. An impaired ability to understand oral communication, for example, will compromise a child's ability to understand and participate in relationships. The specifics will vary, depending on whether the impairment is, for example, in the auditory processing of spoken language or in the decoding of nonverbal movement, gesture, and tone of voice with which the oral communication is sent. If the deficit is in auditory language processing, the child's understanding of what was said to him will be impaired. If the deficit is in nonverbal cognition, the child will not understand the attitude of the communication—what the speaker was communicating about her relationship with the child—and the contextual meaning of the particular spoken words.

Usually, learning disabilities show up in the school performance of children whose cognitive development up to that time has seemed to be more or less within normal limits. Such deficits invariably affect the personal, social, and educational development of the child. When a child in school is unable to learn to read, for example, while all around her other children are learning, it sets her apart from them, making her different and inferior. Often, children are told to "try harder" when they're already trying as hard as they can or to "pay attention" when they are attending but cannot make sense out of the letters by matching them with sounds and seeing how they go together to make words. In such cases, the message that the teacher neither acknowledges nor values the efforts that the child is making is not lost on the child.

When children cannot learn due to learning disabilities, they are often regarded by their teachers, parents, and/or peers as stupid, lazy, or mentally or emotionally ill. They often evoke frustration and resentment in their teachers. Note that, in many or all areas other than those involved in the learning disability, these children may have entirely normal cognitive function and be capable of normal development; indeed, such children may be bright or gifted in some areas. A dyslexic child who can't learn to read with normal instruction might, for example, have outstanding mechanical aptitude or be socially gifted. Typically, such strengths are not identified or encouraged even though cultivating them might balance the shame and pain of the deficit.

Children may have cognitive deficits affecting their expressive spoken or written language even when their physical ability to speak or write is not impaired. Such children are often treated as if they are stupid or retarded, even though they may be socially and/or nonverbally average, bright, or gifted. The potential for damage affecting the child's personal and social development is obvious.

By the time children enter junior high school, relationships with peers and authority figures outside of the home have typically become so important that they compete with parents as role models for behavior, values, etc. Conflicts among the cultures of the family, peers, and school are driven by biological and socioeconomic forces working in and through the child to drive her toward an existence that is more or less independent of her parents and family. The presence of learning disabilities makes it harder for children to negotiate these transitions, thus impeding their development toward independence.

Impact of Learning Disabilities on the Adolescent and His Family

Adolescence is a difficult and trying developmental process for all adolescents and their families. The teenager enters adolescence more or less dependent on the parents and leaves it more or less on his own. Parents have to gradually transfer control to their teenager, so that he can learn how to make decisions for himself, while maintaining sufficient control to protect him from the dangers of the environment and of his immature judgment. The teenager begins to learn about the adult meanings of sexual, economic, and community responsibility. By the end of his teenage years, he will be expected to function more or less as an adult in these realms, although economic independence will be deferred if he remains a student and his parents pay for tuition and/or living expenses.

The child's emergence into adolescence often raises issues that threaten the parents. Since the child's budding adulthood signals his eventual departure from the home of the parents, they face the impending loss of a love object. This may evoke emotional pain or conflict stemming from earlier situations when they lost love objects, including perhaps their parents, in ways that were precipitous or painful. The intimacy of parents with very young children is based largely on the children's utter dependence, a foundation that is eroded and gives way in adolescence. Parents are challenged by their children's emerging adulthood to restructure the nature of their relationship. Personal closeness between parent and child becomes increasingly like that between adults, in which acknowledgment of the separate identity of the individuals is an important part of the relationship. Control issues must be successively renegotiated as the child progresses through the teenage years, with the parents avoiding the temptation to overcontrol or abandon their adolescent child. Successfully parenting an adolescent requires the parents to maintain an empathic connection with him as over a decade he becomes transformed from a household child to an independent adult (Cohen & Balikov, 1974).

This is difficult enough, and our society provides us with little effective guidance—too much information from so-called "experts," much of which is really "fads and folklore," and too few genuinely good role models. Imagine how much more difficult it is for the parents of a child with LD. As the child begins to become more independent but still needs the structure of his parents, his learning disability provides yet another threat to the parent-child relationship. One of two extreme reactions is commonly observed. In the first, the parents are so traumatized by the child's disability that they become overprotective and fail to help him to become as independent as possible. In my practice I have encountered several parents of middle-aged children with severe learning disabilities who not only encourage their children to continue living with them but actually perform the most mundane activities of daily living for them, such as cooking meals and washing clothes, while expecting little or nothing of them in the way of contributing to the household. Such extended dependence is clearly not in the best interests of the adult with LD, who will one day have to get on in the world without his parents' protection. Where parents have encouraged extended dependency in their severely LD child, the intimacy based on dependence that characterizes early childhood has been extended by both children and parents into adolescence and adulthood, becoming an obstacle to progressive independence.

In the second extreme reaction, the child rejects the values of his parents and family and becomes increasingly involved in antisocial behavior, drug use, etc. This may occur because the parents really do reject the child, in some way wanting to get rid of him, so that they can maintain or regain their own balance. Some LD adolescents have the social skills and initiative necessary to succeed in the peer street culture or at work, even though they fail in school. If the parents demand school success as the price of their respect, the child may become prematurely independent, finding acceptance where he can. These issues tend to show up first in junior high school and to be exacerbated in high school, as the child approaches adulthood.

Academic Disabilities versus Life Disabilities

Many people who have learning disabilities in school turn out to be quite successful in life—sometimes more successful than many of their non–learning disabled classmates, if success is measured by achievement in business or other non-academic venues. For example, a dyslexic child who spells phonetically rather than correctly may never do well in school, where the idea of grading for content of writing rather than spelling seems to many teachers to be contrary to the purpose of education. That same child may have capacities of leadership, initiative, and creativity that will enable her to rise to a high corporate position, achieve success in the arts, or start a successful business, where she can employ a secretary to correct her spelling. The learning disability in this case, a deficiency in spelling, is more of a problem in school than beyond it. Such children can go through hell in school for relatively minor cognitive problems, while their strengths go unrecognized and uncultivated and only emerge after the school day, or the school years, are over. Conversely, children without academic disabilities may pass through elementary school, high school, and even college without apparent problems and yet emerge with deficits in ability to identify and solve problems, accept new responsibilities, communicate with others, contribute significantly as team members, or fulfill leadership positions. The fact is that in some ways school prepares children for life, and in other ways it overemphasizes skills that are not particularly relevant and ignores ones that are crucially important.[3] Some learning disabilities are made worse by the restrictive culture of school learning as opposed to life learning. For those who think that education as we practice it represents some sort of pinnacle of training for youth, it should be humbling to remember that some of the worst disasters in history have been engineered by people who were among the cream of the educational crop. The child who is "learning disabled" in school may be more "life able" than another child who is, to all appearances, entirely normal.

Attention Deficit Disorder

Attention deficit disorder (ADD) is another condition that school can improve by early identification and treatment or worsen by providing an environment in which the weaknesses of the child are overemphasized and the strengths ignored. In some cases, the diagnosis is made where there is no real deficit at all, only an extreme mismatch between the nature of the child and the behavioral requirements of school. ADD is not a simple issue. The answer to the question of whether attention deficit disorder is underdiagnosed or overdiagnosed is: both.

Attention is a complex process, as we know from studies of individuals who have suffered traumatic brain injuries. Attention involves the focusing and sequencing of the left hemisphere and the organization and prioritizing of the right. It requires inhibiting distractions that interfere with concentration, whether they arise externally, from the environment, or internally, from thoughts, feelings, and sensations. It is theorized that the reason stimulants help many hyperactive children is that they stimulate the function of inhibitory pathways that are not working as well as they should be. Neurologically, children who are behaviorally hyperactive are not so much hyperactive as underinhibited. Once the cerebral inhibitory pathways are normalized by the stimulant, they can do their job of inhibiting responsiveness to stimuli from the external and internal environments, and the child can attend better and longer in school. For this reason, using an automotive analogy, I've described stimulants for truly hyperactive children as like "brake fluid."

But everybody's brakes are not the same. It makes sense to think about attention as a continuum. At one end is the person who can focus very intently on a single stimulus for a long time without being distracted, but who may not notice much else. I once worked with a teacher who was like that; whatever she looked at was perceived fully and richly, but she hardly noticed anything else that was happening around her at the time. At the other end of the attention continuum is the person who is acutely sensitive to every distraction, who notices everything but may not be able to focus very persistently on anything. When I take a walk with a hyperactive child, I am often stunned by how much he notices that I don't.

Obviously, each kind of attention has its benefits and disadvantages, and most of us are somewhere in between these poles. Someone making a watch or a tool by hand has to be able to concentrate intently on it for long periods of time without being distracted by minor interruptions. A hunter stalking prey in the woods, on the other hand, has to be acutely alert to minute information from the environment. School culture is skewed to regard the former type of persons as "normal" and the latter ones as "abnormal," whereas in fact neither kind of attention is intrinsically superior. Remember that, in cultures where children grew up with their families in farming or hunter-gatherer economies, children minded domestic animals, gathered food plants, participated in hunting when they were older, and had other important responsibilities for the well-being of their families. The idea of separating children from the survival responsibilities of life and instead teaching them mental skills in schools, from early childhood through young adulthood, is quite new, historically speaking, and remains to be evaluated in historical perspective.

There is no diagnostic test that directly identifies ADD; the diagnosis is always a judgment call. In making it, one gathers information from parents, teachers, and others who know the child well. One conducts tests of learning and memory to see how the child responds compared to peers. One may observe the child in school or at home. One office visit is not enough, since most truly ADD children can pull it together for a visit or two; several may be necessary. The criterion for differentiating whether a child is hyperactive rather than just biologically mismatched with the school culture is whether he is attentionally dysfunctional in most other settings as well.

The differentiation between the genuinely ADD child and the merely robustly active one is very important. Children with real attention deficits are impaired as learners and also in their social lives. They often welcome the improvements in learning and self-management that they get from medication and wouldn't want to be without it. On the other hand, the merely robust child who is misdiagnosed as ADD will be given medication to no purpose and have to suffer the effects of being regarded as having a clinical syndrome when none exists. Children with real attention deficits need some accommodation in expectations as well as specific methods to compensate for their attentional lapses. Normal but highly robust children, on the other hand, may need both more stimulation and more structure.

The need for structure and stimulation may be particularly evident among boys (although there are certainly examples among girls too). Joe Griffin and Ivan Tyrrell (1999) of the European Therapy Studies Institute write:

> This tendency (among boys) for risk taking and sensation seeking means that boys need more stimulation in order to focus and structure the way they give attention. This, of course, has an impact on the education styles that boys

and girls respond to best. Typically girls make tremendous strides within the educational system when it is cooperatively based and they are subject to appraisal by continuous assessment. Boys need discipline and a more structured and stimulating approach before they can focus and work well. . . . The statistic that up to 10% of all boys are diagnosed as having attention deficit hyperactivity disorder (ADHD), an extreme form of the need for greater stimulation to focus attention, clearly shows how boys' attention needs are failing to be addressed by current educational practices.

There is no doubt that some children have attention insufficiencies that would present problems for them wherever they were. But there are also many whose learning or behavioral problems in school have more to do with the unsuitability of that environment for those children than with anything inherently wrong with them. Among the adults portrayed in this book, several have had more success after leaving school than they ever had in it. Ask yourself whether their success after school is because their LD or ADD improved, or because their minds were simply better suited to life in "the real world" than they were to school.

As psychotherapists working with persons with learning disabilities, we are presented with the results of the damage due to misunderstanding and mistreatment, and we have to help our clients heal from that damage. Helping our clients to understand what their learning disabilities are, how they have been affected by them, how they have been helped or hindered by the responses of others, how their strengths and weaknesses have helped or hindered them in school, and how they may help or hinder them in life beyond school—these tasks are at the heart of psychotherapy with persons with learning disabilities.

Possible Indicators of Learning Disabilities in Adults

Many indicators of learning disabilities are discernible in an interview or clinical appraisal. When several of these indicators occur together, especially in cases where intelligence is at least in the average range, counselors and therapists are advised to refer the client for a learning disabilities assessment.

Client's Report of the Problem

Does the client report:

_____ a fear of being lazy, crazy, or stupid?

_____ accusations of being shiftless, immature, or impulsive?

_____ berating him- or herself for not trying hard enough, for being irresponsible, or just a loser?

_____ perception by others as unmotivated, as not being able to get his or her act together, as having unrealized potential?

_____ inventing clever or devious ways to hide the problem or cover up incompetence?

Behavioral Observations

Does the client appear to:

_____ be disheveled, have difficulty selecting clothes that go together or problems tying a tie?

_____ have inappropriate or unusual body language, awkward or clumsy body movements?

_____ have difficulty with making eye contact, maintaining the correct social distance, or general social behaviors?

_____ give seemingly tangential responses to questions, have word-finding or syntax problems, impulsively try to say everything at once?

Medical History

Does the client have a history of:

_____ prenatal substance use?

_____ prematurity?

_____ low birth weight ?

_____ birth trauma?

_____ history of otitis media or allergies?

_____ high fevers?

_____ accidents involving head trauma?

_____ headaches, gastric complaints, ulcers, and other correlates of anxiety?

Developmental History

Is there a history of:

_____ immaturity, language delay, or delay in developmental motor milestones?

_____ an erratic, inconsistent school history or comments on report cards such as "could do better," "needs to buckle down," "needs to use the good ability he has," "needs to focus more," "does not live up to potential"? (see Dane, 1990)

_____ retention in one or more grades, frequent attendance at summer school, in-school or after-school tutoring, a referral for any kind of testing, remedial work or special classes, speech therapy, or a history of truancy and dropping out?

_____ frequent switching of schools without accompanying changes of address, or searching for a school that can finally teach the child? Unusual circumstances surrounding the high school diploma? Was it earned on time? Through a GED program? The military?

_____ lack of pursuit of training or education beyond high school? What made the client decide not to continue?

_____ hatred of reading, math, English, or gym, particularly when accompanied by success in some other subject?

_____ discrepancy between the client's learning and school history and that of siblings?

_____ social difficulties, having mostly younger friends, having friends who were considered less intelligent, losers, or undesirable?

_____ problems with the social activities of childhood such as learning to play games or ride a bike?

_____ family conflict over school or social issues?

Adult History or Current Functioning

Is there a history of:

_____ drug or alcohol use or failed rehabilitation programs?

_____ lack of progress in psychotherapy?

_____ difficulty with or avoidance of reading? Do clients read something over and over again? Do they have difficulty with attention or memory while reading? With word attack or comprehension? With using a dictionary or phone book?

_____ problems with daily applications of math, such as balancing a checkbook, figuring tips or discounts, or taking measurements?

_____ problems with daily living skills? What is the level of effort involved in doing daily tasks? Is the quality of the result equivalent to the effort? What tasks do clients avoid doing? What tasks are they afraid that people will ask them to do? How do they learn new tasks?

_____ problems driving, parking, remembering where the car is parked, or taking public transportation?

_____ problems following directions or giving directions to a place, getting lost easily, or having difficulty reading a map?

_____ difficulty with lateness or getting things done on time? Do clients consistently use a watch? An alarm clock? A daily planner?

_____ difficulty participating in activities such as recreational sports, social dancing, or appreciation of the arts?

_____ social inadequacy and isolation, dating or marriage problems?

_____ problems with being left out of social conversations? Do clients have difficulty interpreting humor, sarcasm, or irony? Does group conversation flow too quickly, especially in noisy, crowded environments?

_____ difficulty with communication skills? Do clients misunderstand what is said to them? Do they have difficulty finding the exact word they want, with finishing sentences, or with expressing what they want to say?

_____ underemployment, frequent job loss, or job switching?

_____ difficulties with job search, hiring, training, or promotions?

_____ problems taking phone messages, writing memos and reports, or reading instruction manuals?

_____ difficulty getting along with colleagues and supervisors?

_____ difficulty operating simple office machinery?

_____ difficulty meeting deadlines, getting to work on time, or having appropriate materials at hand?

_____ difficulty with procrastination, making decisions, or adjusting to change?

. . . .

Modifications of Therapy to Accommodate Adults with Learning Disabilities

Oral Language

If the client has difficulty with:	The therapist can:
Understanding complex words and sentences	• Avoid taking comprehension for granted • Simplify vocabulary • Define words and verify that the client has understood them • Decrease complexity and length of sentences • Decrease complexity and number of ideas discussed at one time • Write out a list of important points • Review and highlight key ideas • Use visual mapping (concept maps), i.e., drawing charts and diagrams • Illustrate points with sketches, visual images, or visual analogies

Oral Language (continued)

If the client has difficulty with:	The therapist can:
The rate at which language is understood	• Slow speech down to the client's pace • Repeat frequently
Word-finding problems	• Ask clients if they want help locating the right word • Provide word choices • Provide the first sound of the word
Oral expression	• Do not hesitate to ask for clarification • Check frequently to verify comprehension of what client says • Mirror what client says • Ask client to bring in written or taped notes, questions, and thoughts
Auditory memory	• Reserve a few minutes at the beginning and end of a session to review previous material • Provide continuity by discussing the focus of the next session • Allow client to tape-record sessions or take notes • Provide a simple list or diagram that you have jotted down during the review of the session • Assign "homework" to stimulate the client's memory between sessions

Attention and Organization Problems

If the client has difficulty with:	The therapist can:
Attentiveness, restlessness	• Shorten sessions • Allow for frequent, short breaks
Fidgeting, distractibility	• Remove distracting objects from office

> • Provide a noiseless, malleable object for client to hold or squeeze
> • Allow client to stand, pace, sit in different chairs

If the client has difficulty with:	The therapist can:
Disorganized or associative thinking, wordy or tangential responses	• Be more directive overall • Play a more active role than usual in determining the structure and focus of therapy
Tendency to stray from the topic	• Get therapy started by asking a direct question • Actively weigh what is heard and consider what to focus on and what to let slide by (see Hallowell & Ratey, 1994)

Nonverbal Problems

If the client has difficulty with:	The therapist can:
Establishing rapport	• Avoid assuming that implicit messages are being perceived • Describe feelings and attitudes verbally
"Reading" body language	• Teach body language, describe it explicitly
Catching on to practical concepts	• Use much verbal repetition • Act as partner in the search for solutions to practical problems
Inappropriate behaviors	• Interpret the social world verbally • Teach appropriate behaviors and coach clients in their use

········· ··········

Notes

Preface

1. As in most of this book, I here use the longer phrase "students who . . ." rather than "learning disabled students," for the following reason, already well known to LD specialists but perhaps not to therapists and others reading this book. These students are *persons*, not walking sets of symptoms, and they have a right to be regarded as more than whatever disabilities (or abilities) they might have. However, completely avoiding the adjectival locution might give readers the impression that there is something shameful about having a learning disability; after all, no one objects when the adjective in question is "gifted" or "creative." Hence I have compromised by using terms like "learning disabled adults" occasionally and only when there is no hint of any negative connotation. There are approximately 30 such phrases in this and the following chapters, compared to well over 150 uses of the more felicitous longer phrases such as "adults with learning disabilities." Let us hope that as the general public becomes more aware of what it means to have a learning disability, the need for such linguistic maneuvers will disappear.

Chapter 1. Misunderstood, Misdiagnosed, Mistreated

1. Other studies confirm the high percentage of learning disabled adults who need counseling. Johnson and Blalock (1987) found that 36% of their clinical population of learning disabled adults had received counseling or psychotherapy. A survey of LD adults by a national professional organization revealed that at least one-half of the respondents wanted counseling services, and that help with personal problems ranked third out of ten areas of need (Chesler, 1982). Balow and Blomquist (1965) found that 25% of subjects who were diagnosed with childhood dyslexia showed evidence of psychopathology on the MMPI 10 to 15 years later. Hoffman et al. (1987) surveyed 381 adults with LD and found that 24%

stated that they needed help with personal problems. Most recently, a 20-year follow-up study of adults with LD found that 42% of their subjects reported diagnosed psychological difficulties that were classifiable under the *DSM-IV*. These difficulties included depression, schizophrenia, substance abuse, social phobias, panic disorders, and obsessive-compulsive disorder (Raskind, Goldberg, Higgins, & Herman, 1999).

Chapter 2. Hanging by a Twig

1. Much controversy surrounds the validity of the concept of disorders of cognitive processing. The majority of definitions of LD include the notion that deficits in cognitive processes affect learning, even though there is no agreement among professionals as to how to categorize these constructs or how to measure them. Experts have proposed several models for the diagnosis of LD. All incorporate the notion of depressed achievement (e.g., Siegel, 1990). Most models also incorporate the notion that this depressed achievement is discrepant with intelligence (e.g., Critchley, 1970; see also Stanovich, 1993). Models that attempt to explain this discrepancy in terms of specific cognitive processing deficits that affect achievement in spite of adequate intelligence are also prevalent (Hoy & Gregg, 1994; Johnson & Blalock, 1987; Johnson & Myklebust, 1967; Kavale, 1993). However, while the *DSM-IV* (1994) acknowledges that cognitive processing deficits may be associated with the disorder, these deficits are not specifically addressed. Knowledge in the area of cognitive function specifically in adults with learning disabilities is extremely limited, and there are no nationally accepted criteria for diagnosis of learning disabilities for the adult population. Nevertheless, research such as that of Johnson and Blalock (1987), as well as case studies of numerous adults with LD (see Gerber & Reiff, 1994), including those in this book, indicate that, though academic skills may improve, cognitive processing problems persist into adulthood and resurface in new ways that interfere with social, vocational, recreational, and daily living skills.

2. Of course, learning disabilities exist across the entire range of intellectual ability. Those who are retarded may *also* have unexpected discrepancies between their level of achievement in some specific area(s) and their reduced intellectual level. That is, a mentally retarded person may also have a learning disability.

3. Some theorists have different views. Coles (1987), for example, claims that there is not enough evidence that children have inherent limitations in their ability to process specific types of information. Mann (1979) and Hammill (1990) claim that there is no evidence to suggest that training in "hypothetical processes" is effective. But this chapter and the rest of the book proceed from the notion that specific cognitive process-

ing difficulties exist and that they can and do interfere with learning. In addition, recent research provides strong indications that cognitively-based training in phonological awareness, reading comprehension strategies, writing strategies, and general study strategies can be quite effective. For a good review of this issue see Torgeson, 1998.

4. Theories about the connections between processing deficits and dyslexia are numerous. Currently most hypotheses consider linguistic processing deficits, particularly in phonemic awareness, as the most likely cause of reading and spelling problems. Referring to the widely accepted "phonological core deficit hypothesis" for explaining dyslexia, Mann (1998) summarizes the relevant literature, indicating that dyslexics "tend to have problems with phoneme awareness and also with three aspects of language-processing skill: (1) speech perception under difficult listening conditions; (2) vocabulary, especially when vocabulary is measured in terms of naming ability; and (3) using a phonetic representation in linguistic short-term memory" (p. 190). However, although they are less fashionable these days, explanations for dyslexia that involve visual processing problems must also be given attention, as Mary's example attests. Willows (1998) comments, "Clinical observations and case reports, correlational evidence from studies using standardized psychometric instruments, and visual deficit subtypes from clinical and neuropsychological studies all point to some role of visual processing deficits in reading disabilities. Evidence from information-processing research involving basic visual perception and visual memory also suggest that some relationship exists between visual processing deficits and reading disabilities" (p. 229).

5. Much current controversy exists as to whether or not attention problems are a legitimate type of learning disability or a separate disorder. Many claim that although attention problems are often found along with learning disabilities, an attention deficit is not a learning disability because it concerns not a learning process but a disposition for learning. Many also claim that one can have an attention problem that does not directly affect learning to read or spell, so attention problems are not learning disabilities because they do not affect the acquisition of basic academic skills. However, not all authorities in the field separate attention deficits from learning disabilities. Levine (1998) for example, takes issue with the conceptualization of ADD as a distinct clinical entity. Furthermore, some definitions of LD include attention right along with other processing deficits. For example, "The disorder manifests itself with a deficit in one or more areas: attention, reasoning, processing, memory, communication" (Rehabilitation Services Administration, 1985). Sergeant (1996) even proposes that attention is a cognitive process that cannot be entirely separated conceptually from memory, since his definition of selective attention "places

the locus of the attention limitation in working memory" (p. 57). Obviously, a thorough discussion of this controversy is beyond the scope of this book, and the issue will be left as an open question.

6. We acknowledge the need to identify useful subtypes of attention deficit disorder, especially the presence or absence of hyperactivity. However, for the sake of avoiding such infelicities as AD/HD, we will use the term ADD in this book, with the understanding that it encompasses important subtypes.

7. It is the emphasis in our culture on academic skills that prompts many experts to advocate limiting the concept of learning disability to difficulty learning basic skills such as reading, spelling, and math. Many professionals exclude from the concept problems with less "important" abilities such as social and recreational skills, musical and artistic skills, and even skills of daily living. Others disagree, maintaining that learning is not limited strictly to academics, and this disagreement is one reason that the definition of LD is so controversial. While such conceptual limitations on the definition may be more acceptable when diagnosing children (though I am not convinced it is), this position certainly does a disservice to adults, who typically present with problems in social, vocational, or other adaptive skills.

8. Bipolar disorder is a later name for manic-depression, in which the individual alternates between energetic, grandiose elation and lethargic, hopeless depression. In cyclothymic disorder, states of hypomania (somewhat but not completely manic), agitation, or irritability alternate with moderate depressions.

9. At its worst, psychotherapy has a history of competing dogmas and egos being replaced by new waves of competing dogmas and egos. But that's another matter.

10. Some psychotherapists, however, have made the mistake of misdiagnosing learning disabilities as psychic defenses, for example, a child with a disability in reading may be misunderstood as actively trying to avoid developing proficiency in reading in order to satisfy a need to remain dependent and free of responsibility. Fortunately, as information about learning disabilities becomes more widespread, this kind of error is happening less often.

11. There are a lot of wild claims around about the contribution of biology to individual differences. This follows a period in which there were a lot of wild claims around about how biology didn't matter and human behavior was entirely determined by social conditioning.

12. Usually the two forms of diagnosis are not in conflict, but sometimes they are, as when reviewers for managed care companies refuse to approve psychotherapy for covered persons because they decide that

clients who are not suicidal or who are able to reduce or do without medication must by definition not be severely depressed enough to need continuing psychotherapy.

13. This is not to suggest that these two features are the only aspects of personality in gifted LD persons, just that they are important ones.

Chapter 3. Naked Under the Desk

1. Strauman (1994) provides an enlightening explanation as to why adults with LD feel such guilt and overreact. He builds on the work of Rosenberg (1979), who suggested that self-concepts can be conceived as *actual* self-concepts (more or less accurate knowledge of what we are) and *desired* self-concepts (what we wish to be). Carrying this basic idea further, Strauman (see also Higgins, Strauman, & Klein, 1986) proposes that desired self-concepts are used as "self-guides" and as such are inherently associated with affect and/or motivational outcomes because a discrepancy between desired and actual self-concepts will produce emotional distress. This way of parsing the issue is particularly applicable to individuals with a learning disability, like Mark. If such a person has a self-guide that involves being industrious or intelligent, but actually believes himself to be lazy or stupid, that individual would be likely to experience negative affect in situations that activate the self-guide—intelligence, or in Mark's case, industriousness—even if the individual is not aware of the relationship between the situation and his or her self-standards (p. 297).

Strauman further suggests that these self-guides can be classed as *ideal* self-guides (representations of attributes of the kind of person the individual or some significant other believes that he or she would *like* to be) and *ought* self-guides (representations of what he or she *ought* to be). His research indicates that discrepancies between actual self-concept and ideal self-guides produce depression, while discrepancies between actual self-concept and ought self-guides produce anxiety. (More psychoanalytically oriented discussions of these two sorts of discrepancy see them as producing, respectively, shame and guilt [Piers & Singer, 1953]. Aronfreed [1971] makes the same point from a non-psychoanalytic perspective.) Strauman concludes that, in general, discrepancies in self-concept can "constitute markers of cognitive vulnerability to depression and anxiety" (p. 303) and are "proximal contributory causes for both the onset and maintenance of chronic emotional distress, potentially culminating in clinical disorders" (pp. 303–304). He also finds that "links among self-representations, childhood memories, and emotional vulnerability demonstrate the importance of a developmental perspective on self-evaluative cognition" (p. 304). Although Strauman does not discuss learning disabilities per se, the applicability of his work seems clear, and the parallel between the phenomena of discrepancies in achievement and discrepancies in self-concept is remarkable.

2. Briefly, a thirsty lion is prevented from drinking from a pond by the sight of his own reflection in the water, which he takes to be another lion. There's a lot of metaphoric meaning here!

3. This means that calls for "every child to be able to read by the third grade," or some such benchmark, though politically appealing, are biologically nonsense.

Chapter 4. The Rebel without a Clue

1. Reiff and Gerber (1994) also suggest that social intercourse often depends on a shared knowledge base, and because of her reading problems, Kerry has more difficulty acquiring a broad knowledge base than most people. Thus, social discourse is less fluent.

2. For the person with a learning disability, most problems with daily living skills are related to difficulty processing nonverbal—primarily visual and spatial—information. A syndrome of nonverbal processing problems has been identified and investigated over the last 20 years by a number of researchers. Rourke (1982) provides an extensive discussion of a syndrome of nonverbal dysfunctions, including problems with visual perception, visual attention and memory, oral-motor praxis, prosody, pragmatics, handwriting, arithmetic, social skills, and emotional stability.

3. With respect to health care in particular, nonverbal learning disabilities can make it difficult to establish and maintain adequate physician-patient relationships, which then jeopardizes treatment. Because of the nature of learning disabilities, it is important for all helping professionals to recognize that behaviors such as missing appointments, becoming overly dependent on the service provider, not following a prescribed course of treatment, lack of progress, noncooperation, failure to follow through on referrals, frequent switching of physicians or therapists, quitting and restarting therapy, and so on, may not be the manifestation of a negative attitude but may instead be either the direct result of a learning disability or the indirect result of the frustration, anxiety, and tension that accompany a learning disability (Wren & Smiley, 1995).

4. The European Therapy Studies Institute publishes an excellent journal, *The Therapist*, and has developed an outstanding series of cassettes for therapists and people interested in therapy. The address of ETSI is: 1 Lovers Meadow, Chalvington, East Sussex BN27 3TE, England.

Chapter 5. The Worst Thing . . . and the Best

1. Hooper and Olley (1996) discuss a number of mechanisms that connect neuropsychological dysfunction and psychopathology. They suggest

that these mechanisms may be direct, in which case brain dysfunction directly causes emotional and behavioral disruptions, or indirect, in which case the learning disability sets the stage for other factors that cause emotional and behavioral disturbances. Direct mechanisms include behavioral disruptions that arise from abnormal brain activity and the effects of anomalous neurodevelopment on temperament and personality development. For example, both learning difficulties and abnormal behavior may arise from frontal lobe dysfunction that results in social disinhibition, poor judgment, and impulsivity. Indirect effects include heightened exposure to failure and the social stigma of learning disabilities, adverse family reactions ranging from overprotection to scapegoating, the individual's own reaction to being learning disabled, and adverse effects from treatment or lack of treatment.

2. In addition, Johnson (1981) has found high levels of anxiety, panic responses, and being overwhelmed by stress. Rogan and Hartman (1976) found overcommitment, withdrawal, and mood swings among their subjects. White (1985) reported more dependence within familial relationships and a limited range of social opportunities. Gerber and Reiff's (1991) subjects indicated feelings of isolation, discomfort in social gatherings, and a sense of boredom and frustration with recreation and leisure time.

3. It is not the purpose of this book to provide an extensive discussion of ADD or to elucidate the distinction between LD and ADD or ADHD. Indeed, some scholars question the value of conceptualizing ADD as a distinct clinical entity. Levine (1998), for example, maintains that such a distinction leads therapists to neglect the extreme heterogeneity of individuals who are having problems with attention and to separate attention from other relevant areas of developmental function. He suggests that it is more desirable to view attention as one of several neurodeveopmental processes and to consider the powerful effects of various neurodevelopmental functions on attention instead of allowing the condition to be defined by a list of traits. Thus, in Dominic's case I focus on the interactions between his attention problems, his other cognitive processing difficulties, and his emotional reactions.

4. From a developmental perspective, unresolved pain in people with LD may be connected to arrested psychosocial development. Pickar and Tori (1986) used Erikson's developmental theory to investigate the emotional status of learning disabled adolescents. Their results support the notion that arrested affective development may be due to emotional wounds occurring because of LD-related school failure. They found that the stage of industry (competence) vs. inferiority was affected more deeply in learning disabled students than in normal ones. They suggest, not surprisingly in light of Dominic's interview, that since school is the "work" of

childhood, school failure due to LD directly affects the development of a sense of competence.

Chapter 6. We Had You Tested and Nothing's Wrong

1. It is worth noting that even parents who come to understand the nature of learning disabilities find it difficult to avoid producing oppositional behavior on the part of their LD children. As parents recognize the permanent nature of learning disabilities, they try to protect their children from lifelong failure by shielding them and preparing them to use various compensatory strategies. However, a frequent by-product of such protection, even when successful, is that the parent-child relationship becomes more entangled, making it harder for the LD children to establish autonomy and self-control. Then, because the children can't foresee how difficult adult life will be, they interpret their parents' concerns as intrusive and overcontrolling, and react accordingly.

2. It is important to note that the distractibility factor on the WAIS is not fully researched and is currently not a reliable predictor of ADD in adults. It is not clear which subtests would load on the factor or how low a subtest score must be to be significant.

3. The evaluation report illustrates how very difficult it is for anyone, even psychologists, to avoid negative judgments and attributions of poor character. The evaluator refers to Sonja as not only *careless* but also, and even worse, as *negligent* in information-processing. If it is this easy for supposedly objective professionals to draw such moralistic conclusions, should we be surprised that Sonja's parents had the same thoughts?

4. An excellent source of questions that can be asked while taking a case history can be found in Appendix B of *Adults with Learning Disabilities,* by Johnson and Blalock (1987). Additional diagnostic questions that thoroughly and systematically explore cognitive processing problems, as well as vocational difficulties, can be found in Appendix C of that book.

5. The results of many standardized tests can yield rich information about a patient if test performance is analyzed from multiple perspectives. Just as the Wechsler intelligence tests can yield indicators of both social/emotional and cognitive dysfunctions, so other tests can provide a variety of information about a patient.

Unusual performance on projective tests may indicate processing problems, either verbal or nonverbal. Subtle oral language problems (particularly with syntax), as well as other *verbal* problems in reading, spelling, or handwriting, may be picked up from oral or written sentence completion instruments. Responses from the Rorschach may yield clues to oral vocabulary or retrieval problems, since patients with LD may pull from memory an incorrect word or association, or patients with expressive language problems may not be able to provide convincing explanations for the figures they perceive. TAT stories may point to oral expressive problems as well.

Similarly, in the *nonverbal* realm, idiosyncratic responses to the Rorschach or TAT may be the result of difficulty with visual attention or perception. Some individuals with visual processing problems may have specific difficulty with visual scanning, with attention to detail, or with interpreting the line drawings of the TAT, thus providing what appear to be eccentric, inappropriate, incomplete, or poorly sequenced stories. Visual-motor problems may be evident on tests requiring copying geometric shapes and in human figure drawings. Furthermore, resistance to engaging in any of these projective tasks may not be reluctance to express emotion, but rather reluctance to produce a poor product, to reveal processing problems, or to engage in cognitive activities that are difficult and distasteful. Such resistance should be sensitively pursued, as it may be the first clue to an underlying learning disability.

6. Lawrence Lieberman (1987), a wise advocate for the learning disabled, raises the question of whether the label "learning disabled" is helpful or detrimental to adults with LD. For some, adult society is more tolerant than school and they are able to fade into the adult world and lead successful lives. Others find that without advocacy and support their lives are filled with pain and frustration. Then, says Lieberman, there is the hook. "The hook is what is used to hang every failure on; every perceived injustice, every reason for not maximizing one's own potential," and learning disabilities can be a powerful hook (p. 64). He goes on to say that the label LD is only meaningful in adulthood if it helps people live more satisfying lives. "Some people should be LD adults. It will help them live. Others who are LD should stay a million miles away from it. Some should beware of the hook" (p. 64).

7. Cognitive tests should include tests of memory and learning and neuropsychological screening tests, which Sonja apparently did not receive during her evaluation. A single non-testing clinical diagnostic interview is not enough, since an ADD subject can often keep it together well enough to avoid obvious symptoms in a single interview, and subjects who look like they have ADD may really have other problems, such as nonverbal learning disabilities or personality or anxiety disorders, or may have these variables as well as ADD, as in Sonja's case. In the past, ADD has tended to be overlooked in favor of personality/emotional diagnoses. Now that it is becoming better known, we begin to see the reverse oversight, as personality and emotional disorders are overlooked in the diagnosis of ADD. A good case history, so often necessary to make an accurate diagnosis, is often not taken.

Chapter 7. I've Been Seeking Information All My Whole Life

1. According to Rourke, primary neuropsychological deficits exist in right-hemisphere functions, especially tactile and visual perception and complex psychomotor skills. During infancy, these deficits limit the capacity to deal adaptively with novelty in its many forms and result in secondary disorders of tactile and visual attention and markedly decreased exploratory behavior. These deficits in turn affect intermodal integration, concept formation, and problem-solving (Rourke, 1982; Rourke, Del Dotto, Rourke, & Casey, 1990).

2. Barton and Fuhrmann (1994) have found an eclectic, integrative approach to be effective in helping clients understand and adjust to their learning disability. They suggest that four approaches (psychoanalysis, cognitive therapy, behaviorism, and humanistic, person-centered therapy) can be integrated to provide what they call "a comprehensive picture of clients who are influenced by their early learning, by what they think, by what they do, and by how they feel." If therapists "think about human beings as composed of unconscious motives, and by thoughts, behaviors, and feelings," they can intervene with a particular client in any of those realms (p. 86).

Barton and Fuhrmann suggest that therapy begin from a person-centered perspective, in order to establish trust and support and to forge the therapeutic alliance. Early parts of the reframing process can be addressed from a person-centered perspective. Helping clients develop a deeper understanding of the learning disability itself can be addressed from a cognitive psychology perspective, since it involves becoming aware of and adjusting one's thoughts and beliefs about the self. Clients can be helped to find a way to live with the conflict of being both smart and dumb, lazy and industrious, perhaps by conceptualizing this "tension of opposites" as an energizing force. Cognitive therapy can be used to reduce the magnitude of the discrepancy as much as possible, adjusting the client's self-concept in some ways, modifying the client's standards in others, and realigning perceptions of the world when they are unrealistic (Strauman, 1994).

To address the emotional impact of the disability, Barton and Fuhrmann suggest that psychoanalytic techniques may be useful in helping the client explore the past with an eye to gaining a greater understanding of early patterns of family behavior, especially the family's reaction to their disabled child. Then, as clients begin to accept responsibility for change and start to plan how to move forward, cognitive therapy may be used to help them confront a variety of erroneous beliefs and perceptions, plan and organize for change, learn needed skills, and challenge assumptions about the world. Behavioral techniques can help clients learn specific social skills or eliminate dysfunctional behaviors. Many with LD could benefit from stress reduction therapy as well.

Chapter 8. Psychotherapy of Two Invisible Sources of Distress

1. The terms "patient" and "client" are used interchangeably here. Neither one is altogether satisfying to describe the person participating in psychotherapeutic healing, since "patient" denotes a medical relationship in which a passive person receives a physical treatment rather than being an active participant with a major role in the outcome of a healing relationship, and "client" denotes a business relationship equivalent to that which a customer has with a lawyer or accountant.

2. The concept of the three-level brain can be a helpful one (see Maclean, 1990). As a useful oversimplification, these three major levels of the brain are often characterized as the "reptilian" (central core), "mammalian" (limbic system), and "human" (neocortex).

3. James Burke, star of the BBC "Connections" series, once said that education does a wonderful job of preparing children for the 18th century.

References

Abbott, R., & Frank, B. (1975). A follow-up of LD children in a private school. *Academic Therapy, 19,* 291–298.

American Psychiatric Association. (1994). *Diagnostic and statistical manual of mental disorders* (4th ed.). Washington, DC: Author.

Aronfreed, J. (1971). *Conduct and conscience: The socialization of internalized control over behavior.* New York: Academic Press.

Balow, B., & Blomquist, M. (1965). Young adults ten to fifteen years after severe reading disability. *Elementary School Journal, 66,* 44–48.

Barkley, R. (1996). Critical issues in research on attention. In R. Lyon & R. Krasnegor (Eds.), *Attention, memory, and executive function* (pp. 45–56). Baltimore: Brookes Publishing.

Barton, R., & Fuhrmann, B. (1994). Counseling and psychotherapy for adults with learning disabilities. In P. Gerber & H. Reiff (Eds.), *Learning disabilities in adulthood: Persisting problems and evolving issues* (pp. 82–92). Stoneham, MA: Butterworth-Heinemann.

Bender, M. (1994). Learning disabilities: Beyond the school years. In A. Capute, P. Accardo, & K. Shapiro (Eds.), *Learning disabilities spectrum: ADD, ADHD, and LD* (pp. 241–253). Baltimore: York Books.

Bogen, J. (1969). The other side of the brain: An appositional mind. *Bulletin of the Los Angeles Neurological Societies, 34*(3), 135–162. Substantially reprinted in R. Ornstein (Ed.), *The nature of human consciousness: A book of readings.* San Francisco: W.H. Freeman, 1973.

Bogen, J. (1977). Split-brain evidence for complimentary hemispheric specialization. Paper presented to the Institute for the Study of Human Knowledge, Chicago, IL.

Brown, D., & Gerber, P. (1994). Employing people with learning disabilities. In P. Gerber & H. Reiff (Eds.), *Learning disabilities in adulthood: Persisting problems and evolving issues* (pp. 194–203). Stoneham, MA: Butterworth-Heinemann.

Brown, D., Gerber, P., & Dowdy, C. (1990). *Pathways to employment for people with learning disabilities.* Washington, DC: President's Committee for the Employment of People with Disabilities.

Bryan, T. (1998). Social problems and learning disabilities. In B. Wong, *Learning about learning disabilities* (2nd ed., pp. 237–275). San Diego: Academic Press.

Buchanan, M., & Wolf, J. (1986). A comprehensive study of learning disabled adults. *Journal of Learning Disabilities, 19*(1), 34–38.

Casey, J., Rourke, B., & Picard, E. (1991). Syndrome of nonverbal learning disabilities: Age differences in neurological, academic, and socioemotional functioning. *Development and Psychopathology, 3,* 329–345.

Chesler, B. (1982). ACLD vocational committee survey on LD adults. *ACLD Newsbrief,* No. 145.

Cohen, R., & Balikov, H. (1974). The impact of adolescence upon parents. In S. Feinstein & P. Giovacchini (Eds.), *Adolescent psychiatry: Vol. III. Developmental and clinical studies.* New York: Basic Books.

Coles, G. (1987). *The learning mystique: A critical look at "learning disabilities."* New York: Pantheon.

Critchley, M. (1970). *The dyslexic child.* Springfield, IL: Charles C. Thomas.

Cruikshank, W., Morse, W., & Johns, J. (1980). *Learning disabilities: The struggle from adolescence to adulthood.* Syracuse, NY: Syracuse University Press.

Dane, E. (1990). *Painful passages.* Silver Spring, MD: NASW Press.

Deikman, A. (1976). *Personal freedom.* New York: Grossman.

Deikman, A. (1979). Sufism and psychiatry. *The world of the Sufi.* London: Octagon Press.

Deikman, A. (1982). *The observing self: Mysticism and psychotherapy.* Boston: Beacon Press.

Frank, J. (1974). *Persuasion and healing.* New York: Shocken Books.

Garber, B. (1989). Deficits in empathy in the learning-disabled child. In K. Field & B. Cohler (Eds.), *Learning and education: Psychoanalytic perspectives.* Madison, CT: International Universities Press.

Gardner, H. (1985). *Frames of mind.* New York: Basic Books.

Gazzaniga, M. (1967). The split brain in man. *Scientific American, 217*(2), 24–29. Reprinted in R. Ornstein (Ed.), *The nature of human consciousness: A book of readings.* San Francisco: W.H. Freeman, 1973.

Gerber, P. (1978). *A comparative study of social perceptual ability of learning disabled and nonhandicapped children.* Doctoral dissertation, University of Michigan, Ann Arbor.

Gerber, P., & Reiff, H. (1991). *Speaking for themselves: Interviews with learning disabled adults.* Ann Arbor, MI: University of Michigan Press.

Gerber, P., & Reiff, H. (1994). *Learning disabilities in adulthood: Persisting problems and evolving issues.* Stoneham, MA: Butterworth-Heinemann.

Ginsberg, R., Gerber, P., & Reiff, H. (1994). Employment success for people with learning disabilities. In P. Gerber & H. Reiff (Eds.), *Learning disabilities in adulthood: Persisting problems and evolving issues* (pp. 204–213). Stoneham, MA: Butterworth-Heinemann.

Griffin, J., & Tyrrell, I. (1999). *Psychotherapy and the human givens* (Monograph). Chalvington, East Sussex, UK: European Therapy Studies Institute.

Grigar, M. (1994). *A day to cry.* Chicago: Grigar Graphics and Publishing.

Hallowell, E., & Ratey, J. (1994). *Driven to distraction: Recognizing and coping with attention deficit disorder from childhood through adulthood.* New York: Simon & Schuster.

Hammill, D. (1990). On defining learning disabilities: An emerging consensus. *Journal of Learning Disabilities, 23,* 74–84.

Higgins, E., Strauman, T., & Klein, R. (1986). Standards and the process of self-evaluation: Multiple affects from multiple stages. In R. Sorrentino & E. Higgins (Eds.), *Handbook of motivation and cognition: Foundations of social behavior* (pp. 23–63). New York: Guilford Press.

Hoffman, J., Sheldon, K., Minskoff, E., Sautter, S., Steidle, E., Baker, D., Bailey, M., & Echols, L. (1987). Needs of learning disabled adults. *Journal of Learning Disabilities, 20*(1), 43–52.

Hooper, S., & Olley, J. (1996). Psychological comorbidity in adults with learning disabilities. In N. Gregg, C. Hoy, & A. Gay (Eds.), *Adults with learning disabilities: Theoretical and practical perspectives* (pp. 162–183). New York: Guilford Press.

Hoy, C., & Gregg, N. (1994). *Assessment: The special educator's role.* Pacific Grove, CA: Brooks/Cole.

Johnson, C. (1981). LD adults: The inside story. *Academic Therapy, 16,* 435–442.

Johnson, D. (1987). Principles of assessment and diagnosis. In D. Johnson & J. Blalock (Eds.), *Adults with learning disabilities: Clinical studies* (pp. 9–30). New York: Grune & Stratton.

Johnson, D., & Blalock, J. (1987). *Adults with learning disabilities: Clinical studies.* New York: Grune & Stratton.

Johnson, D., & Myklebust, H. (1967). *Learning disabilities: Educational principles and practices.* New York: Grune & Stratton.

Kanner, L. (1943). Autistic disturbances of affective contact. *Nervous Child, 2,* 217–250.

Kaplan, C., & Shachter, E. (1991). Adults with undiagnosed learning disabilities: Practice considerations. *Families in Society: The Journal of Contemporary Human Services, 4,* 195–201.

Kavale, K. (1993). A science and theory of learning disabilities. In R. Lyon, D. Gray, J. Kavanaugh, & N. Krasnegor (Eds.), *Better understanding learning disabilities: New views from research and their implications for education and public policy* (pp. 171–195). Baltimore: Paul H. Brookes.

Kelly, G. (1963). *A theory of personality: The psychology of personal constructs.* New York: Norton.

Kelly, K., & Ramundo, P. (1993). *You mean I'm not lazy, stupid or crazy?* New York: Fireside.

Kirk, S. (1963). Behavioral diagnosis and remediation of learning disabilities. *Proceedings of the Conference to Explore the Problems of the Perceptually Handicapped Child, 1,* 1–23.

Kohut, H. (1977). *The restoration of the self.* New York: International Universities Press.

Kohut, H. (1984). *How does analysis cure?* Chicago: University of Chicago Press.

Larson, K., & Gerber, P. (1987). Effects of social metacognitive training for enhancing overt behavior in learning disabled and low achieving delinquents. *Exceptional Children, 54,* 210–212.

Lerner, J. (1993). *Learning disabilities: Theories, diagnosis, and teaching strategies.* Boston: Houghton Mifflin.

Levine, M. (1989). *Developmental variation and learning disorders.* Cambridge, MA: Educators Publishing Service.

Levine, M. (1998). *Developmental variation and learning disorders* (2nd. ed). Cambridge, MA: Educators Publishing Service.

Lieberman, L. (1987). Is the learning disabled adult really necessary? *Journal of Learning Disabilities, 20*(1), 64.

Maclean, P. (1990). *The triune brain: Role in paleocerebral functions.* New York: Plenum Press.

Mann, L. (1979). *On the trail of process.* New York: Grune & Stratton.

Mann, V. (1998). Language problems: A key to early reading problems. In B. Wong (Ed.), *Learning about learning disabilities* (2nd ed., pp. 129–162). San Diego: Academic Press.

Maslow, A. (1968). *Toward a psychology of being.* New York: Wiley.

Merriam-Webster's Collegiate Dictionary (10th ed.). Springfield, MA: Merriam-Webster.

Modell, A. (1998). *The transformation of past experience.* Paper presented at the conference on Psychoanalysis, Neurobiology, and Therapeutic Change, Chicago, IL.

Myklebust, H. (1954). *Auditory disorders in children.* New York: Grune & Stratton.

Nadeau, K. (Ed.). (1995). *A comprehensive guide to attention deficit disorder in adults: Research, diagnosis, and treatment.* New York: Brunner/Mazel.

Nicholas, M. (1994). *The mystery of goodness.* New York: Norton.

Orenstein, M. (1992). *Imprisoned intelligence: The discovery of undiagnosed learning disabilities in adults.* Doctoral dissertation, The Institute for Clinical Social Work, Chicago.

Ornstein, R. (1993). *The roots of the self.* San Francisco: Harper.

Ornstein, R. (1996). *The mind field.* Cambridge, MA: Malor. (Originally published by Grossman, 1976)

Ornstein, R. (1997). *The right mind: Making sense of the hemispheres.* New York: Harcourt Brace and Company.

Pickar, D., & Tori, C. (1986). The LD adolescent: Eriksonian psycho-social development, self-concept, and delinquent behavior. *Journal of Youth and Adolescence, 15*(5), 429–440.

Pickering, E., Pickering, A., & Buchanan, M. (1987). LD and nonhandicapped boys' comprehension of cartoon humor. *Learning Disability Quarterly, 10,* 45–51.

Piers, G., & Singer, M. (1953). *Shame and guilt: A psychoanalytic and a cultural study.* Springfield, IL: Charles C Thomas.

Raskind, M., Goldberg, R., Higgins, E., & Herman, K. (1999). Patterns of change and predictors of success in individuals with learning disabilities: Results from a 20-year longitudinal study. *Learning Disabilities Research and Practice, 14*(1) 35–49.

Rawson, M. (1968). *Developmental language disability: Adult accomplishments of dyslexic boys.* Baltimore: Johns Hopkins University Press.

Reber, A. (1985). *The Penguin dictionary of psychology.* New York: Viking Penguin.

Rehabilitation Services Administration. (1985, January 24). *Program policy directive P.D.-85–7.* Washington, DC: U.S. Office of Special Education and Rehabilitation Services.

Reiff, H., & Gerber, P. (1994). Social, emotional, and daily living issues for adults with learning disabilities, In P. Gerber & H. Reiff (Eds.), *Learning disabilities in adulthood: Persisting problems and evolving issues* (pp. 72–81). Stoneham, MA: Butterworth-Heinemann.

Rogan, L., & Hartman, L. (1976). *A follow-up study of learning disabled children as adults.* Final report. Project #443CH60010, Grant #OEG-0-74-7453. Washington, DC: Bureau of Education for the Handicapped, U.S. Department of Health, Education, and Welfare.

Rosenberg, M. (1979). *Conceiving the self.* New York: Basic Books.

Rourke, B. (1982). Central processing deficiencies in children: Toward a developmental neuropsychological model. *Journal of Clinical Neuropsychology, 4,* 1–18.

Rourke, B. (1989). *Nonverbal learning disabilities: The syndrome and the model.* New York: Guilford Press.

Rourke, B., Del Dotto, J., Rourke, S., & Casey, J. (1990). Nonverbal learning disabilities: The syndrome and a case study. *Journal of School Psychology, 28,* 361–385.

Schechter, M. (1974). Psychiatric aspects of learning disabilities. *Child Psychiatry and Human Development, 5*(2), 67–77.

Selye, H. (1952). *The story of the adaptation syndrome.* Montreal: Acta, Inc.

Selye, H. (1977). *The stress of my life* (2nd ed.). Toronto: Van Nostrand Reinhold.

Sergeant, J. (1996). A theory of attention: An information processing perspective. In R. Lyon & R. Krasnegor (Eds.), *Attention, memory and executive function* (pp. 57–70). Baltimore: Paul H. Brookes.

Shah, I. (1986). *The book of the book.* London: Octagon.

Shah, I. (1993). *The exploits of the incomparable Mulla Nasrudin/The subtleties of the inimitable Mulla Nasrudin* (double volume). London: Octagon.

Shah, I. (1998). *The lion who saw himself in the water.* Boston: Hoopoe.

Sheridan, R. (1897). *The rivals: A comedy.* London: Dent.

Shreve, J. (1993). *Square peg in a round hole: Coping with learning differences at home, in school, and at work.* San Diego: Square Peg Enterprises.

Siegel, L. (1990). IQ is irrelevant in the definition of learning disabilities. *Journal of Learning Disabilities, 22,* 469–487.

Sigman, M., & Capps, L. (1997). *Children with autism: A developmental perspective.* Cambridge, MA: Harvard University Press.

Silver, A., & Hagin, R. (1985). Outcomes of learning disabilities in adolescence. In M. Sugar, A. Esman, J. Looney, A. Schwartzberg, & A. Sorosky (Eds.), *Adolescent psychiatry: Developmental and clinical studies* (Vol. 12, pp. 197–211). Chicago: University of Chicago Press.

Smith, S. (1989, April). The masks students wear. *Instructor,* pp. 27–32.

Spekman, N., Goldberg, R., & Herman, K. (1992). Learning disabled children grow up: A search for factors related to success in the young adult years. *Learning Disabilities Research and Practice, 7,* 161–170.

Stanovich, K. (1993). Discrepancy definitions of reading disability. In R. Lyon, D. Gray, J. Kavanaugh, & N. Krasnegor (Eds.), *Better understanding learning disabilities: New views from research and their implications for education and public policy* (pp. 273–307). Baltimore: Paul H. Brookes.

Strauman, T. (1994). Self-representations and the nature of cognitive change in psychotherapy. *Journal of Psychotherapy Integration, 4*(4), 291–316.

Strauss, A., & Lehtinen, L. (1947). *Psychopathology of the brain-injured child.* (Vol. 1). New York: Grune & Stratton.

Torgeson, J. (1998). Learning disabilities: Historical and conceptual issues. In B. Wong (Ed.), *Learning about learning disabilities* (2nd ed., pp. 3–34). San Diego: Academic Press.

Tzelepis, A., Schubiner, H., & Warbasse, L. (1995). Differential diagnosis and psychiatric comorbidity patterns in adult attention deficit disorder. In K. Nadeau (Ed.), *A comprehensive guide to attention deficit disorder in adults: Research, diagnosis and treatment* (pp. 35–57). New York: Brunner/Mazel.

Westman, J. (1990). *Handbook of learning disabilities: A multisystem approach.* Boston: Allyn & Bacon.

White, W. (1985). Perspectives on education and training of learning disabled adults. *Learning Disabilities Quarterly, 8,* 231–236.

Williams, P. (1997). *Developing emotional intelligence.* (Cassette). Worthing, West Sussex, UK: European Therapy Studies Institute.

Williams, P. (1998). *How stories heal* (two cassettes). Hailsham, East Sussex, UK: European Therapy Studies Institute.

Willows, D. (1998). Visual processes in learning disabilities. In B. Wong (Ed.), *Learning about learning disabilities* (2nd ed., pp. 164–189). San Diego: Academic Press.

Winn, D., & Tyrell, I. (1999). Treatment on trial (an interview with Iain Chalmers and Clive Adams). *The Therapist, 5*(2), 24–32.

Wren, C., & Smiley, T. (1995). *Treatment of adults with learning disabilities: The patient's perspective.* Chicago: DePaul University.

Index